1914–1918
AN ANATOMY
OF GLOBAL CONFLICT

JAGIELLONIAN STUDIES IN HISTORY

Vol. 4

Andrzej Chwalba

1914–1918
AN ANATOMY OF GLOBAL CONFLICT

Translated by Teresa Bałuk-Ulewiczowa

Jagiellonian University Press

This publication was financed by the Jagiellonian University in Krakow – Faculty of History

REVIEWER
Tomasz Schramm

SERIES COVER DESIGN
Jan Jacek Bruski

COVER DESIGN
Agnieszka Winciorek

Cover photography: The fortress of Przemyśl (Galicia). One of the destroyed forts, 1915; Courtesy of the National Digital Archives (Narodowe Archiwum Cyfrowe) in Warsaw.

JAGIELLONIAN UNIVERSITY PRESS

www.wuj.pl

ISBN 978-83-233-3638-9
ISSN 2299-758X

Jagiellonian University Press
Editorial Offices: Michałowskiego 9/2, 31-126 Kraków
Phone: +48 12 663 23 81, +48 12 663 23 82, Fax: +48 12 663 23 83
Distribution: Phone: +48 12 631 01 97, Fax: +48 12 631 01 98
Cell Phone: + 48 506006 674, e-mail: sprzedaz@wuj.pl
Bank: PEKAO SA, IBAN PL 80 1240 4722 1111 0000 4856 3325

Table of Contents

Author's Preface

We know more or less all there is to know about the way the hostilities of the 1914–1918 war developed. What's still left to be cleared up are just a few details which will not have much of an effect on the general picture of the armed conflict. At the most they'll help to nuance the chronicle of the war. Of course, we won't manage to explain or sort out all the problems. We certainly won't ever be able to establish the precise figures for losses sustained by the belligerents in particular clashes and battles. There will just be estimates. On the other hand, better prospects for research are opening up for historians interested in the soldiers' predicament, in what was going on behind the front lines, in the role civilians, communities, and nations played in the war, in the war economies and everyday life, or in the role of the women who made an energetic entry into a "man's" story. It will be worthwhile to study the stories of individual soldiers and what they suffered, of heroism and treachery, of people losing and recovering their faith in God, of struggling to survive and growing accustomed to death. An area which offers promising horizons for research is historical anthropology, which has the cognitive instruments needed to embark on new paths of study and the effective verification of what has been accomplished hitherto. Another opportunity to enhance our knowledge of the Great War are the case studies being conducted in many of the world's academic centres, examining the inside story of the war from the point of view of its rank-and-file participants. Yet another prospective area for study are the attempts to classify the different types of armed conflict. In a word, research on the fabric of the war and its participants offers the chance for progress on the way to a global understanding of the nature and essence of the Great War.

The hundred years that have elapsed since the Sarajevo assassination on the 28th of June 1914 and the outbreak of war are an incentive to search for new areas of scholarly exploration.

This book is an attempt to embark on fresh paths of research using new instruments of cognition. It searches for answers to questions in historical anthropology. It contains a clinical review of a collection of diverse source materials from all the important fields of battle and their aftermaths, as well as from the civilian background. It makes use of a variety of resources relating to the Eastern, Western, and Southern European fronts, as well as fronts beyond Europe. To make the book more readable I have decided to break free of the usual academic custom of footnoting and have put only a selected bibliography at the back.

I would like to thank Professor Michał Baczkowski, Professor Tadeusz Czekalski, and Professor Tomasz Gąsowski of the Jagiellonian University in Kraków for reading the book *in statu nascendi* and sharing their opinions and comments with me. I am indebted to Professor Tomasz Schramm of the Adam Mickiewicz University in Poznań, whose suggestions helped to verify some of my judgements and ideas, and improve the quality of my narrative.

Andrzej Chwalba
Kraków, April 2014

I. The War Starts

1. Sarajevo

Sarajevo, capital of the Austro-Hungarian province of Bosnia-Herzegovina, lay on the peripheries of the Habsburg Empire and was not remarkable in any way except for its population of many cultures and religions, and its variegated architecture. Its modern districts held a central position and were built according to imperial standards. It was a city of the administrative and business *nouveaux*, with a cosmopolitan class of state officials, representatives of many nations, but dominated by native speakers of German, loyal to the House of Habsburg and the Roman Catholic religion. The new town with its cafés and restaurants, theatre and cinema, fashionable shops, elegant streets and promenade, was encircled by squalid and impoverished districts, with no running water or sewerage, cluttered up with cheap tenement houses, shacks and shanties, more reminiscent of the Ottoman Empire. Herds of animals roamed the streets, women covered up from head to toe in traditional Muslim apparel shuffled along, and child beggars, many of them disabled, loitered on street corners, while the menfolk, clad in loose-fitting woollen trousers, spent their days in the cafés, drinking Turkish coffee. The landmarks of each district were their places of worship. Muslim mosques were the predominant edifices, often in close proximity to Orthodox Christian churches used by the Serbs, and Roman Catholic churches which served the Croats.

But the impression of drowsiness was only superficial. In fact, there was a strong undercurrent of tension between the Habsburg authorities and the Bosnian Serbs, who deeply resented and could not be reconciled to foreign occupation. It had aggravated during the Balkan Wars. The Serbs had been roused by the Serbian victories in the First Balkan War against Turkey, and the Second Balkan War against Bulgaria, and they were proud of Serbia. In 1913 Sarajevan schoolchildren had paraded in the streets with ribbons on their caps with the names of cities occupied by the Serbian army, publicly declaring that Bosnia should be part of Greater Serbia. Anti-government activities proliferated. Propaganda materials were smuggled in from Serbia, urging the Serbs of Bosnia and Herzegovina to engage in acts of violence against the "Habsburg invader," as they called Austria-Hungary. The government in Vienna was alarmed and on 2nd May 1913 introduced "exceptional powers," partially suspending the 1910 Constitution of Bosnia-Herzegovina, replacing civilian with military authorities, bringing in military courts, and imposing border control to confiscate newspapers smuggled in from neighbouring Serbia. Another part of its preventive measures were army manoeuvres, to be held in June 1914, intended to stress the Habsburg resolve to keep Bosnia and Herzegovina. They were to be led by the 84-year old Emperor Franz Joseph, but when he fell ill with pneumonia, his doctors advised him not to travel. He was to be replaced by the heir to the throne, the Archduke Franz Ferdinand, who was Inspector-General of the armed forces, commander-in-chief in the event of war. Nonetheless, in view of the tense situation General Oskar Potiorek, the military governor of Bosnia and Herzegovina, was considered as an alternative to the Archduke. In the event neither were the manoeuvres called off nor did the Archduke withdraw from the visit. The manoeuvres were scheduled to finish on 28th June – hardly a randomly chosen date, Vitovdan (St. Vitus's day), the anniversary of the Serbian defeat in the Battle of Kosovo Pole in 1389. Serbian nationalists took it as an outrage to have their national day of mourning profaned.

The Archduke arrived in Bosnia straight from his favourite residence at Konopiště near Prague. On 24th June he sailed on the battleship Viribus Unitis to one of the Dalmatian ports and on the 26th

started the manoeuvres. Local newspapers had been writing about the visit for weeks. The people of Sarajevo decorated their houses with flowers and flags, as recommended by the authorities. Six Serbian conspirators from Bosnia and Herzegovina, members of an organisation called Mlada Bosna (Young Bosnia), decided to spoil the holiday atmosphere. Their aim was to kill the Emperor's nephew. It wasn't the first Serbian plot against him. The conspirators were convinced Franz Ferdinand was one of the most anti-Serbian politicians, and for them a symbol of a monarchy they hated. The Archduke was indeed in favour of the occupation of Bosnia and Herzegovina and did not hide his dislike of Serbia, which he called a land of cut-throats, fools, and plums, or pig-breeders. On the morning of 28th June Franz Ferdinand, his wife, and entourage alighted from the train. The city welcomed its illustrious guests with fine, warm weather. From the railway station the motorcade of six cars, which the tight-fisted Archduke had "hired" from his subordinates, headed for the city hall. The cars took the route which had been announced to the public, for the spectators lining the streets to express their respect and admiration for the Archduke. At 10.15 a.m. one of the plotters, the typesetter Nedeljko Čabrinović, threw a bomb at the Archduke, but it exploded under the following car, injuring one of its passengers, who was taken to hospital. "I come here on a visit, and they throw bombs at me. It's an outrage!" Franz Ferdinand is reported to have shouted. Nevertheless he and his wife continued the visit. After about an hour the cars set off on the next part of the visit. Gavrilo Princip, the last plotter stationed along the route, did not miss his chance, though the Archduke's car passed by him only because the driver made a mistake and had to turn back. "Suddenly I heard people shouting, 'Long live!' Immediately I saw the first car… When the second car came up I recognised the heir to the throne with a lady next to him and I started having second thoughts whether or not to shoot. But all at once I was overwhelmed by a strange feeling and I aimed at the heir to the throne. The car was taking the corner at a slower speed," Princip later declared in court. It was 11.30 a.m. He had fired two bullets from his Browning: one for the Archduke, one for the hated Potiorek, but perhaps he had closed his eyes and hit the Duchess instead, as he later confessed. She died on the spot. Her husband expired somewhat later.

Princip did not run away. He swallowed a suicide pill, but the cyanide in it had evaporated and it failed to work. The local Serbs did not hide their delight over the assassination, while the Croats, who were favoured by the Austrian authorities, and the Islamic inhabitants loyal to the monarchy expressed solidarity with the Habsburgs and called for severe punishment for the assassins. "Down with the Serbs, down with murderers," they shouted. Alongside the Austrian Germans, the Croats, whom Vienna treated preferentially, were the most outraged. The reaction of the Hungarians, who did not like the Archduke, was satisfaction. Franz Ferdinand had held the Hungarian upper classes in contempt, calling them an "oligarchic clique," and was against making Hungarian the second official language in the military. Not surprisingly Hungarian officers shouted, "That pig is dead." There were even rumours that the movers behind the plot were Hungarian officers led by Prime Minister Tisza. The Polish upper classes of Galicia were not too worried by the death of the Archduke, who did not like Poles, particularly Polish aristocrats. Some Czechs were shocked, chiefly on account of Duchess Sophie, who was a Czech, but others could not conceal their satisfaction while still others couldn't care less. It was not their problem, just as it wasn't for numerous Czech Soldier Švejks. "So they've done it to us," said the cleaning lady to Mr. Švejk. "They've killed our Ferdinand." "Which Ferdinand, Mrs. Mullerova?" asked Švejk as he continued to rub his knees, "I used to know two Ferdinands. One works for Pruša the chemist, and once drank a bottle of hair lotion by mistake, and the other's Ferdinand Kokoška, the dog-turd collector. Neither'd be much of a loss." That is how the Good Soldier put it in the opening scene of Hašek's novel.

It certainly wasn't the first attempt by Southern Slavs to assassinate an Austro-Hungarian official. Conspiracy and terrorism had been strong traditions among them since Ottoman times. Of course more plots were planned than accomplished, and more were foiled than succeeded. In 1910 there had been a Serbian plan to kill the Emperor but it was not carried out; and in 1912 some Croats attempted to murder the Ban of Croatia. There had been several plots to kill Franz Ferdinand: in 1902 in Italy, in 1906 in Slovenia, in 1910 at Ostrava in Moravia, and in 1913 in Vienna. Numerous conspiracies had been planned in Sarajevo against Potiorek. All unsuccessful. In 1912 a Bosnian Croat had intended to kill Leopold von Berchtold, the Minister of Foreign Affairs.

By the late 19th century assassination had become a way of conducting politics. Bombs were thrown at kings and premiers, guns aimed at presidents, ministers, and other state officials. Those who died included two presidents of the United States, the king of Italy, the tsar of Russia, the king of Serbia, and the consort of the Austrian emperor. Death was supposed to speed up history and help to achieve otherwise unattainable goals. Ever since the times of Mikhail Bakunin and Peter Kropotkin anarchists had been resorting to violence in the belief that the tyrant's death would disintegrate the state. Conspiracies were hatched to punish insolence and avenge the offended, to seize power, to chastise those the conspirators thought worthy of discipline. Assassination excited the young imagination, arousing fanatical fighters ready to die for the cause, whose deaths served as a legacy for future generations.

Assassination attempts were facilitated by inefficient security systems. Monarchs and ministers often failed to appreciate the risk of assassination in the belief that hiding behind the backs of the military was demeaning to themselves and their country. That's what happened with the Archduke, who ignored warnings from counterintelligence and the police. In 1918 General Maximilian Ronge, head of the Austro-Hungarian military intelligence service, observed that he had never considered security as vital as during those manoeuvres, yet to his disappointment the Archduke turned down his suggestions – why or what made him do so was a mystery to Ronge. In June 1914 the secret police had hard evidence that there was trouble brewing and wanted to protect the heir to the throne. But they did not do much. They only ordered secondary school students not from Sarajevo to leave the city. In outcome there were only 112 local policemen and 6 detectives, none of them Serbo-Croat speakers, protecting the Archduke. One policeman for every 100 m of the route. In those days there were no armoured, fast-moving vehicles for VIPs. Franz Ferdinand was travelling in a Gräf und Stift cabriolet with a 28 HP engine, which made the assassin's task all the easier.

Who was Princip? He was born into a poor family, his father was a postman. Thanks to his ability and hard work he completed a secondary school education in Sarajevo and went up to study in Belgrade. He was short and frail, had a lean, pale yellow face, and one could hardly imagine how such a skinny and lowly individual could have resolved to perpetrate such an assassination, as the investigating magistrate wondered. Historians are still wondering, since he wasn't the ringleader and didn't stand out in the group. No doubt he and the other conspirators were deeply convinced they were doing the right thing. So who were they? What was their motive? They were a unit of an underground liberation movement operating on a broad territory and comprising young Southern Slavs, mostly Serbs, with some Croats and Slovenes. The borders between different units in the organisation were flexible, hence the difficulty in establishing who belonged to what, complicated by the fact that they left no written records. Their aim was the secession of the Slavic lands from Austria-Hungary and the creation of a South Slavic state. Apart from two sovereign states, Serbia and Montenegro, the lands inhabited by Southern Slavs were under Austrian rule (this included Dalmatia, Styria, and Carinthia); or (like Vojvodina and Croatia) belonged to Hungary. Then there was Bosnia and Herzegovina, long occupied and eventually annexed by Austria-Hungary in 1908. Serbs considered it a "still un-liberated" Serbian territory. The conspirators were highly critical of the Austro-Hungarian regime, which they saw as demoralising and promoting foreign officials and merchants at the expense of locals. They took this as a grave affront and an expression of the government's colonialist policy. They were disparaging about the Western Latinate tradition. "Syphilis and clericalism is the infelicitous legacy of the Middle Ages from which modern civilisation cannot break free," as Princip is reported to have said.

Members of Young Bosnia included school and university students, workers, young people in rebellion against staid parents. Most came from rural backgrounds. In 1913 only 50 individuals in Bosnia were university graduates, and a few hundred had completed secondary education. Bosnia had no university, and only 5 *Gymnasium* secondary schools. Some in the upper strata of Viennese and Budapest society thought even that was too much. Since Bosnian students were denied the right to associate, they went underground. The conspirators were supported ideologically and financially by the Serbian diaspora. Already on 3rd December 1913 a Serbian paper published in Chicago announced that the heir to the Austrian throne would be visiting Sarajevo in the spring, and urged Serbs to take up arms – knives, guns, bombs, dynamite, anything they had. "Death to the Habsburg dynasty!" it rallied them. Politically and militarily they were aided by Lieutenant Colonel Dragutin Dimitrijević, head of the Serbian intelligence service in Belgrade, who used several pseudonyms, mainly Apis. "War between Serbia and Austria is inevitable," he wrote in a newspaper he controlled. "The war will be determined by our commitment to our tradition and culture, and rooted in the destiny of our race, which cannot allow itself to be assimilated. The war must bring freedom for Serbia, the Southern Slavs, and the people of the Balkans. Our entire race must stand up together to stop the invasion of enemies from the North." Not surprisingly, his staff, Serbian intelligence officers and members of an organisation called *Ujedinjenje ili Smrt* (Unity or Death), which had probably been operating since 1909 and was called "the Black Hand" by its opponents, trained the conspirators, armed them with 4 Belgian revolvers and 6 bombs, and helped them to cross the border between the sovereign Kingdom of Serbia and Austro-Hungarian Bosnia. Apis pursued his own policy with no consultation with either the king or the prime minister, who were both opposed to such risky moves. He and his political associates saw Serbia as the Yugoslav Piedmont – the spark to set alight war with Austria. Effectively, Princip and the other young plotters were just tools in their hands.

Apis was convinced that Russia would not leave Serbia in the lurch, and that Russia would not be left without the support of France. Hence he pursued a deliberate policy for the outbreak of a war which would lead to the emergence of a Great Serbia. In this sense his activities can hardly be regarded as anything but provocation. His close contacts with the Russian intelligence and secret services, which had a considerable influence in Belgrade, were intended to guarantee Russia's solidarity. Some historians believe that ultimately Apis was guided by the German intelligence service, which was carrying out Berlin's policy to trigger the outbreak of war and manoeuvre Vienna into military engagement. But this is only one of the six most frequently cited hypotheses on the links between the Sarajevan conspirators and the outside world. Another theory says that Princip's hand was steered by those Viennese politicians who did not want to see Franz Ferdinand on the throne, which is why they deliberately chose the day, 28th June, to provoke the Serbs, and and were deliberately negligent about having the route properly secured.

The conspirators were not cold-blooded implementers of someone else's orders; neither were they hired killers, but romantics, deeply convinced that violence could and should be used to achieve superior aims. They did not calmly reckon up the odds. Like the Russian anarchists, they said killing tyrants was worthwhile to liberate the people and make them happy. They belonged to a generation of fanatics ready to set the world on fire to get what they wanted. In their private lives they practised the revolutionary code of asceticism. Some were teetotallers and abstinent in matters of love, treating a declaration of love for a woman as a sign of weakness and a slur on female dignity. After the assassination they claimed they did not regret it. On being sentenced, Čabrinović wrote that if the heir to the throne had not come to Bosnia, he would have found and slain him in Vienna. He stressed that for Serbs the visit had been an overt provocation as Franz Ferdinand had come to observe manoeuvres held on Serbian soil, and against the Serbian people.

The Archduke and Duchess had a quiet funeral, with no military honours, and no pomp and circumstance. The Emperor's decision irritated the friends of the deceased, but the government in Vienna was reluctant to lavish special tributes to an individual who was unpopular at Court and had married a Czech countess. As she was not of the royal blood, their children were debarred from the succession to the throne and used her surname. Due to the morganatic marriage Sophie was looked down on, both in life and after death. Later the car in which the couple made their last journey, along with their blood-stained clothes, Sophie's hat and lace gown, and her husband's green-plumed hat and field-marshal's uniform, were put on display in Vienna's military museum as Habsburg relics. The Austrian postal service issued a memorial stamp for the third anniversary of the assassination.

In the aftermath the Austrian authorities dealt bloodily and brutally not only with the conspirators but also with the other South Slavic underground youth organisations, most of which were annihilated. The assassination provided an opportunity to subdue the Slavic territories of Austria-Hungary. The trial of the conspirators and their accomplices lasted from 12th to 23rd October 1914. 25 persons were charged. On 29th October the Sarajevo court delivered the verdict. On 3rd February 1915 three of the arrested were executed. They did not include the assassin himself, whose age on arrest was 19 years and 11 months, one month of the age of majority, which prolonged his life. He was sentenced to 20 years in prison and sent to the infamous Terezin gaol near Prague, fit only for rats, as inmates used to say. Princip and the other incarcerated conspirators were maltreated. On the 28th of every month they got no food, and each year on 28th June were locked up in an unlit dungeon. Princip died on 28th April 1918 of tuberculosis, which found excellent conditions for rapid development. Only five of the accused in the Sarajevo trial survived to the end of the War and the emergence of the new Kingdom of Serbs, Croats, and Slovenes. The rest died of hunger or disease. In 1920 the assassin's body was exhumed, transported to Sarajevo, and buried there. After 1918 many of the schools, streets, and institutions in Serbia and Bosnia-Herzegovina were named after Gavrilo Princip, as was the bridge over the Miljacka in Sarajevo. In Communist times a plaque with an inscription in Serbian was put up on the spot from which he had fired the fateful shots. It read, "From this place on 28th June 1914 Gavrilo Princip gave expression to the national defiance against tyranny, and to the many centuries of our nations' struggle for freedom."

From the outbreak of the War to the end of 1914 the Austro-Hungarian authorities arrested over 5,000 Serbs in Bosnia. Some of them were charged with crimes against the dynasty. 150 were hanged, 37 of them in Trebinje, where the biggest demonstrations against the heir to the throne had taken place in 1906. The arrested were put into three concentration camps, set to hard labour, and died off at a fast rate. Serbian associations and church schools were closed down. Some Serbian property was confiscated. Food rationing was introduced in Bosnia already in the autumn of 1914. Not surprisingly for Serbians, the Austro-Hungarian regime left a bitter memory of foreign occupation. On 3rd November 1915 a trial of 156 Bosnians, mainly from the educated classes, started in Banja Luka. They were accused of favouring terrorism. The verdict was delivered on 22nd April 1916. 16 were sentenced to death, but the Emperor Karl exercised his right to clemency and commuted the death sentences to life imprisonment. Over 80 were jailed.

Apis did not live to see the end of the War. The wide-ranging political influence enjoyed by the Serbian special services was becoming a nuisance for the king and court, and the government of Serbia. He was never forgiven for helping the conspirators without Belgrade's consent and for the consequences of Sarajevo. He was suspected of plotting against the king. In the summer of 1915 he was dismissed from his post as head of the intelligence service and in December 1916 he and his friends were arrested. He was court-martialled in Salonica, where the Serbian civilian and military authorities in exile had their headquarters, sentenced to death by firing squad, and executed on 26th June 1917.

The Sarajevo assassination was no harbinger of war. For decades there had been no dearth of assassinations in Europe, but none of them had turned into a *casus belli*. It was thought that this time it would be the same, the excitement would fade and things would return to normal. The European ruling classes carried on in a sense of security they felt they had a right to. However, this time history was about to take a different course.

2. The last hours of peace

The Great War started on 28th July 1914, from what looked like a local, peripheral quarrel between Serbia and Austria-Hungary, between the Karađorđević dynasty and the Habsburgs, soon – within the first few days of August – to turn into a war between the Dual Alliance and the Triple Entente, and thence, within the next few weeks of 1914, to bloat up into a world war. The outbreak of war was preceded by a spate of mobilisation, full or partial, carried out by the belligerents. Mobilisation was a transition phase between peace and war. The men subject to mobilisation, draftees or called up from leave, as well as volunteers, had draft cards delivered to their homes, summoning them to report to specified units. They packed, said their prayers and good-byes to their families and went off to their military draft centres. Within a few days army barracks filled up with thousands of young men. But while some were in a hurry to be conscripted, others were rushing to the altar. Churches of all denominations were crammed with newlyweds and their families. Only on the Saturday and Sunday, 31st July and 1st August in Berlin alone there were two thousand weekend weddings. It was the same in other countries and cities of Europe setting off to war, as conscripts and volunteers alike hastened to tie the knot.

Once in barracks, the young men were given medical tests and had their hair cut. Next uniforms, equipment, and weapons were issued to them. Having received their uniforms and arms, they were allocated to a company, companies were allocated to a battalion, battalions to regiments, and regiments to divisions. Infantry divisions had ancillary units – supply units, sanitary units, kitchens, cavalry units, cyclist units, and postal services – attached to them. Divisions were loaded up onto festively decorated rail carriages and transported to rally points where they joined a corps, which joined up with other corps to form an army. It all proceeded according to a detailed schedule. The French and German armies mobilised and concentrated their units in the most efficient manner. In France only 1.5% of the men called up did not report for service, and in Germany the figure was even less – 0.9%, demonstrating the efficiency of the state authorities and perhaps also the general acceptance of war by the men who were mobilised. Even in Russia mobilisation went pretty smoothly, despite the vast distances and meagre communications network. Only 4% of the Russian conscripts never reached barracks. Mobilising cavalry divisions was a problem though, as transportation for just one of them required 40 trains – as many as for an infantry division five times the size. Trains were used to transport troops to the front. A German infantry corps consisting of two divisions needed 170 carriages to transport the officers, 965 carriages for the men, and 1915 carriages for its artillery and engineers – a total of over 3,000 carriages and 80 trains, and on top of that an analogous number of trains for equipment and victuals. Mobilisation plans had to be precise. That is why the German and French plans entailed data even on the number of axles that had to roll over a given bridge in a given time.

The men setting off for barracks were given a hearty send-off with church bells ringing, and military bands welcomed them on arrival with boisterous tattoos. Enthusiastic crowds cheered them at railway stations and on the streets of festively decorated cities with houses draped with the national colours and portraits of the head of state. Words of welcome, gestures of admiration, and community singing of national anthems and patriotic folk songs were showered on them in town and country alike. Hats flew up in the air and handkerchiefs waved to greet them, and girls put flowers – roses, lilies, cornflowers and evening stock – into their gun barrels. The enthusiasm must have had its effect on the soldiers, even those who were leaving for the front with a heavy heart and anguish on their faces, and those who just a day or two before had taken part in a sad farewell ceremony at their local church or synagogue, saying good-bye to their community, crying with their wives, mothers, and sisters. "Soldiers were sent off to the sound of the balalaika, conscripts danced on crowded platforms beating up clouds of dust, and their relatives bade them farewell, making the sign of the cross and weeping," a Russian shopkeeper recalled. The sunny weather must certainly have contributed to the air of optimism, good humour, and even better expectations. It was all so impressive: never since the Napoleonic Wars had the streets been so full of soldiers and civilians.

Festooned with decorations like a honeymoon couple's car, the train carriages enhanced the soldiers' sense of optimism. Slogans encouraging them to battle and mocking the enemy were plastered on the walls. German posters read "Every bayonet thrust means one Frenchman less" and "To Paris for breakfast." The pleasant atmosphere was dubbed "the August experience" and enhanced by uplifting and morale-boosting songs like "It's a long way to Tipperary," which eventually became one of the most popular wartime tunes. Over the next days and weeks censored papers and picture-houses conveyed a propaganda image to the public of happy, smiling soldiers full of romantic and patriotic excitement – an idealised, very one-sided picture. Many photographs from this period preserved in private collections and made public later show sad, anxious, or even terrified soldiers. Those leaving heavy-hearted and full of foreboding did not get into the propaganda pictures of a happy army going to war. Another group the propaganda failed to display were those who just a day or two before had taken part in anti-war demonstrations.

The positive attitude to the war was patent in the work of the writers who had signed up or been conscripted. They wrote that war meant the affirmation of vitality, energy, the power of the spirit, virtue, that it "had made the world beautiful." War was an act of creation, "the rising shape of a new era," "a marvellous wonder," "a sacred moment," "a war of purification," the start of "a new life." War was "the only life..., a ripple of excitement, and nothing in the whole world could match it." The "time of triumph had come for the most splendid values." It was the "hour of youth." People prayed earnestly to be able to contribute to the war effort, to swap civvies for a glorious army uniform.

The biggest support for the war was indeed observed among the writers and artists, intellectuals, academics, and students, as the armies of all the belligerent countries reported. Opinion polls carried out among the students showed that the overwhelming majority of them were happy to go to war. Civil servants, administrative staff, teachers, and representatives of the legal professions who were called up showed a good deal of understanding and approved of the war. In the French department of Charente an opinion poll was conducted among teachers. They were asked for their attitude on mobilisation and the war. Initially, out of 330 respondents 188 did not approve of mobilisation, 66 had reservations, and 76 responded with patriotic enthusiasm. But after a few days, once they were in their army units, they succumbed to the "charm of war" and the pro-war climate. As many as 131 of the 288 respondents said that they were going to war with patriotic enthusiasm, 103 out of a sense of duty, and only 54 reluctantly. Most of the students of the Sorbonne taking part in the opinion poll approved of the war and agreed that "we experience our greatest power in camp life and under shellfire."

Students and many others treated the war as an exciting adventure or as sports rivalry. War carried a promise of something new, it meant turning over a new leaf, it offered new prospects. "Young men marched triumphantly; now they were being cheered, though before they had been just ordinary people no-one respected or took any notice of," wrote Stefan Zweig. Soldiers recalled how proud they were to put on a uniform, in which they felt useful and appreciated, after all, they were being cheered by the crowds. Never before, in civvy street, had anyone hailed them like that. They knew that such a lot – the future of their countries and nations – depended on them, the young generation. "This is a time when it's worthwhile being a soldier! Cannon fire rules the world's destiny. Civilians seem useless, and women are an obstacle, a nuisance," wrote the Polish Princess Maria Lubomirska on 31st July 1914. But what was the reaction of the countryfolk, who made up the majority in every army except for the British Expeditionary Force? As a rule they were unsympathetic or hostile. But the enthusiasm of the crowds changed their attitude. Nonetheless a substantial number of them were dissatisfied with their lot. You could hardly expect people who were their families' sole breadwinners to be pleased. Their wives and mothers applied to the local authorities, or directly to the military, for their discharge, saying that without them farming would grind to a halt. Usually their petitions came to nothing. So they consoled themselves that the war would not last long. "Home for Christmas," they wrote.

Even in multinational states like Austria-Hungary, Russia, or Germany, mobilisation went fairly smoothly. Conscientious objectors on ethno-national or religious grounds were few and far between. This was an opinion confirmed by the inhabitants of Polish territories. Polish men serving in the German army felt solidarity with the Germans; Poles serving in the Austro-Hungarian army felt solidarity with that army; and Poles in the Russian army felt solidarity with the army of Russia. "Men went to war gladly and prayers were said in the churches for an Austrian victory," said the peasant leader Wincenty Witos, future prime minister of a free Poland. Lithuanians from the Russian part of Lithuania and from the part under Prussia behaved in the same way; and so did Ukrainians under Austro-Hungarian or Russian rule. They went with their own. Everyone felt the same happiness, and the sense of discipline and solidarity with "one's own" king and country turned out to be strong. Moreover, Polish, Lithuanian, or Ukrainian soldiers under the colours of "their own" armies did not have much of a choice, since they did not have a national army of their own in which they could serve, and they saw no reason to commit themselves to one of the powers that had partitioned their country against another.

The fighting spirit displayed by the crowds, soldiers, and artists passed on to the politicians, including those who were apprehensive of, or against war. Nearly all parliamentarians, including those in the British dominions, acquiesced and acknowledged the war as a sacred act for the defence of their country, and readily voted in favour of their respective war budgets and wartime legislation granting governments special powers. Only a few individuals like Karl Liebknecht in the Reichstag had the courage to vote against. "Peace on the home front" and "a holy alliance" reigned supreme. No longer were there any left-wing and right-wing Frenchmen; neither were the Germans and the British divided nations. Even in Russia deputies to the Duma overwhelmingly acknowledged the war as a war of defence for their country, voted in a war budget, and reacted to the Tsar's address with an ovation. Very few indeed, like the Bolsheviks, did not concur. But it was in Russia in fact that the first cracks started to appear within a few weeks, and opposition parties came out strongly against the tsarist regime. In the other countries, too, dissenting politicians emerged after some time. By the end of the war support for them had risen considerably, but nowhere except in Russia did they dominate the political stage.

The countries which mobilised and subsequently entered the war imposed a series of typical measures, only to be expected in such circumstances, with the aim of making things easy for their own, and difficult for the enemy. They closed their borders and introduced censorship: newspapers could no longer publish war correspondence from the frontline unless they obtained permission from the military authorities. Munitions and fuel stores were safeguarded, especially against spies and sabotage; and persons the authorities suspected of disloyalty were arrested. But the scale of these detentions was much smaller than what had been envisaged before the war. In the general enthusiasm for the war in France and Germany the plan to arrest those blacklisted as "enemies of their country" was withdrawn. It turned out that nearly all the pre-war suspects marched off to war without demur, some had even volunteered. We can only guess what Jean Jaurès, the French anti-war socialist, would have done if he had lived to the patriotic time of trial – he was assassinated just a few days before the outbreak of the war by a pro-war extremist.

In August 1914 the military of the belligerent countries took control of the railway lines and inland waterways, and were granted the right to shoot at anyone who defied them. Sentry-posts were set up along the roads, manned by soldiers to control travellers' documents.

In border zones the police took hostages, and civilians were evacuated to prevent sabotage. Austria put a prohibition on church bell-ringing and cattle-grazing on mountain slopes within a 30-km frontier zone along her southern and eastern borders, and ordered all windows shut after dusk. The belligerents made it difficult for enemy states to communicate with each other and with their special agents in neutral countries. Just a few hours after declaring war the British cut the Transatlantic submarine cables the Germans had been using, forcing the latter to switch to the radio broadcasting station at Bremen and the American lines.

3. Could war have been avoided?

During the War and in its aftermath the opinion circulated that it could have all taken a different course, that war could have been avoided. That one should not succumb to the influence of a deterministic view of history being inexorable, and say that since war did break out therefore it was inevitable. So was it possible to preserve peace? Could war have been averted? The chances to preserve peace were based on a couple of premises which soon turned out to be illusive. First there was the belief that the monarchs of Europe were united by bonds of solidarity and an aversion to war. The monarchs were indeed interrelated by consanguinity and kinship, making up one big family. Kaiser Wilhelm II and the Tsarina were cousins through their mothers, so as were Nicholas II of Russia and George V of the United Kingdom, what's more, they were each other's spitting image. Edward VII was uncle both to the German Kaiser and to the Tsarina, while the latter was the sister of Irene of Prussia, who in turn was the Kaiser's cousin and sister-in-law. Nearly all the monarchs reigning in large and small states alike were related to or descended from the Saxe-Coburg-Gotha dynasty, which Bismarck had maliciously called "the breeding stallions of Europe." In letters they addressed each other as "Dear Cousin," "Dear Brother," and "Friend." One of the signs of solidarity between the "Cousins," the emperors, kings, and princes, was their mass attendance at the funeral of Queen Victoria in 1901, who was the aunt of some of them, and the grandmother of others. In 1914 seven of her descendants were on the thrones of Europe. 1910 witnessed a parade of monarchs, the most spectacular public show of monarchical solidarity, at the funeral of Edward VII, "the uncle of kings." Relations between the monarchs were based not only on their family ties, but also of their shared traditions, similar values, and court etiquette. But even families occasionally go through tiffs, feuds, and wars, and so even in the family of monarchs tension erupted time and again, despite the veneer of fraternity. There was no guarantee that the monarchs' Europe, grounded on a mutual legacy, would not allow a war to break out. Even had the monarchs all come out in opposition to war, there would still have been no certainty that they could have prevented it. None of the reigning monarchs had absolute power; none could impose his will; they all had to listen to their advisers, ministers, generals, and – in the age of the European constitutions – also the voice of their people, the nation, even though the monarchs were the symbols of their states, emblems of sovereign statehood, and their portraits were displayed in public buildings. So they could not have stopped a prospective clash of arms even if they had wanted to. But did they want to? That is a question which is hard to answer unequivocally.

Once war had broken out, the monarchs were compelled to make a dramatic choice between solidarity to their royal relatives and to their own nation. Or, in fact, they were deprived of the choice, since they could not come out in opposition to their subjects. Under pressure from his British subjects George V changed his German surname to the English name Windsor, which is still the surname of Britain's monarch today. He also deprived the German Emperor of the honorary title of commander of the British army, and struck German and Austro-Hungarian officers off the British register of the officers' corps, and removed several knights of the Garter belonging to enemy countries from the Order. His monarchical cousins in belligerent countries did likewise.

The second hope for the prevention of war was confidence in the diplomats, who had always found ways to deflate even the most dangerous tension without resorting to war. They had always striven to reconcile antagonists, exercising the difficult art of effecting a compromise. Usually they would call a conference with the "concert of powers," and that would be enough. In 1913 the Chancellor of Germany warned that in the next war, which would erupt on trivial grounds, not only the Hohenzollern crown would be at stake, but also the future of Germany, and he cautioned that trying to set off a war was not only imprudent but also criminal. Nevertheless in 1914 neither monarchical nor diplomatic solidarity proved sufficient to stop the War.

The third source of confidence in the impossibility of war was the position of the socialist parties congregated in the Second International. Their view was that armed conflict was beneficial for international capital, imperialist states, and nationalistic governments, but not for the proletariat, which had to strive under a socialist leadership to maintain peace. The socialists threatened to bring the workers out on a general strike if war broke out, and they thought this would be enough to restrain warmongers. This, too, turned out to be illusory: the anti-war demonstrations organised on the eve of the outbreak of the War did not stop it. Anti-war feelings were particularly high in Britain. The prospect of dying for "stinking Serbians" and "drunken Russians" (as the British press wrote) was not encouraging. But when war did break out, the pacifist socialists, including the British ones, vanished from the streets in solidarity with their own nation. National solidarity won over class solidarity, which was a shock for many.

Fourthly, the military alliances, the Triple Entente and the Triple Alliance, were intended to act as an insurance policy against the outbreak of war. Yet they failed. Neither were the political and economic relations between countries in the opposing blocks any use. These ties, many of them reinforced by treaties, could have given rise to hopes for peace. But the yearning for war proved stronger than the desire for peace.

Fifthly, hopes for peace were pinned on the pacifists. Their works commanded a substantial readership. Norman Angell's best-selling pamphlet, *The Great Illusion,* argued that European integration had reached a point when a war which would dismantle the bonds would be traumatic for all. Another widely read work was a six-volume elaboration by Jan Bloch, a Polish Jew and one of the wealthiest industrialists in the Kingdom of Poland under Russian rule. It was published in Paris in 1898 and translated into several languages (English version: *Is War Now Impossible?*). Karl Kraus was yet another author on the impossibility of war; his work was popular in Austria and Germany. Yet neither he nor Angell, nor any other pacifist devised a practicable scheme to prevent war, or established an effective pacifist movement. Pacifists tended to be socially isolated and politically insignificant. The German Kaiser contemptuously called them eunuchs. Soon it turned out that pacifists were most outspoken on peace in times of peace.

A sixth chance to save peace was envisaged in the pressure exerted by international business, which had good reason for apprehension, since war would mean the breakdown of their hitherto commercial and financial connections, and instead preferred to negotiate deals for the allocation of economic spheres of interest. Just two weeks before Sarajevo British and German businessmen reached an agreement for the building of a railway from Baghdad to Basra. Two British members were to join the board of the German-controlled Baghdad Railway Company. In February 1914 a similar settlement had been arranged between French and German entrepreneurs. However, the influence of big business proved too weak to avert war. At any rate the arms and munitions industry was generally in favour of war.

The political tension, growing year by year especially between the great powers over dominance in Europe, the recovery of lost territories or the acquisition of new lands, influence in the Balkans and the Near East, for the re-allocation of colonial land and for predominance on the seas and oceans led to an unprecedented arms race. But did armaments inevitably spell war for Europe? They may have done, but it is hard to tell with certainty, though of course there are such opinions. They were definitely conducted on an unparalleled scale. All European countries, big and small, not excluding Montenegro, were increasing their defence budgets, which showed that the idea of war was popular in the parliaments, too, and a means of assimilating public opinion with the real prospect of war. Spiralling war budgets indicated that most parliamentarians accepted government plans to escalate expenditure on arms. Only in 1909–1914 arms budgets rose by an average of 50% in the countries of Europe. In 1913 they accounted for 3.5% of GDP, and 5% by 1913. Armaments led to a substantial rise in the burden of taxes imposed on society – serious enough in Germany for fears of state insolvency to emerge. The only chance envisaged to halt such a gruesome prospect was to sidestep it – start a war during which the state's liabilities to its own citizens could be put on ice. Especially naval budgets rose at an astronomical rate. Scores, and sometimes hundreds of associations and organisations supported naval shipbuilding, effectively making up a strong pressure group.

The country most interested in a colonial reshuffle was Germany, while Austria-Hungary had no such ambitions. The Germans considered they had got less than their fair share of the colonial cake. They did have about 3 million square kilometres of colonies on two continents, inhabited by 13 million people, which officially they called "protected areas," but it was not much either as prestige or economic assets. Already in 1900 in a book on the great powers (*Die großen Mächte: ein Rückblick auf unser Jahrhundert*) Max Lenz had forecast that war was unavoidable for the redistribution of the declining British Empire, which would be replaced by a German empire. He argued that colonies would change hands in line with the principle of Social Darwinism: weaker proprietors like the French, Portuguese, and British, would drop out, and more powerful masters like the Germans would come in. In 1913 Heinrich Claß, president of the Pan-German League, predicted that Germany's future would be secure once it gained predominance not only in Europe but also wherever it could be victorious overseas. He saw territorial enlargement as the basis of Germany's national existence. This idea may be read as containing the seeds of war, but an idea is not the same as its practical hatching.

The Germans were not happy with their position in Europe, either. Holding the central place on the continent, they were obsessed with the notion of being wedged between the devil and the deep blue sea – Russia and France. In reality they did not have very much to fear from these neighbours, at least not for the time being. It was more of an artificially prompted psychosis rather than a real threat, but it helped to enhance pro-war attitudes.

The arms race was goaded on by imperialist propaganda and war rhetoric. Nationalism gradually turning into chauvinism was another factor preparing nations for the challenges looming ahead. Alongside love of one's own country and nation and national pride, it also contained another ingredient – contempt of and hostility to other nations, and a national arrogance which sanctioned the claim of a national right to rule other nations. Nationalists maintained that the road to national unity and solidarity led through war. War, they said, would be a catharsis cleansing the nation of its weak points and shortcomings. Italian nationalists stressed that war was the fastest and most heroic means to building up wealth and willpower. Viktor Adler, one of the leaders of the Austrian anti-war Social Democrats, observed on 29th July 1914 that for the nationalists war was like a means to salvation promising hope of a change for the better. But nationalism did not become the prevailing mode of thinking, and nationalist parties and associations did not dominate the political scene. Liberal and conservative parties on the one hand, and socialist parties on the other, continued to be the strongest political organisations, although the influence of nationalist ideas could be observed in all of them, not excluding the socialist groups. Liberals proved the most susceptible to the whispers of nationalism. The main strength of the nationalists were their organisations and associations: small numerically but vociferous, disciplined, hierarchically structures and amply financed. Such were the German associations – the *Deutscher Ostmarkenverein* (German Eastern Marches Society), the Army League (*Deutscher Wehrverein*), the Navy League (*Deutscher Flottenverein*), and the Pan-German League (*Alldeutscher Verband*); the British organisations – the National Social Purity Crusade, the

National Service League, the British Navy League, and the Imperial Maritime League; the French organisations – the *Ligue des patriotes* (League of Patriots) and *Action française* (French Action); the Russian Black Hundred (*Chornaya sotnya*); and the Italian Nationalist Association (*Associazione Nazionalista Italiana*). These organisations were capable of rallying public opinion to their cause, promoting war and the arms race, and impacting on governments, parliaments, and monarchs.

Nationalism fed on a corrupted version of Social Darwinism intended to raise awareness of a need for military confrontation for the sake of glory and national values. Social Darwinism was popular especially in England, disseminated by Benjamin Kidd, author of *Social Evolution* (first published 1893). Similar views were promoted by Harold F. Wyatt, one of the founders of the Imperial Maritime League, who wrote of war being a test "which God has given for the trial of peoples."

There was a cultural atmosphere conducive to war. The late 1890s had initiated a farewell to positivism and scientism and ushered in Neo-Romanticism. By the early 20th century millions had come to believe the artists, writers, and intellectuals that they were living non-descript, prosaic lives, full of consumerist boredom, with no greatness, loftiness, or spirituality about it. There was no point to such a bourgeois lifestyle, apparently. War was expected to bring purification, liberation, and demonstrate the nation's stamina, as Thomas Mann wrote. It was claimed that war brought nobility and taught the virtues of discipline and obedience. The humdrum life of drudgery could only be transformed by something that was lofty and invigorating, and that something was war. What mattered was the hero's active life of martial exploits. The Neo-Romantics and adherents of the Avant Garde perceived war as a manifestation of spiritual strength, vitality and creativity. War was a life-giving principle, an expression of the supreme culture, as Friedrich von Bernhardi wrote in 1911 in *Deutschland und der Nächste Krieg* (Germany and the Next War), a book which went through six editions in Germany in just two years. In 1912 the French painter Pierre Bonnard wrote that in the vortex of war it was not just the instincts that were rediscovered, but the virtues that were renewed. In 1891 the French writer Emile Zola observed that only warlike nations developed, and that a nation died as soon as it disarmed; according to him war was the school of discipline, dedication, and courage. Another group of artists enthusiastic about war were the Italian Futurists; Filippo Marinetti dubbed war "the world's only hygiene." In general the Avant Garde, in permanent rebellion and summoning others to throw off the straitjacket of morality, stand up in defiance against the old world and replace it with a new, better, and more noble reality – ought to have acknowledged that much of the blame for evoking the War was theirs.

The renowned historian David S. Landes has pointed out that many thought of war being rather like a picnic. The tragedy of the War was due to people's credulous vanity. They thought it would be a kind of social event – a kaleidoscope of elegant uniforms, magnificent courage, admiration from women, parades and a sense of felicity. The War broke out because there was not enough foresight. The diagnosis of the causes of the outbreak of the War put forward by ex-President Theodore Roosevelt were not very different: Europe had not engaged in fighting for a long time and decided to awaken its spirit of action. In the circumstances war became acceptable and even desirable.

The fashionable historians and philosophers of history produced more arguments in favour of war. In 1887 Heinrich von Trietschke wrote that the justifiability of war was founded directly on the awareness of its moral inevitability. Since history was in a permanent state of flux, therefore war was justified and had to be regarded as one of the orders sanctioned by God. People took to heart what he had to say, and also the words of the early 19th century conservative thinker Joseph de Maistre, who maintained that war was the normal condition of mankind. The intellectual preparation for war was attended by the ideas of Henri Bergson, who said that Europe needed spiritual revival by a strong clash of its component parts; and by the philosophy of Friedrich Nietzsche, popular throughout Europe. Nietzsche called for action and violence, and a struggle against sloth, bourgeois philistinism and middle-class hypocrisy, and his slogans attracted many followers. One of them, "war and courage have done more great things than charity," was printed on propaganda leaflets which soldiers of diverse armies found in their kit. Nietzsche summoned them to lead a life full of risk, to rise up in rebellion against liberalism and the established standards. Ideas directly or indirectly eulogising war appealed to millions, especially to the young, and of course they would be the ones marching off to war.

The fiction written at the time also exerted a certain influence on the psychological and emotional preparation for war, which tended to be portrayed in contemporary novels as an exciting adventure. Espionage and visions of the future were popular subjects. Novels were published in instalments in newspapers, on the Germans landing on the British coast, or on British forces arriving on German soil. The boys' books, magazines, full of the adventures and exploits of brave soldiers ready to die for their country, were another form of preparation for the war looming on the horizon.

Another factor contributing to the war preparations was the official policy on history the various states pursued, chiefly through the schools. School curricula put special emphasis on the principal battles the nation had fought, both to honour victories as well as to recall defeats in an effort to stir up a desire for revenge. Celebrations were held for the anniversaries of the nation's important wars, or of the birth and death of its heroes. For the French this meant Napoleon's victories, while Germans commemorated the Battle of Leipzig, in which Napoleon had sustained defeat. In 1913 the German authorities staged a grandiose event held at the Leipzig Memorial, a celebration of national unity coinciding with the festivities for the twenty-fifth anniversary of the accession of Kaiser Wilhelm II. The Russians commemorated Napoleon's retreat from Moscow, while in July 1914 the French honoured the seventh centenary of the Battle of Bouvines.

Schools held patriotic events and propagated negative stereotypes of enemy nations, particularly in school magazines. Pupils were taken on outward-bound courses organised in a military manner, and mustered for military and civil defence training during P.E. classes. All of these activities exerted a fundamental impact on the mental preparations for the conflict. Textbooks instructed pupils on patriotism and the sense of making a sacrifice for one's country. War was not likely, but it could not be ruled out, as one French schoolbook informed pupils in 1912. That was why France was armed and ready to fight at any time, it told them. By defending France they would be defending the land of their birth, the richest and most beautiful country in the world. Another way of mobilising and educating students and pupils were mass patriotic events, such as Britain's Navy Day or the youth festivals held in Germany.

A factor which helped to intensify the atmosphere leading to war was the series of crises starting with the annexation of Bosnia and Herzegovina. Next came the Agadir or Second Moroccan Crisis (the *Panthersprung*) in 1911, followed in Germany by a wave of anti-French pro-war hysteria. The mob called the Kaiser a coward, clamouring for him to abdicate and for the Chancellor to resign. There was also the Pig (or Customs) War between Belgrade and Vienna, 1906–1909; the war between Italy and Turkey over Libya, 1911–1912; and finally the Balkan Wars, which upset the existing balance of powers. The fact that every year witnessed a new crisis heightened the tense atmosphere and encouraged hot-headed behaviour. Prejudices proliferated, along with mutual resentment, distrust, and nationalistic phobias. The permanent state of tension turned into a veritable tightrope-dance over a precipice. Each new crisis added to the already accumulated charge until a critical mass was reached. A large-scale armed conflict could have erupted at any moment. A spell of cold war set in. Successive crises only spiralled the scale of armaments even more, "rehearsed" the militarisation of national economies, and induced the foundation of more "defence unions." Anxious citizens asked questions about the coming war. Daisy Hochberg, Princess von Pless wrote in her memoirs for 1911 that she was continually thinking about the coming war and whether there was a chance of avoiding it. In her recollections the Polish aristocrat, Princess Matylda Sapieha, noted that by the beginning of the winter of 1912 to 1913 there was more and more talk of a war breaking out between Austria-Hungary and Russia. In Poland there was an undercurrent of turmoil. The atmosphere in independence groups was near to boiling point. Tension was mounting so much that in Galicia in 1912–1913 more and more volunteers were joining Polish and Ukrainian paramilitary riflemen's organisations. When the immediate danger had passed the rate of recruitment fell.

However, none of these factors need have precipitated a global conflict. Successive crises could have continued to come and go, resolved by well-tested procedures; the world could have continued to arm; armies to train and parade; and war plans to sleep in closely guarded safes. Life could have continued in peace; although under constant tension from crisis to crisis it would have certainly not have been comfortable. For how many years can you sit on a powder keg? Not long. So it comes as no surprise that more and more often people realised that despite the risks war brought and the uncertainty of its final outcome the attempt should be made. According to Joseph Conrad, war was inevitable and could not be halted, as the consequence of the motives that determine the conduct of nations and peoples, like a tempest which Nature itself must discharge. So if war was inevitable, there was no sense in putting it off. This argument was like the surgeon's line of thinking: if an operation is the only chance to save a patient's life, the sooner it is done, the better the odds for its success and the patient's survival. That's how the British journalist Sir Sidney Low put it on the eve of the War's outbreak: a justified and necessary war was no more brutal than a surgical operation. It was better to cause the patient pain and get blood on one's fingers than to let the disease spread far enough to be a threat to oneself and the world at large. After all, war was just another way of pursuing policy. Something that might be called the obligation of war had emerged. All that had to be done was to choose a date. The vicious assassination in Sarajevo on 28th June 1914 seemed to meet all the expectations and triggered a chain reaction.

II. Land Warfare

1. Manoeuvre warfare

The 1914–1918 war was conducted primarily on the land, but there was also war on the oceans and seas, as well as airborne warfare. However the crucial form of warfare which determined the final outcome was the action undertaken by land forces. Before August 1914 the generals had imagined that they would be able to achieve the aims the politicians set them by manoeuvre warfare. This was the type of war they had been preparing for, studying its potential variants and checking its diverse scenarios for years. Its success would be determined by the rapid movement of troops and the chief part in combat was to be played by the infantry. The first weeks of the war confirmed these expectations as well as the role ascribed to cavalry, which was useful in reconnaissance and for carrying out raids on communication lines, and efficient in combat as a "mounted infantry." On the Eastern front there were a few heroic cavalry charges at enemy forces. However, in the autumn of 1914 manoeuvre warfare petered out on the Western front, turning into trench warfare. On the Eastern and Balkan front it took a mixed form in view of the vast distances and scattered distribution of forces. At times it was more reminiscent of manoeuvre warfare; at other times it resembled trench warfare. On the Alpine front it was trench warfare from the very start. The military action conducted in the deserts of the Near East, Mesopotamia, Egypt, and Palestine had some of the features of manoeuvre warfare, and some of trench warfare, carried out in extreme desert conditions with limited access to water and communication lines. A very different type of combat was conducted in winter conditions with snow blizzards and temperatures well below freezing point. Yet another kind of warfare involved landing operations, often of a combined nature from the land and sea, and sometimes with the use of aircraft. In 1914 the generals had not anticipated the use of alternative models of warfare other than manoeuvre warfare. The emergence of several basic types of warfare as the war progressed was due to the dynamics the course of action took, and for many it was a surprise. If the war had finished after a few weeks, or even after a few months, there would have never been a division into the different types of warfare which developed after some time.

Towards the end of the War in the autumn of 1918 the type of warfare conducted on the Western front changed when the front was breached in several places, and returned to manoeuvre warfare. This happened because the Allies had gained decisive superiority over the German forces in terms of resources and personnel. At this time fast-moving units such as motorised troops, motorcyclist and cyclist units demonstrated their advantages. Just as it had begun with manoeuvre warfare, so too the First World War came to an end with the manoeuvre method.

2. Trench warfare

Trench warfare has become the symbol of the First World War. But the soldiers engaged in it had to learn its rules as they went along, or in fact as they stood or squatted, since the theoreticians of the art of war and the chiefs of staff had not expected that there would be a need to abandon manoeuvre war for war in the trenches, which was little known at the time. In 1907 a British officer had heralded that in practice every army would turn into a garrison in a very extended fortress, but his was an isolated opinion. The pacifists, too, had been warning that the forthcoming war would be like a permanent clinch, exhausting but hard to resolve. But the military commanders and politicians treated their opinions as pacifistic propaganda. The Polish financier, industrialist and pacifist Jan Bloch was one of those who foresaw the coming of trench war.

In trench war technology gained the upper hand over the art of war, and the word "battle" acquired a new meaning. The British historian Basil Liddell Hart wrote that the period from 1915 to 1917 did not deserve much attention as regards strategy, since strategy became subservient to tactics, and tactics were lame. In trench war the infantry, and above all the artillery and engineers rose in importance, while the role of the cavalry diminished, though it was still useful for reconnaissance and cover operations. If it took part in combat, its operations were like those of the infantry. Horses were used as a means of transport, not for battle.

How did soldiers take trench war? They could hardly have been expected to like it. They did not care for the role of trench rats fighting off real rats – often their chief enemy. They bolstered morale with jokes and irony. In the trains taking them to the front they could read that if the weather was bad, the war would be conducted indoors. The generals did not take to trench war, either. Lord Kitchener, the British Secretary of State for War, did not consider it proper warfare, but was at a loss what to do. Another general accused the Germans of behaving like frightened moles, refusing to fight like men. The military liked action and hated inaction. They wanted warfare conducted by soldiers, not by technology and an anonymous crowd. One of the soldiers wrote from the trenches that they had a dehumanising effect, turning people at best into efficient machines mindlessly carrying out orders.

Trench warfare originated in circumstances that enforced it. In October 1914 the Germans attacking on the Western front stopped to rest, collect their thoughts, rally their reserves and top up on ammunitions before striking again. To avoid enemy fire and sallies both the Germans and the Allies started entrenching, which they treated as a temporary measure. Officially trenches were regarded as a way to spend winter in combat conditions and their aim was to save lives.

In the early spring of 1915, after wintering in the trenches, the troops left their dugouts to face the enemy but sustained heavy losses and ran back the trenches for shelter. After a while they tried again, with the same result. Over the next months and years both sides tried again and again, but nothing much changed. There was stalemate on the front. Not surprisingly, the title of Remarque's famous novel, *All Quiet on the Western Front*, comes from German staff reports. Beating the enemy entrenched in their defence line turned out to be impossible. In 1914 Field Marshal Sir John French, Commander-in-Chief of the British Expeditionary Force, wrote to a friend in London that the war was nothing like what they had been used to, and that battle meant one side carrying out a siege, and the other defending a besieged fortress, only on a gigantic scale. Both sides would agree with the opinion of Erich von Falkenhayn, Chief of the General Staff of the German Army as of the autumn of 1914, who observed that the first rule of trench warfare was not to lose even an inch of ground, and if that happened, to recover it immediately in a counter-attack, even at a cost of fighting to the last man. The trench war went on and on, and the trenches became the main theatre of war and their environs the killing-fields, for first of all the front usually took the form of a straight line, which ruled out attacks from the flank. Secondly, for years neither side managed to gain material superiority or enough manpower to break the deadlock. Thirdly, thanks to the dense network of roads and railway lines the side under attack could obtain reinforcements, supplies, and ammunition fairly quickly. As a result for nearly four years neither side won very much but both sustained huge losses.

In these circumstances the only thing the armies in the West could do was to work assiduously to reinforce their defence lines over a stretch of about 800 km, which was to make for more effective defence and give them better conditions to make a surprise attack. Already in the spring of 1915 work started on the digging of new trenches parallel to the existing ones. Sometimes enemy trenches were only 100–150 m away from each other. Trenches were dug in the war in the Near East as well. On the hilly terrain of Gallipoli the distance between the Australian and Turkish trenches could be as small as 20 m. Soldiers would post their opinions of each other up on boards, and these could be ironic or humorous, but not necessarily hostile. There were instances of soldiers from enemy forces meeting for a drink, and on the Western front there were even football matches played on no-man's land by ad-hoc teams spontaneously made up from opposing trenches. At such times there were numerous friendly gestures between soldiers from mutually hostile armies, which seriously worried their commanding officers. In the first months of the war there was even an informal, unwritten rule not to fire from a hiding-place, during mealtimes, when the men on guard duty changed, or during patrols along the barbed-wire lines. It was not fraternisation, the men said, but self-preservation, in accordance with the principle of "live and let live."

This climate could well have prompted the idea to celebrate Christmas together. The first fraternal gestures of this kind were met with diffidence by both sides, suspicious that they concealed a ruse, a Christmas prelude to an unexpected attack. But it turned out this was no trick. Soldiers exchanged Christmas greetings with no hostile feelings, celebrating together and forgiving each other. Such behaviour was an expression of religious feelings, the desire to live in peace, the need to feel accepted in the midst of a brutal war, and a sign of homesickness. The Christmas Eve truce applied to about 2/3 of the French and German troops, and 4/5 of the British and German troops. In 2005 Christian Carion made a film entitled "Joyeux Noël" on this subject. The guns went silent, just as the film shows. Those taking part were astonished and excited. Soldiers from hostile armies met on no-man's land, put up and decorated Christmas trees, lit candles and even fireworks, embraced each other, had drinks and Christmas specialities together. It was the beginning of a ball, one of them commented. Some visited enemy trenches. They talked, said prayers together, and exchanged presents such as watches, tobacco, bottles of alcohol, tinned beef, chocolate, socks, biscuits, crucifixes and medals, barrels of beer, and even took each other's autographs, which they sent home to their families. They had plenty of gifts to exchange, as their HQs had provided a large supply of presents. They also exchanged newspapers. Those who knew the language of the enemy could compare the information in their own and the enemy press on the same events, and discovered what wartime manipulation and propaganda means.

On Christmas Day soldiers continued to meet each other and sing carols. They wrote in letters to their families how extraordinary it was. One British soldier wrote it was the most wonderful Christmas he had ever had and that he would have never believed it if he had seen it in the cinema. On some sections of the front the truce lasted until the New Year. Another British soldier wondered what would happen if the spirit that had overcome the trenches overcame the people in the whole world: instead of insulting each other people would start singing Christmas carols together, and instead of taking revenge, they'd be exchanging presents, and wouldn't the war come to an end immediately? Naturally enough, the commands decided to stop this. They imposed a ban on holiday meetings, which damped down the men's fighting spirit, demolishing the image of the enemy as monsters. Many refused to obey orders to fire on the enemy lines. On some stretches of the front whole units infected by the Christmas spirit had to be withdrawn and replaced with new units. The press rallied to the assault, warning of the fatal consequences of mutual revelling, which the papers said was a sign of weakness on the part of the enemy, if they had to call for a Christmas truce. A few cases of an Easter truce were reported in the spring of 1915, but this time on a much smaller scale. In the next years as hatred of the enemy grew in line with what the war propaganda prescribed it became harder and harder to hold meetings and conversations with the enemy and treat them like gentlemen. The soldiers' behaviour became more and more brutal. A soldier who had seen his friend killed stopped having second thoughts and shot to kill. Having learned what contact with the enemy could do to their men's morale, the authorities of the belligerent sides gave orders for the system of trenches to be laid out in a way to make such contact impossible.

As of 1915 trenches were being dug on all the fronts. They were used for protection against enemy attacks, and facilitated, or indeed made attacks against the enemy possible. They were intended to enable machine gun, light mortar, grenade, and sniper's posts to be positioned up to a few score metres forward. Trenches were 1–2 metres wide, but at intervals of a few score metres had wider stretches, going up to 3–4 metres in places called "nodes of resistance" where ammunition, food supplies and medical equipment was stored. Between trenches there were narrow communication ditches for runners carrying messages. Usually a pair of messengers would be sent, in the hope that at least one of them would reach the destination and deliver the message on time. Where technical conditions allowed, trenches would be dug to a depth of at least 2 metres, or more, in two storeys, down to 8–9 metres. The trenches in Gallipoli and mountainous regions were shallower, as the rocky terrain made digging difficult.

Shooting platforms would be installed about a metre below ground level. The front of the trenches would be protected with sandbags or stones, and the sides would be boarded up with planks. There would be loopholes left between them for observation with a periscope. There were many kilometres of fortification lines, so to assist communication trenches were given street names such as Haig Street or Avenue Joffre, in honour of the commanders.

Different construction types and techniques were employed in mountain areas and, for instance, in Flanders, where the water table was not very far down below ground level and the irrigation system had been destroyed. The trenches of Flanders were like muddy ponds or quagmires. To make things easier, wooden floors were put down in them, and pumps fitted with rubber hoses were in operation. But there were even reports of men drowning in the mud when it happened to rain during combat.

Minefields and barbed wire, known as "the devil's rope," "the steel fence," or "the barbed garden fence," were an important component of the defences. Barbed wire was the soldier's bane. When barbed wire went up on the front the techniques and effects of warfare changed, and the memory of it would haunt veterans for a long time. Barbed wire was invented by the Americans for fencing fields and pastures. In 1898 the British used it in the Boer War. In successive armed conflicts it was used more and more. During the First World War barbed wire was laid out at ground level on a network of steel pins. This had to be done at night, as quietly as possible so as not to arouse the vigilance of enemy snipers. The British designed a supporting pin in the shape of a corkscrew, which could be screwed into the ground with hardly any noise. Other activities conducted at night included burying the dead, evacuating the wounded from the trenches, and conserving, repairing, and reinforcing shelters.

To secure the best effects for attack and defence there had to be a good system of communication and observation. This could be achieved by a network of wires running in tubes at about 2 m below ground level. Wires laid out on the surface deteriorated soon and were destroyed. Other communication systems included the wireless telegraph and reconnaissance patrols sent out to no-man's land and enemy trenches. Observations were carried out and information sent from church and mine shaft towers. Even the services of dogs were employed. On the other hand, trees – and especially the stumps of trees left standing in the areas under shellfire – were no good either for observation or for transmitting messages. A soldier serving in the Battle of Warsaw in 1915 wrote that the forest had been devastated for kilometres on end and looked as if it had been struck by a hurricane; the boughs hanging down from shattered trunks and the scattered branches marked the places hit by shrapnel. Within the trenches these methods were not very reliable means of communication between officers and men, and the use of coloured flags, whistles, bugles, and firework rockets proved much more effective.

Not all the trenches played the same or a similar role. Some were hardly ever troubled; others were constantly scenes of battle, especially where big battles were fought using material resources. Some soldiers spent a few years in the trenches (with intermissions); while others never experienced an enemy attack and never themselves attacked. They had the luck to spend their entire time in service in the rear, at a safe distance away from the front line. All they knew about the war was what they were told or read. Some were wounded several times; others finished their service with no injuries at all or with just a scratch. For the latter the main problem was how to kill time, how to go home with money in their wallet, how to overcome the deadly boredom and banality; and their officers' chief worry was how to keep the lethargic sitting around in the trenches from having a destructive effect on the men and their morale and mentality.

Trench war gave rise to serious problems with supplies, sleeping, washing, eating, and performing the call of Nature. Complaints about the food were ubiquitous, but it was hard to deliver hot meals if neither fires could be lit nor cookers installed in the trenches, to prevent the smoke and flames from giving away positions to the enemy. The predominant fare in the trenches was dry rations and cold of necessity: bread, tinned provisions, and sporadically fruit and vegetables. Bread, which was the basic food, was supplied from field bakeries situated at the rear. The most efficient bakeries were the ones the Americans brought from home, which by the end of the war were producing a daily quota of 54 thousand loaves, each weighing 5–6 kg, baked in 8 huge ovens. The worst times for food supplies were during periods of prolonged combat and in the autumn and winter. A report from the Western front said that at such times you could see plenty of masklike faces, starving and pale with cold; what most people had on their minds was where to get their next meal. Alongside food, victuals also included water, beer, wine and spirits, depending on the national tradition. British and Australian soldiers brewed tea whenever they got the chance.

It was not until fortresses were built along lines of permanent resistance that conditions improved somewhat. These structures were huge reinforced concrete bunkers of several storeys, containing stores, hospitals, munitions stores, toilets, and canteens, with long communication tunnels lit up with electric lighting and equipped with subterranean telegraph lines. Life became easier and more lives could be saved. To all intents and purposes they were underground cities, and most of them were on the Western front. Next to them there were dugouts supported by tree trunks going down to a depth of 4–6 m, and covered with corrugated iron roofing. They were lit up with candles, paraffin or acetylene lamps. But dugouts offered protection only against minor shells. Well camouflaged shelters prevented enemy aircraft and observation balloons from identifying them. At a certain distance behind the trenches and shelters for the men there were special shelters for commanding officers, fitted out with armoured observation points. They were well camouflaged and fairly well equipped, rather like hotels, with beds, carpets, toilets, water wells, stoves, chairs, furniture, portable bath-tubs, and thermos flasks.

It was the duty of the engineers to protect the officers and men against the terrible consequences of intensive shelling. Alongside the subterranean cities miles of tunnels were dug to shelter whole regiments and divisions. Such tunnels were constructed on all the fronts, even in the Near East, where on General Allenby's orders they were built with underground electric lighting and even a narrow-gauge railway. Allenby managed to hide over 30 thousand soldiers away from the enemy's gaze and artillery. On the Western front the Canadians had a team of engineers who proved their high level of professional skills in tunnel construction. In 1918 they built 12 tunnels, the longest was 1,722 m. They managed to accommodate most of their forces in these tunnels. The Germans turned out to be even more effective in the construction of state-of-the-art underground forts, keeping them in contact with neighbouring forts and with the rest of the country. The best known of these networks was the famous Hindenburg Line (*Siegfriedstellung*), 143 km long.

In the hot and dry areas, the Balkans and the Near East, the main problem was providing the soldiers with enough water. But the main annoyance in everyday life in the trenches on all the fronts were the plagues of rats, lice, cockroaches, fleas, ticks, insects and mosquitoes. This was due to the bad sanitary conditions and the large numbers of corpses. In January 1916 one of the soldiers on the Western front wrote that when lights went out the rats and lice came out and were masters of the place. You could hear rats gnawing, scuttling and thudding along the planks, giving out muted squeals. They worked very hard, and within a few days any bodies left unburied would be reduced to a skeleton clad in a uniform. These four-legged gate-crashers were the most difficult enemy to beat. Rat-hunts were held regularly. According to one soldier, on one night alone he and his mates killed nearly a hundred rats, not counting the ones in the mud and water, which they had to drown using stones. Rat-hunting was another remedy against boredom and hopelessness, for sometimes fighting on the front could come to a standstill for weeks on end. Rats were Enemy Number One, and Number Two were lice. The trenches earned the nickname of "Liceland." "When we entered our dugouts and our bodies warmed up, the lice would come out of hiding in our clothes, line up in columns of four and start marching over our bodies. They were our constant companions," a British soldier wrote.

A rota system operated in the trenches: it could hardly be any otherwise. In the Allied armies it was usually a three-shift system: 3 days in the trenches, 3 days training, and 3 days in the rear. In the German army it was a four-day system: 4 days in the trenches and 4 days off. Soldiers did not get much sleep, and sometimes hardly any sleep at all, as they had to do certain duties during the night which they could not do in daytime. Hence the opinion that they were dying for lack of sleep, dead-beat, or looked as if fast asleep. On their days off in the rear they could use the shops and canteens offering hot meals, to taste an unknown cuisine. They could visit soldiers' reading-rooms, mess-rooms, or brothels. They could paint, draw, or sculpt. They could make crucifixes and little altars out of shell fragments. Time spent in the rear was a good opportunity to write home. The letters they wrote were very similar to each other, regardless of nationality or front. "I received your card and the letter from home, too. They wrote about the cow and the calf. My best regards to you and to everyone at home too," wrote a Polish soldier to his family near Bochnia. Writing was an inner compulsion. Soldiers knew that families suffered if they got no letters from them, and they suffered, too, if they had no news from their family.

Both sides worked hard to find the best way to destroy the enemy's defence system, asking again and again what should be done to dig in and keep their hard-won positions, to gain the upper hand strategically. One of the methods which was to lead to success was digging tunnels under enemy trenches. Already in 1915 British engineers were digging at depths of scores of metres below ground level. They employed miners who used the techniques applied to make pit shafts. When they finished the job the engineers installed a large amount of explosives at the end of the tunnel, and when they set it off the enemy forces in the trench above them were blown up along with their trench. This is what happened at Mesen and at Ypres in July 1917, when the British attack started with the explosion of 19 mines. "The ground began to tremble. My body went up and down, as if carried by an ocean wave," wrote one of the British engineers, observing the effects of his work at Ypres. "Suddenly I saw the biggest ever, most terrible firework display... It was a veritable volcano, as if spitting out a huge tongue of fire," wrote a Belgian witness of the Mesen operation. The explosion could be heard in London, 200 km away! A crater 69 m in diameter and 24 m deep was formed. 10 thousand Germans were killed. In the environs of Mesen and Ypres the British dug 24 tunnels of lengths from 180 m to 1,800 m in two years. In fact, both the Allies and the Germans were sapping, using pickaxes and shovels, and passing buckets of earth from hand to hand along a line up to the surface. Sometimes sappers from opposing sides would meet, and close combat would ensue with the use of pickaxes, shovels and spades. Both sides used the most up-to-date precision instruments such as tapping systems equipped with microphones, and the most primitive but still effective tools like buckets turned upside down, which helped them discover and destroy sappers. If this did not succeed they would quickly evacuate the trench and set up machine-guns in a safe place, as straight after the explosion the enemy infantry would attack. So tunnels were not always a foolproof measure, especially as Nature often proved a formidable adversary of sappers, preventing digging and allowing water to seep in and flood the tunnel. Another obstacle was carbon monoxide. That is why diggers were accompanied by animals such as rabbits or canaries. If the animals became restless it was a sign of serious danger. The miners' war did not turn out to be a military panacea.

Hence the principal weapon in the struggle to destroy enemy defence lines was artillery, the maker of "hurricanes of steel." However, in the first months of the war the predominant types of guns were ones which shot shells over an almost horizontal trajectory and proved ineffective. This forced the belligerents to design and produce guns and shells capable of hitting and destroying enemy defences. The new guns, powerful mortars and howitzers, shot shells which destroyed targets with a very strong force of explosion. However, transporting them over terrain riddled with shell craters, barbed wire, and trenches was not easy. Heavy artillery destroyed both enemy defences and the delicate psyche of the men that operated it. Under a barrage of shellfire all that a soldier whose resistance had sunk to a low thought of was to put up a white flag as soon as possible and march off into captivity. "The entire mountain seemed to be shaking in its foundations… huge lumps of rock were ripped off and tumbled into the Russian trenches below. I had never seen such a display of firepower before," recalled a soldier in the Russian army who had fought in the Battle of Gorlice.

Fortunately for soldiers, artillery was not always effective. In 1914–1915 only two out of every hundred shells fired landed straight in a trench, and by 1918 it was only four in every hundred. Many shells never exploded. Those which hit the mud usually failed to explode. Often as many as 30 out of every hundred fired never exploded. Their poor quality was chiefly the result of the low quality of the materials and the imperfection of the machines used to produce them. Over five days on the Somme in June 1916 the British fired 1.5 million shells out of 1,500 guns, nonetheless before the offensive the German barbed wire defences remained "virtually untouched and very dense" and for all practical purposes were still serviceable despite the artillery fire. The attacking soldiers found as much, thinking the enemy defences had been destroyed and there would be no problem with crossing them. However, it often turned out that attackers were gunned down as soon as they started to leave their trenches.

Sometimes soldiers were killed by their own artillery. This happened mostly in the second phase of the war, once a developed form of moving barrage known as the *Feuerwaltz* ("fire waltz"), a more effective type of artillery fire, had been introduced. Its invention is attributed to two generals independently of each other, the German Hans von Seeckt and the Pole Tadeusz Rozwadowski. But there was a snag about moving barrage, which was supposed to advance just ahead of its own infantry advancing behind it. However, perfect co-ordination was hard to achieve. If the barrage moved too slowly, its own men were hit. One of the Canadian officers instructed his men that they should advance behind the barrage fire as casually as if they were riding a bike along a beach, screened off by a bus. When they got to the enemy line and the Germans put their hands up they were to send them to the rear. But he was being too optimistic. According to French estimates about 75 thousand soldiers could have been killed or wounded by their own artillery fire. One of the French officers owned up to belonging to the regiment which had killed the most Englishmen. To avoid losses from their own artillery, the Austrians put pieces of white cloth on their kitbags, and had grey and red-and-white flags to mark the extreme positions of their attacking forces. So the ambient theory on the Western and Italian fronts, that the artillery captured a position and the infantry held it, all too often did not work. It was hard to surprise the enemy, who always had enough time to bring in reinforcements and deploy them in the rear.

Trench lines were breached on all the fronts except the Western front. On the Eastern and Balkan fronts artillery proved the critical factor. The Eastern front was far more extended than the Western front, and owing to shortages the Russians had not been able to build an effective line of gunners' trenches and shelters. But to breach enemy lines the attackers had to have a clear advantage in terms of materials and manpower, as happened in the Battle of Gorlice. In 1915 some of the Balkan lines were breached, for example in Rumania and at Caporetto in Italy, thanks to the attackers' overwhelming advantage in manpower and materials. They made a quick advance, preventing the defenders from gathering reinforcements, which in Russia, the Balkans, and Rumania, were slow to arrive due to defects in the railway network.

On the Western front, too, it was believed that the success of an attack depended on its speed, hence soldiers were ordered to leave behind in the trenches all accessories which would be of no use during an attack. Whole weeks were spent on training leaving the trenches, running and jumping, and the soldiers were kept fit. In practice, however, rapid attack was out of the question over a shell-pocked field riddled with anti-personnel mines and laced with barbed wire. To make an assault feasible at all at least some of the mines and barbed wire had to be cleared. There were men specially trained to cut the wire with shears. For protection against machine gun fire they carried shields like medieval knights, and when they had done the job, put up white tape to guide the attackers. However, vigilant defenders fixed bells on the barbed wire to warn of the approach of intruders, or they might connect up a live wire or set up a dense mesh net against grenade attacks. Even the successful defusing of the mines and removal of the barbed wire did not mean that the road to the enemy lines was clear, for beyond the barbed wire there might have been an earthwork, a series of wooden fences, low-lying trip-wires, and camouflaged pits waiting to catch potential attackers in traps like the ones for hunting big game. Some laboured to defend themselves, and others to outsmart them.

To beat the barbed wire broad planks or mattresses were put on it, but the task required time and a lot of luck, since enemy soldiers were waiting for any who dared to attempt it. In the late phase of the war attackers were aided by the Bangalore torpedo, a tube filled with strong explosives inserted in the wire. It was first developed by the British Indian army. In 1917 the Germans introduced barbed tape (razor wire), which could not be cut or destroyed, since it could not be snapped and was rolled up into an entanglement, but it turned out that all the barbed wire could be negotiated by tanks.

The most difficult tasks were building trenches, laying mines, and spreading out barbed wire in the marshy, wet and rainy terrain of Flanders. The soldier's worst enemy there was the rain, water, and mud. This was a subject that appeared in hundreds of memoirs and commentaries. Some even said that after their Flemish experience they "had a favourable attitude to English weather." They remembered the rain which soaked the trenches and made them disintegrate, and rendered guns useless. Their primitive pumps and ad hoc irrigation systems were not much help. War veterans had really bad memories of Flanders.

"Rain, midnight rain, nothing but the wild rain," wrote Edward Thomas in the poem "Rain."

The rain did not cease to pour down, and the vast fields of craters turned into a sea of stinking, asphyxiating mud in which men, animals, and tanks struggled hopelessly and stuck. The few roads which could still be made out amid the mud were constantly under German artillery fire, under which endless supply columns wandered intrepidly all night long. Such were Winston Churchill's recollections of the autumn of 1917. A German wrote that it was not war, but more like messing around in the mud. As they plodded through the mud, some soldiers lost their socks, shoes, and even their trousers. So they put empty sandbags on their shoes, and tied them up above the knee. They marched with their heavy kitbags over wooden platforms. If any of them fell into the mud it was hard to pull him out. "We were loaded like Christmas trees, so any explosion nearby made soldiers lose their balance and plunge straight into the mud." It was even harder to transport artillery and drive carts carrying provisions pulled by horses or oxen. It took a soldier 3 to 4 hours to cover a kilometre, a distance he normally did in 20–25 minutes. None of the battles fought in the mud ended in success for the attackers. All the attacks launched by both sides drowned in the sea of mud and water. "The mud! We slept in it, we ate in it. Stinking mud everywhere. The bodies of the dead sank in it. Wounds festered in it. There were also the carcasses of horses and mules in it, with guts bursting out of their bloated bellies. It was a nightmare," a British soldier recalled.

But even in Flanders some attackers managed to reach enemy defences. In the fighting in and around the trenches they used hand-grenades, knives, revolvers, sappers' daggers, steel-tipped clubs, knuckledusters, and sharp-edged pickaxes. Long bayonet rifles turned out not to be of much use for fighting in the trenches, so the soldiers were issued shorter rifles. Those who made it to the enemy lines and took the front trenches ran on, fewer and fewer in number, to the lines further back. Those who got furthest were completely exhausted when the defenders turned their reserve forces on them – and the attack petered out. Success was transient. Experience of trench war showed that defence was easier than attack. Defenders could react faster to a changing situation than attackers.

Diverse methods of attack were tried in trench warfare, in search of gaps through which it would be possible to pass. Some generals were in favour of mass charges, others preferred single file. Some pretended to launch attacks at various points along the front to divert the enemy's attention and prevent him from identifying the real location of the assault. Others trusted to combined attacks: poison gas, the use of mines to blast enemy trenches, and attacks by reserve units from the far rear. Work was going on all the time to improve mobility for infantry assaults. Good mobility was to be secured by elite stormtrooper units by the Germans in 1915, and later deployed by the Allies as well. The best and most experienced soldiers were consigned to these units. They were given additional food rations, longer leave, and were relieved from kitchen duty. Their job was to infiltrate enemy territory in small squads in order to spread panic, disorganise the enemy's defence, and get him to retreat. Stormtrooper units destroyed command posts, communication systems, and supply depots. Their soldiers were equipped with hand grenades and cluster hand grenades, knives, portable mortars, nail-studded wooden pikes, flexible clubs on a wooden handle, and fire-throwers. They wore protective helmets and steel collars to protect the throat, and bulletproof vests reminiscent of medieval breastplates. Only in 1918 the Germans produced 500 thousand such vests, but not all stormtroopers put them on, since they impeded mobility, which was to be their main advantage. The units which availed themselves of these vests were the snipers, observers of artillery fire and others, and a bulletproof vest saved many of them from serious injury. However, such security measures were virtually unknown outside the Western front.

In 1917 the Italians formed storming battalions known as *Arditi* (the Daring Ones), but they did not make a significant contribution to the action, since no modifications were introduced in the tactics used hitherto to accommodate them. On the other hand, German stormtroopers scored successes at Caporetto. Oskar von Hutier's stormtrooper units did very well, a model example of which was their capture of Riga. In 1918 the Allies' storming units were to prove effective. They were deployed in offensives carried out simultaneously at several points. Short attacks with the use of a small force often proved more effective than long-lasting single assaults. On the Western front storming units often managed to penetrate quite deeply into enemy lines, but were unable to permanently breach the front.

What were the trenches like in the aftermath of a battle? An anguishing and terrible sight. The dead would tumble down into the trenches. If there were large numbers of corpses not all of them could be removed, especially as the wounded had to be given priority. Whenever combat continued for longer, the stench of decomposing corpses became intolerable. Stench and nausea made up one of the most frequent recollections of those who defended the entrenched fortresses. The sight of the heaps of wounded jumbled up with the dead gave rise to similar experiences of shock and disgust. Many went ill. Those who survived compared trench war to a cemetery with bodies left unburied. Sometimes defenders would demand extra rations of tobacco and face-masks to offset the stench of rotting human and animal bodies.

It left a deep mark on their psychology. "What was human life in that heartless world, a world full of the stench of thousands of rotting bodies? Death lurked at every step and divested those who had survived of their human instincts," Ernst Jünger recorded his experience. Soldiers had to quickly learn to live with all this by activating adaptive strategies. They became immune to brutality, death, and obscenity. They assimilated turpitude and agony. They grew indifferent to the fate of others. "You become absolutely indifferent to everything the world has to offer except the duty to fight. You're eating a slice of bread while someone is hit by a bullet and drops down next to you. For a moment you look at him, then you carry on eating. ... Eventually talking about your own death affects you as little as a discussion on an invitation to an official lunch," an Austrian soldier wrote. The monotonous routine of repeating the same activities and sitting in the trenches waiting for an attack or being attacked had a negative psychological effect as well. On 25th December 1914 Tom was writing to Janet in London that "the first battles of the war left so many dead both sides have held back until replacements could come from home. So we have mostly stayed in our trenches and waited." The enemy was not keen on fighting, either. "But what a terrible waiting it has been! Knowing that any moment an artillery shell might land and explode beside us in the trench, killing or maiming several men." They knew very well that silence in the trenches might be a silent prelude to a tempest of fire and death.

Waiting to leave the trenches must have been extremely stressful. "A couple of hours of waiting in suspense made some fill their time with prayers, while others cursed, and still others thought and talked of home and their dear ones. The silence of the grave, the calm before the storm, which always attends the order to prepare for attack, can throw anyone off-balance," says one of the soldier's memoirs. Those who had served for longer had it easier thanks to their experience. But not all of them. Some developed a state of oblivion akin to a narcotic trance, under the influence of strong emotions, or perhaps opium and cocaine. So they waited tensely for the signal to exit. They left as soon as the commanding officer gave the sign with his cap, baton, cloth, or whistle. There was nothing left but to climb up the ladder and attack. "Anyone who went through the moment of leaving the trenches never again had to face such danger and dread," wrote one of the survivors.

The sight of the craters and pits, of which there were hundreds of thousands, stayed in the soldiers' memories. It was estimated that only the Battle of Ypres in 1917 left over a million of them on a surface area of two and a half square kilometres. Craters facilitated decoying, hiding, and attacking, as they were safer than the trenches. Enemy artillery did not aim at craters, and aircraft could not detect men concealed in them. Usually deep craters soon filled up with water to the size of Olympic swimming pools, which did not stop them from being good decoys, naturally above the water table.

3. Alpine warfare

"Almighty God, Who rulest all things, save us from the unrelenting cold, from the whirling blizzard, from the fall of the avalanche, and guide our feet to a safe place. Protect us on the crags that make the head reel, on the vertical rock-face, over the treacherous precipice." That was the prayer of the Italian Alpine riflemen. Alpine warfare, also referred to as mountain warfare, was essentially a type of position warfare, but special in that it was conducted in extreme conditions, at high altitudes, in a mountain landscape with numerous obstacles in the form of sharp peaks, sheer precipices, rapid mountain rivers, in a rare atmosphere and often at low temperatures. Another hindrance was the drastic temperature swing: at midday it would be hot, but by night at high altitudes the temperature would drop to below freezing point. Mountain warfare was the most bizarre, absurd, and unimaginable kind of war – a war against the forces of Nature. The weather and the mountains were an additional enemy. In the upper regions of the mountains there were winter conditions for most of the year, with blizzards and snowstorms even in summer. In the highest parts of the mountains combat was conducted above the permanent snow line. Visibility in the mountains could be next to nil due to snowfalls, mists, or sharp sunlight. Soldiers had to learn to live with all this and bear in mind the risk of frostbite, avalanches, and the need to carry through snow tunnels kitbags weighing 30–40 kg. They had to acclimatise to the thin air conditions, which exhausted them quickly. Fortunately, most of the combat was not in winter, for the snow, ice, and avalanches ruled it out. The locks of their rifles and the barrels of the big guns froze up. Usually armies waited till spring to attack, but often winter conditions would surprise them during combat in spring or autumn. Mountain warfare called for the right equipment and the right personnel. In the Italian army there had been training for Alpine riflemen (*Alpini*) since 1872. Eight regiments had been created by 1915. Germany had an *Alpenkorps*, and Austria-Hungary had mountain companies. There were also mountain units in the

French, Rumanian, and Bulgarian armies. The men who served in mountain units were recruited mostly from the inhabitants of the highlands, qualified skiers and climbers. They were equipped with skis, ice-axes, ice grippers for their boots, hooks, ropes, and snowshoes. They had warm uniforms with protective devices. During the War the belligerents ran numerous training courses for those interested in the art of Alpine war.

The war was conducted at higher and higher altitudes on account of the advantage of controlling areas overlooking valleys and lower summits, hence also over the heads of the enemy. A mountaineer in a good position armed with a machine gun on a rocky ledge could stop an attack of enemy infantrymen, inflicting heavy losses. He could pelt the enemy with barrel-shaped rolling bombs, with a fuse timed to go off when it reached the enemy position. Alpine warfare gave defenders even more of an advantage than lowland war did, since virtually every attack had to be directed upwards. If both combating sides were situated at the same height, they often engaged in close combat on the ledges, which were nicknamed "walls of death." In the mountains trenches tended to be so close to each other that you could hear enemy conversations, pots and pans jangling, and the wounded groaning. There was combat only during the daytime, which is hardly surprising. Fighting went on even on glaciers, such as in the Passo Tonale in June 1915, at an altitude of 1,895 m, on the Marmolada Glacier (3,243 m), in the Adamello-Presanella Alps, and in the Ortler Alps. Both attackers and defenders moved about on skis.

The soldiers marching up into the mountains were accompanied by mine-setters, engineers, miners, and prisoners-of-war. Some of the miners were in uniform, some wore civvies with armbands and a military cap. They built the roads leading up to the summits. They used explosives to clear the ground for night shelters, stores, canteens, hospitals, and artillery positions. The shelters were built of concrete and waterproofed with bricks, corrugated roofs and tarpaulin. They were connected to each other by means of underground corridors and ventilating shafts. Stoves were installed inside to dry the damp air. Entrances to shelters would lead along winding passages to prevent shrapnel and, to a certain extent, poison gas from getting inside. Mountain units made an effort to instal a telephone network and electricity supply throughout the territory they held; they also set up alarm bells, signalling systems, and reflectors. The industrial war and the technological race had moved up into the mountains.

Once the shelters had been built the men, equipment, artillery, and barbed wire had to be transported up. It was a big job for the ancillary services. For every man out on the front there were 5–7 working in the rear. The hardest task was getting a fortnight's fuel and food supply up. Soldiers in the mountains had tinned food only, as there was no way to transport field kitchens, and the use of heaters was the height of luxury. But occasionally the supply system failed and soldiers went hungry.

Bringing water supplies was not easy. Beasts of burden were used to transport water, carrying it in tanks fitted into baskets. Water pipes were constructed to carry water over long distances, into pits hollowed out on the campsite. Lighter equipment and soldiers were hauled up on a system of cable hoists; or mules, donkeys, and horses laden with baskets were used for transportation. In the lower parts of the mountains the men marched over the newly laid roads and embankments, or were transported by rail on newly built narrow-gauge lines and on the ordinary railway lines. Higher up they had to march along marked trails which could be secured with rope or steel ladders if required. One such trail was 3,000 m long and earned the epithet of "the Italian ladder to heaven."

Once the soldiers were up at their posts they set about the construction of firing positions to defend themselves against enemy artillery and machine-gun fire. Their hit range was longer than in the lowlands: sometimes pieces of rock ripped out of the mountainside reached targets better than artillery shells did. Building conditions depended on the season. They were worst during the spring and autumn blizzards. "There's a blizzard; we take the planks and metal stakes to build the shacks... For cover I have sacks full of snow and an iron shield. In front of our ditch there is barbed wire, most of it snow-covered… It's freezing cold. We're completely out in the open air," wrote Benito Mussolini. In summer they had to build, or rather gouge out defences in the rock, and make use of the natural caves. Instead of full-fledged trenches they dug ditches and used the debris to erect a parapet in front of the ditch, reinforced with sandbags. But in highland conditions the force of the backdraft from artillery fire was so big that these structures proved unstable, which increased casualties. Another factor which made for a higher fatality rate was the difficulty of transporting the injured to the medical centres which were situated at lower levels. Many of the wounded died through loss of blood before they could receive treatment. Burying the dead was difficult for lack of space. "Men spend whole days lying next to the wounded and the dead; graves, which may be quite close to defence positions, are being ripped open by grenades, which send decomposing corpses flying about the place… The men are overwhelmed with disgust, lose their appetite, and cannot wash for lack of water," one of the Austrian generals reported.

There was a risk of rock avalanches, and avalanches of snow in winter. Luckily for the soldiers, shells that fell into deep snow usually did not explode. The percentage of undetonated shells was considerably higher than in normal conditions. But even if it did not detonate, a shell could start an avalanche. "The most terrible enemy was Nature herself… whole platoons were wiped out without trace, noiselessly, without the slightest sound except that which the gigantic white mass itself gives out," an Italian Alpine rifleman recollected. The avalanches were huge, because there were huge masses of snow in the Alps. They were death-traps. In winter at 2,000 m the snow was about 5 m deep, and at 3,000 m it was 9 m deep. Avalanches carried away entire units, stores, field hospitals, firing positions, and massive guns along with the men attending them. 150–180 thousand were killed on the Tyrolean front, about 60 thousand of them snatched away by avalanches – over twice as many as were victims of poison gas on the Western front. The most tragic memories are of the winter conditions that came suddenly during the autumn of 1916. There was snow and frost alternating with thaws and avalanches. In December

1916 about 10 thousand men were lost on both sides through avalanches. It was probably the biggest disaster of its kind on record. Bodies were still being brought down when the spring thaw came.

In winter most of the soldiers moved down towards the valleys. However some spent winter at high altitudes guarding the alarm systems and equipment, maintaining and repairing guns and rifles. "The blizzard was so strong, and the snow so deep, that having covered a few score metres on foot with the utmost difficulty, as the muscles in my shins had been stretched to the point of exhaustion, I tried to go on on my knees, but I couldn't manage even that. For three days we were completely cut off from civilisation," Polish General Jan Romer recalled. The bad experience of avalanches made the belligerents develop their rescue services and employ meteorologists and geologists to forecast the times and directions of avalanches. Special anti-avalanche barriers were built, or at least attempts were made to build them, as they were not very effective. In summer storms were dangerous, for even small pieces of metal could attract thunderbolts. During storms soldiers would put down their weapons and pick-axes, take off their helmets, leave steel shelters, abandon metal ladders and telephone cables. Thunder hitting rocks could kill or maim, and some who fled in panic, fell into precipices or ice cracks. The storms came with hurricane-like winds which swept up campsites and demolished wooden huts.

Once the men were in their positions, the guns were installed, usually on ledges prepared by the mine-setters and engineers. The parts of the guns, which had been brought up on ropes and hoists, had to be assembled. Some guns had armoured domes set up above for protection against enemy artillery. It took a few days to instal the guns, not always successfully. Sometimes this could be done only at night, though that did not make it safe, as the enemy lit up the rock face with reflector beams and rockets, which did not make the job easier. Many a soldier was killed, many a gun fell into a ravine. Despite the difficulties both sides scored successes. The Italians were happy when they managed to set up six guns on the Tofana di Fuori peak (3,237 m); and the Austrians were even happier when they managed to pull a 149 mm calibre gun up to the top of Mount Ortler (3,905 m). 600 men had worked on the job. It was the wartime record. The heavy 240 mm and 280 mm mortars were not brought up to such heights. The high trajectories of their shells made it possible for them to be deployed from the valleys and still hit targets high up in the mountains. Gun positions were protected by barbed wire, concrete, and steel obstacles.

Often the miners and engineers dug tunnels under enemy lines to blow them up. The Alpine tunnels were 80 cm wide and up to 180 cm deep – narrower and lower than their lowland counterparts. A maximum of 30–50 cm could be dug a day, using simple tools such as pickaxes and drills, as using drilling machines which gave off harmful gases would have been dangerous. There were teams trying to locate enemy digging. There were cases of enemy tunnel-diggers meeting. When this happened, they engaged in close combat, using mining equipment and revolvers, after which the old tunnels would be plugged up and new ones dug. In July 1916 Italian mine-setters made a shaft under Mount Batognica, but the Austrians managed to get through to the chamber in which the Italians had deposited two tonnes of explosives ready to be detonated, and cut the detonating wires at the last moment. However, a few months later the Italians managed to detonate four huge mines, bringing down the summit by a few metres. Whenever the dull sound of digging and hacking stopped, you knew that the explosives were ready to be detonated. In April 1916 the Italians blasted off part of the peak of Col di Lana near the well-known skiing resort Cortina d'Ampezzo. 200 enemy soldiers were killed, but the Austrians remained in control of the valley. The Italians named Col di Lana the blood mountain, because they had attempted to storm it 97 times. In March 1918 the Austrians blew up an Italian unit near Trent by detonating 55 tonnes of explosives.

4. The winter wars

On the lowlands combat continued in winter as well, though not as intensively as in other seasons, and effectively petered out on many fronts and sections. Some campaigns started in the very early spring, although often sleet and snow made action difficult. In general, winter offensives ended in failure, for example the offensive of the Russian Carpathian army against Austro-Hungarian forces, which was conducted in January – March 1915. The Russian command decided to launch an offensive even though their men were not ready for a winter war. They were not equipped with winter gear in time and were still in their worn summer uniforms, which afforded no protection against the cold. "I was being overcome by an absolutely intoxicating drowsiness and warmth, even though the temperature was well below freezing point." This was the effect of exposure to the severe cold. Soldiers were suffering from frostbite and literally freezing to death. General Vladimir Sukhomlinov, the Russian minister of war, thought the campaign unfortunate and absurd, an example of disregard for the soldiers and lack of consideration of likely losses. The Russian supply system failed. Russian soldiers were quite glad to surrender, in the hope that they would fed and given warm conditions. But neither were the Austro-Hungarian soldiers prepared for a winter war, since their planners had forecast the war would end before the onset of winter. As a result both sides together are estimated to have lost about 800 thousand men in the space of a few winter months. The Russians sustained greater losses and were deemed defeated. The chief factor determining the magnitude of losses was the effectiveness of logistic planning for action under extreme conditions, since "no artillery fire could have broken our resistance as totally as the damp, the cold, and the freezing conditions did," one of the Austrian soldiers wrote. Still in March night temperatures went down to minus 20°C. "On 1st March there was fog and a snowstorm, ruling out any kind of orientation whatsoever. Whole regiments went astray, and as a result losses were huge. For weeks on end on the entire area of combat and in the quarters no-one changed their clothes, which for many became a stiff coat of ice adhering to their body… It was white hell," wrote the Austrian Colonel Georg Veitl.

Another action which failed owing to winter conditions was the Austro-Hungarian expedition sent to relieve the besieged fortress of Przemyśl. It was beaten by temperatures going down to minus 30⁰C at night. "The temperature was so low that when by accident I touched a steel telescope stand with my bare hand, a whole patch of skin came off. I saw that whenever a soldier stopped for a rest or could not go on because of a wound, after a half-hour at most of immobility he would freeze to death before our very eyes," one of the soldiers recollected. In the next years there was combat in winter, too, with similar problems and little effect apart from human losses. But the winter of 1915/1916 was hot for the Balkans, when the Central Powers launched an offensive against Serbia. It was the final part of the campaign, terminal for Serbia. Photographs of King Peter of Serbia on a peasant's cart pulled by oxen, and later on a peasant's sleigh, have gone down in history. The heroic winter passage over the mountains of Serbia and Albania made a lasting record in the national memory of the Serbs.

The winter of 1914/1915 impaired the Turkish offensive against Russia. Temperatures went down to minus 26⁰C. The Turks had planned for a quick victory, and hence did not equip their forces for a winter campaign. They issued food rations for four days; however, not only did the soldiers not get a sufficient quantity of warm clothing and tents, but in addition the Turkish Commander-in-Chief Enver Pasha ordered them to leave their winter overcoats and kitbags in the base camp so they could march faster. As a result thousands froze or starved to death, also because it was hard to light up campfires in winter conditions. Overall more Turkish soldiers froze to death than were killed by enemy fire.

Problem number one in the winter wars was transport. Owing to difficulties created by natural conditions, the heavy guns often had to be left behind. Horses were used to transport lighter guns and machine guns; while horse-drawn carts were fitted out with runners and turned into sleighs to carry equipment, supplies and food provisions. Since army regulations did not envisage winter camouflaging, soldiers had to use their own initiative for ways to survive. The more ingenious sort put white sheets on their uniforms. It was not until the bad experience of the winter of 1914/1915 that armies started to issue skis, white camouflaging capes, warm clothing, woollen socks, warm vests and kaftans. In addition soldiers insulated their uniforms with layers of newspapers. But it was not enough whenever combat went on for many weeks. When temperatures slumped tea and coffee, and even wine froze up within minutes, and not surprisingly people were reluctant to play the war game. It was hard to keep fighting when your bread, tinned food, and sausages turned into lumps of ice. "Before you can get to the drink you have to break the layer of ice, your meat and potatoes are frozen stiff, and even hand-grenades are all lumped together. Nice weather for polar bears," were the comments. Quite understandably the general atmosphere could not have been good. There was widespread apathy, which inevitably affected the outcome of action. Generals who had a better knowledge of their men ordered a rest and promised they would start up in spring, when the sun came out and the grass was green. "That's when life is full of delight. Like a picnic. You stroll along the trenches, the air's brisk and the sun's shining brightly," one soldier noted.

Winters were so cold that the lubricating grease in their guns froze solid. The quartermasters' services had the hardest job. It was their toughest test, which they failed as a matter of course, since it was impossible to pass it. In winter digging trenches was hardly imaginable, and sleeping in them was preposterous. Many of those who managed to fall asleep never woke up. The long winter nights aggravated the suffering, pain, fear, and dread. Those in the trenches only thought of how not to succumb to the cold and prayed that the enemy would attack at last, or that they would be sent out into combat.

5. Landing operations

The landing operations associated with covering distances by sea, land, and air, and carried out jointly by naval, infantry, and (to a modest extent) air forces, constituted a special kind of warfare. Landing operations usually led to trench war. This was true of the biggest landing operation, in the Dardanelles, co-ordinated with the landing of Allied troops in Gallipoli. The Royal Marines, a British special unit for landing tasks created in August 1914 and composed chiefly of sailors, took part in the operation. Like other divisions, the Royal Marines were transported to the destination on amphibious assault carriers escorted by a fleet of anti-torpedo monitor vessels. Monitors characterised by their shallow draught and good armour plating were ideal for such tasks. Minesweepers also participated in the operation. The defeat in the Dardanelles and Gallipoli made the Allies withdraw from conducting a couple of similar operations which had been planned. This was also due to an insufficient number of ships, amphibs, and units like the Royal Marines. The British project to construct amphibs failed – the Admiralty found the drawing board designs unsatisfactory.

Far more operations were planned than carried out. The idea of a landing operation in the Dardanelles won the day over a plan for a Baltic landing operation which was to lead to Allied control of the Danish straits by a combined British and Russian naval force. It was associated with a completely unrealistic plan for Russian forces to land in Pomerania and quickly march for Berlin. Another operation which never materialised was a British landing at Ostend in Belgium to disrupt German U-boat movements and to land British troops in the region of the Kiel Canal. If successful it could have changed the nature of the war, opening up a new front. Winston Churchill wondered whether the only option for British forces was shifting barbed wire in Flanders, and answered the question for himself with the idea to land troops on the German coast. But the madcap concept was rejected at the preliminary stage. The Italian chief-of-staff considered the idea of a landing in the region of Trieste and Fiume, but there were neither the material means nor the enterprise to try it. It was decided that the losses would be vast, with little prospect of success.

Another major landing operation, albeit not on a comparable scale with the Dardanelles in terms of forces involved or consequences, was carried out by the Germans landing troops in the Bay of Riga. Code-named Operation Albion, its aim was to gain control of the ports and islands and was conducted on 12th–21st October 1917. Tens of thousands of German soldiers and sailors, as well as 100 aircraft, took part. The Germans destroyed the extensive barrier of naval mines and the Russian batteries, and sank a number of ships. It was an exceptionally opportune time for an assault, as the Russian forces were dispersed and demoralised, and their units were under the command of representatives of soldiers' revolutionary committees. Within just a few days the attackers took four islands including the strategic Oesel and Moon, sustaining a minimum of loss. They dubbed their success a blitzkrieg.

Other landing operations were not as complex as these two. The first chronologically was the landing of British ground forces on the French coast in August 1914. It went smoothly and according to plan, since it was on Allied soil and the German navy was not interfering. Another unobstructed landing took place in November 1914, of a British and Indian force in the Basra region off the Persian Gulf. There were no Turkish forces in the area to impede a successful landing. Another successful landing, by a small Russian force on the Persian coast, took place in September 1915. The plan was to launch an attack on the Turks, but its outcome was not successful. Fully successful landings were accomplished by the French in the Levant in October 1918, when the Turkish army was already in a state of disintegration. The objective was to give France control of the region, which they hoped to annex. Towards the end of the war the American William Mitchell, supported by Commander-in-Chief John Pershing, put forward a plan to land a division and its weapons and equipment by air in Belgium. In view of the shortage of aircraft the operation was postponed to the spring of 1919. The idea itself was a harbinger of the air operations of World War Two.

6. The war of the secret services

It was generally realised that the outcome of any war, and particularly a world war, depended on the use of a variety of means and types of services. Important tasks were assigned to the secret services, intelligence and counter-intelligence, including the collection of information on the enemy's forces and his potential, disinformation activities, and countering enemy intelligence.

To obtain the information they needed on the enemy, all the belligerents availed themselves of the services of deserters and gleaned knowledge from prisoners-of-war, who were interrogated, but also had bugging devices recording their conversations. In 1916–1918 61% of the information the British secret services obtained on the movement of enemy forces came from interrogating prisoners-of-war and deserters, and 18% came from procured documents. The use of radio bugging was widespread; telegrams were intercepted; the movement of forces was observed from immobilised balloons and from aircraft; and homing pigeons were used. If it did not perish, a pigeon might have carried 50–60 thousand messages in the course of the war. But the adversary was vigilant and undertaking countermeasures, damaging balloons, shooting down aircraft, training hawks to deal with pigeons and harassing pigeon owners. There is a list of names of pigeon owners executed by the Germans for helping the Belgian resistance with communication. The belligerent countries went as far as to issue pigeon licences. The Austro-Hungarian authorities bought pigeons from breeders, paying 1 crown for a bird. The French made the best use of pigeons; they recruited 130 thousand birds, 20 thousand of which perished. The Germans had even more – nearly 300 thousand. After the war a monument of a wounded pigeon was put up in Lille, in honour of the pigeon who carried the last message from Fort Vaux during the Battle of Verdun. He arrived at his destination and died of poison gas. The French decorated him with the Legion of Honour and had him stuffed. In October 1918 another famous pigeon, in American service, dispatched information from besieged

American forces despite being wounded. He was given a posthumous distinction, stuffed, and sent to Washington.

Important information was obtained thanks to the work of cryptographers to break the enemy's codes. Throughout the war cryptographers in the service of belligerent countries vied with each other over the encryption and decryption of each other's messages: some strove to design the ultimate code, others to break it. And it was certainly not a marginal issue. The fact that the British discovered the contents of German telegrams had a decisive impact on the United States' decision to enter the war. Thanks to having cracked the Italian codes, Germany and Austria-Hungary scored a brilliant victory at Caporetto. "The enemy knew all our codes, even the most secret ones," the Italian generals admitted helplessly. Austrian cryptographers could read strictly confidential Italian plans like a children's book. At the beginning of the war Russian intelligence saved its fifth army thanks to one of its officers disguised in an Austrian uniform providing false information to the command of one of the Austro-Hungarian armies. The best cryptographers were in British service. They were able to crack virtually any code, including the most secret ones, and learned in advance of the enemy's intentions and potential.

Thanks to codes, important messages could be sent via newspapers. Both belligerent parties were aware of this, and their secret services assiduously went through all the classified ads in the papers as well as soldiers' letters. Even apparently innocent weather forecasts and matrimonial offers could be encoded. "Swiss man, 35, perfect at book-keeping and correspondence, working for a year in a managerial post in Vienna, excellent references" turned out to mean that the Austrian 35th infantry division was going to leave for Italy ("Swiss man" stood for "heading for Italy"), while "managerial post in Vienna" meant the observer's location. If there was no other way of getting a message across, agents would carry it just as in the films and crime stories – in the heels of their shoes, inside watches, in suitcases with a false bottom, in wigs, umbrellas, ladies' gloves, in suit collars, under the lining of a hat, or in texts written in an invisible ink. They also carried microfilms made with cameras reminiscent of a watch. The microfilms could be amplified thirtyfold.

Another important task for the secret services was the surveillance of communities regarded as hostile or disloyal, and individuals suspected of working for the enemy. Lists of persons suspected of treachery had been drawn up even before the war started. When it broke out, some of those suspected of espionage were imprisoned or ordered not to leave their place of residence. In Russia individuals from the German minority or with German-sounding names were dismissed from the army and administrative posts. A ban was put on the use of German in public places. The change of name of the capital city, from "St. Petersburg" to the more homely "Petrograd," which took place on 31st August 1914, was symptomatic of the anti-German obsession on the tide of patriotic feelings. Some Germans, who were Russian citizens, were deported to Germany and their property was confiscated, while larger numbers were interned and sent into distant parts of the Russian Empire. On several occasions the authorities encouraged mobs to conduct pogroms, devastate German houses, shops, workshops, and factories. To save themselves from deportation and protect the family fortune accumulated over many generations, many Germans changed their name, adopting a Russian surname and converting from Lutheran Protestantism to the Russian Orthodox religion. Another large group of suspected persons were Jews, many of whom were indeed quite willing to work for the Central Powers as they hated tsarist Russia, which was notorious for pogroms of Jews and atrocities against them. Many of the Jews in Russia considered espionage on behalf of Germany respectable and rational. In Austria-Hungary the list of suspects included Russophile Ruthenians from East Galicia and the Bukovina, and later on Italians and Rumanians. The Austrian authorities were diffident about the loyalty of the Czechs and Poles, and kept an eye on them. In Germany the suspected groups were the Poles and the Francophone inhabitants of Alsace and Lorraine. Additional security measures were taken against them, curtailing their activities and personal freedoms. The Italian secret services kept pacifists and left-wing groups under surveillance, arresting some of them already in the first days of the war. In Turkey the non-Turkish communities were under suspicion, especially the Christians. Already in the opening days of the war numerous Greeks and Armenians, and smaller numbers of Jews and Arabs were arrested.

Citizens of foreign countries who happened to be on enemy territory when hostilities began found themselves in a difficult position. Every one of them was treated as a potential spy. Usually no effort was made to verify such suspicions and all, or almost all citizens of enemy countries were told to leave, though there were exceptions. Some were interned and subsequently deported. Britain pursued the most liberal policy. When the war broke out, there were 35 thousand German and a few thousand Austro-Hungarian citizens on British territory. For the secret services they were suspects; they were put under surveillance and subjected to repressive measures, but not listed for deportation. Nonetheless all citizens of enemy states had to register and as of October 1914 they could not change their surname. But there were exceptions to the rule. A sign of the atmosphere of war came in 1917, when the royal family changed its German name to the English name Windsor, which it still has today.

Repressive measures against citizens of enemy states were also undertaken in immigration countries such as the British dominions and the USA. In Australia persons of German origin were put under surveillance; later they were deprived of the right to vote, and 3,500 were interned. Australian newspapers disseminated allegedly reliable information that German settlers in Australia were working for the German intelligence service. The Australian authorities wanted to incite hatred of Germans and encourage Australians to join in the war. Similar measures were adopted in New Zealand and Canada; in the latter several hundred Germans and smaller groups of Ukrainians and Hungarians were arrested.

Things were no different in the USA. Nearly half the states banned the use of German in public, including the teaching of German in schools. Bars and restaurants had to remove "Frankfurter sausages" from their menus and replace them with "Liberty sausages," which were exactly the same product. German shepherd dogs met with reprisals, too: they were deprived of their hitherto name. Americans with German roots became an object of special attention for the secret services. They were accused of defeatism and espionage, and made to kiss the Stars and Stripes in public to prove their loyalty. There were lynchings. These activities were to make the war, which many Americans found strange and hard to understand, more popular and motivate them to take action. The American Protective League, which had a membership of a quarter of a million, played a signal role in the hunt for enemies.

In belligerent countries there were reprisals on works of art by citizens of hostile nations. At the request of the secret services the bookshop sale of the literary works of an enemy country could be suppressed, and copies withdrawn from lending facilities in public libraries. The works of Victor Hugo and Emile Zola were banned in Germany, and the works of Goethe and Hegel in France. Citizens' organisations appealed for a ban on the performance of music by composers from enemy countries, theatre productions of plays by dramatists from enemy states, and discouraged the reading of literary works by writers from hostile nations.

Citizens' organisations were often the initiators of spy-hunting projects, which turned into a symbol of mass war psychosis. The inhabitants of Europe, hitherto quiet citizens, succumbed to an obsession with spies, and called upon their authorities to intern all foreigners as potential or actual spies. There was no limit to the fantasies conjured up on the ubiquity of spies. People kept an eye on suspects, watching how they opened and closed their windows, whether they were not sending light signals. Apparently there were spies lurking at every street corner and virtually under every bed. Many an innocent individual was killed or arrested merely on the grounds of a denunciation. The military, which had no qualms about severe retribution and was quick to hang suspects, received strong civilian support. The Germans in occupied Belgium, and the Austrians and Hungarians in Galicia and the Bukovina became notorious for excessive severity. In the latter case the Emperor Franz Joseph intervened. On 17th September

ber 1914 he issued a declaration that he did not want unwarranted arrests to push loyal subjects in a direction that was dangerous for Austria-Hungary.

Work had been going on since before the war to build up such an atmosphere. Newspapers and political commentators had been warning readers of alien infiltration and reporting arrests; literary fiction was full of spy stories. Journalists and novelists reflected the paranoid fear of foreign espionage, while at the same time endorsing it as a genuine threat. William Le Queux's renowned novel *The Invasion of 1910* tells the story of an invasion of the British Isles prepared by a host of German spies. In France books by Léon Daudet worked the same effect, which earned the epithet of "spy mania" for itself. In August 1914 millions of Frenchmen were led to believe that posters advertising a well-known soup concentrate contained important secret information for Germany. A factor which contributed to this climate were the soldiers' magazines warning against spies and posters put up in barracks reading "Beware of spies!"

Citizens of neutral countries were put under special police surveillance. The police were well aware that many a Spaniard, Dutchman, or Swede had been recruited by belligerent states. As citizens of neutral countries they had unrestricted passage all over Europe working as company representatives. Some of the diplomats employed in the embassies, legations, and military or commercial attaché offices of neutral countries had also been recruited. The secret services tried to control their correspondence.

Neutral countries were a good base for the activities of belligerent countries' agents, whose task was to get the government of the neutral state to join their side of the war, or at least to pursue a policy of friendly neutrality. Their second job was to collect data on their host country's economic and commercial relations with enemy states. Thirdly, they were to infiltrate enemy spy networks. The best location for such activities, traditionally the meeting-place for all sorts of rival intelligence organisations, was Switzerland. It was the ideal place for starting up spy affairs, the headquarters of international espionage. The chief belligerents availed themselves of the services of

Swiss politicians and agents (at a price, of course). Another good place for agents was Spain. Under the cover of a Spanish company German agents published two pacifist magazines in French, *La Paix* and *La Vérité*, which were smuggled across the Pyrenees. Both sides' agents observed shipping movements in Spanish ports and Spain's exports and re-exports; they kept a lookout for submarines entering Spanish ports, and paid the local press and journalists to influence public opinion. German agents like the promising young intelligence officer Wilhelm Canaris were supplying arms to Moroccan insurgents fighting against French forces. In Holland British agents were particularly active, under cover of bogus shipping companies in Rotterdam and other places. In the USA Franz von Papen, then German military attaché and future Chancellor of the Weimar Republic, pursued particularly intensive and ingenious espionage activities.

To make things more difficult for spies in belligerent countries, soldiers' and prisoners'-of-war letters, and telegrams and telegraphs were censored. The Germans, Austrians, and Russians had been censoring correspondence already before the war, setting up "black offices" – discreet workplaces in post-offices, where postal employees supervised by counter-intelligence men opened and read letters arriving from abroad. During the war in Vienna secret service staff checked half a million letters a month, and up to quarter of a million in Budapest. By the end of 1917 ten and a half million telegrams had been inspected in Austria-Hungary, of which 43 thousand had been detained for a closer review, and 1,375 handed over to the police for an investigation. To carry out the task, the authorities needed a large group of linguists, so the armies established schools to train translators. By the spring of 1918 only on their Italian front the Austro-Hungarian forces were employing 220 officers and 1,000 private soldiers for language services. Naturally, they could only control a certain percentage of all the mail. In 1916 Britain's Royal Mail handled 12.5 million letters a week; 2 billion items passed through the German *Feldpost* service in the course of the war. Passports were made obligatory on all border crossing points; and efforts were made to limit travellers' movements as much as possible by introducing rigid controls. Travellers had to have special permits authorising them to travel.

Another important task for the secret services was subversion and sabotage. Saboteurs destroyed, or tried to destroy warehouses, ships in ports, and telegraph lines; they disrupted the work of munitions factories, set fire to factories and warehouses, damaged locomotives, spread livestock diseases, and poisoned wells. Both groups of Italian, and their adversary Austro-Hungarian saboteurs worked efficiently in the Adriatic ports, attacking naval and merchant vessels in dock. In 1915 the Benedetto Brin, an Italian battleship, was scuttled by Austro-Hungarian saboteurs. A sabotage network consisting of German and Irish dockers set fire to ships in American ports ready to sail with military equipment to Europe. German saboteurs in Britain and the USA organised strikes in ports and dockyards, set up pacifist organisations, and destroyed installations in power stations and oil depots. One of the most spectacular sabotage operations was carried out by a British team at Ploieşti in Rumania. They destroyed storage tanks containing 800 thousand tonnes of oil to prevent it from getting into German hands. Subversion and sabotage were becoming more and more important, and colleges were set up to train saboteurs, especially in the art of mine-setting.

The agents of belligerent states reached Poles, Czechs, Croats, Serbs, Irishmen, Finns, Lithuanians, Ukrainians, Indians, Persians, and Arabs, in attempts to instigate local uprisings against the incumbent state. They also worked among their enemies, trying to diminish their will to resist and showing how pointless it was to continue fighting. A special task was attributed to internationalist revolutionaries. The Allies were counting on German Communists in Germany and Austria, and the Germans on the Russian Bolsheviks.

Working for the secret service was dangerous, a kind of adventure sport. Agents risked their lives. If arrested they ended up in jail or on the gallows, only rarely were they exchanged for agents from the opposite side. When Carl Hans Lody, first on the list of German spies held in London, was executed by firing squad in the Tower of London, they knew that there would be no mercy. During the spy hysteria of the first months of the war large numbers of real and presumed spies were arrested, and there was a similarly large number of convictions. By the end of 1915 the Viennese police had conducted 1,479 searches in the houses of persons suspected of contact with the enemy and arrested 1,069 persons charged with sedition, including 185 charged with espionage. The Hungarian police instigated inquiries against 2,000 persons suspected of spying, of whom 1,506 were arrested, 5 interned, and 20 deported – all before the end of 1915. During the whole of the war the Germans arrested 1,200 real or presumed British agents, 120 of whom were shot by firing squad. Most of the arrests occurred in the first year of the war. The Russians were proud of their spy-catching successes. Still in the autumn of 1914 they discovered a spy ring working for Germany, which had probably been set up before the war. It was allegedly headed by Sergey Myasoyedov, a lieutenant colonel of the gendarmerie and head of intelligence in the Russian 10th Army which the Germans had easily crushed. Myasoyedov was a handy scapegoat turning attention away from those responsible for the Russian defeat in East Prussia. He was arrested, sentenced to death, and executed in Warsaw on 10th March 1915.

But as time went on there were fewer arrests of spies. The anti-spy hysteria petered out after the first few weeks. And spies learned not to leave tell-tale signs of their activities, perfecting the art of conspiracy and caution. They achieved better results at a cost of fewer losses. In 1915 197 sentences were passed for espionage in Austria-Hungary, but only 12 in 1918. Nonetheless persons suspected of spying continued to be arrested and punished until the end of the war. Even on 10th November 1918 four German spies in American uniforms were executed.

Repressive measures had been employed against spies even before the war. Undoubtedly, the most serious case in the history of counter-espionage activities occurred in May 1913, and involved Colonel Alfred Victor Redl, chief-of-staff of the 8th Corps of the Austro-Hungarian army stationed in Prague, who turned out to be spying for Russia and France under the pseudonym Nikon Nizetas, transmitting strictly confidential material. Redl was discovered. An inquiry was conducted by Captain Maximilian Ronge. It turned out that he had been operating on his own. He was left in his room with a loaded revolver to end the affair on his own. The Emperor took it badly, unable to come to terms with such an affair happening in his army. The Redl affair undermined relations between Vienna and Berlin for a time. However, confidence was restored, Vienna resumed close co-operation with Berlin, and intelligence and counter-intelligence was modernised and developed. Redl was a homosexual who followed an adventure-packed lifestyle and needed much more money to maintain his numerous lovers than his earnings provided. France and Russia decided jointly to foot his bills. Love letters to his male lovers were found in his room, along with a large collection of ladies' underwear, which he put on for dates. Redl's sexual orientation reinforced the belief that homosexuals were more likely to become traitors and therefore were not suitable for work in the secret services. The fact that the Austrian authorities wanted to focus on Redl's sexual orientation rather than on the documents he passed on also underpinned this belief. Redl's story has fascinated writers, journalists and film-makers. In 1984 the Austrian actor Klaus Maria Brandauer played Redl in a film, and the well-known Austrian writer Stefan Zweig mentioned him in his book *Die Welt von Gestern* (English translation: *The World of Yesterday*).

One of the tasks agents were expected to perform was to control popular newspapers by paying them to disseminate defeatism and a sense of moral disarmament among readers. However, infiltrated newspapers soon became exposed, as their adulterated contents would be quickly noticed by both secret services and readers, who boycotted such papers. One example was the French paper *Le Journal*, bought up by undercover German agents with the support of Louis Tourmel, a French parliamentary deputy who had his right to immunity revoked and was arrested in 1916. He died in prison in January 1919, a year after the execution of Paul Bolo Pasha, the Lyon journalist who had bought up *Le Journal* with money advanced by Deutsche Bank. The German secret services also financed the defeatist *Le Bonnet Rouge*, which was soon exposed. Its chief editor died in jail in unclear circumstances. Louis Malvy, the French minister of internal affairs, who had been his protector, was in trouble. However, the French parliament did not consider him guilty of treason. Nonetheless he lost his parliamentary immunity and was sentenced to 5 years' deportation. In January 1918 there was another arrest: of the former prime minister Joseph Caillaux, a defeatist and supporter of a quick peace with Germany who had voiced his opposition to Georges Clemenceau's policy. Yet another journalist who did harm to the French cause, this time on a fairly minor scale, was Ernest Judet, chief editor of the Parisian newspaper *L'Eclair*. The Allies attempted to take over German newspapers, too, but they were not successful and eventually acknowledged that it was too risky and not very effective. However, they did purchase the sympathy of individual journalists.

Women played an active part in the secret war, although they never accounted for more than 10% of all the agents of the belligerent countries. Although few in number, nonetheless they were invaluable in view of the tasks they were required to perform, and also because they rarely came under suspicion. One of the top German agents was Klara Benedix. There were networks with a more than average female membership, such as the Belgian La Dame Blanche which co-operated with British intelligence, where women made up 1/3 of the agents. Another spy ring with a high ratio of women was a Jewish network operating for the British in Palestine and known as NILI (a Jewish name, an acronym for the Hebrew phrase "The Glory of Israel will not lie", 1 Samuel 15:29).

The most famous and certainly the most beautiful agent of the Great War was Margaretha Geertruida Zelle, Mata Hari ("The Eye of the Day"). On 12th February 1917 she was arrested by the French and executed at Vincennes on 15th October, but it has never been proved whether she was an agent, or maybe a double agent. Did she work only for the Germans under the cryptonym H21, or did she also work for the French? She was 41 when she died. She was a dancer and courtesan, and she seduced men with her flimsy, extravagant costume, her sex appeal and erudition. Enamoured French officers passed on information to her, which she then transmitted to

Germany. Her legend has been kept alive thanks to numerous films and novels, and is still regarded as the prototype female secret agent gathering information in bed. In reality she was more of an adventuress in pursuit of sensational experiences and treating her job more like a game, rather than a professional spy. She did not understand the mechanisms of out-and-out war. In 1916 the career of Gabrielle Petit, a first-rate Belgian and British agent, came to the same end. She was executed by the Germans. Gender was no advantage in the event of exposure and arrest. But the work and fate of female agents went counter to the stereotypical image of women and contributed to an increase in their status with the male part of society.

7. Psychological warfare

Propaganda was an active participant of the world conflict. Hans Thieme, an eminent legal historian, dubbed war propaganda "the world war without weapons." It was to help win the victory. It was hard for the recipients of propaganda to figure out what was true and what was false, if often the truth was represented as false and falsehood presented as true. In 1914 the belligerents realised that to win the war it was necessary to manipulate public opinion, although their propaganda machines were not yet ready to operate on the scale expected of them. They were only growing and experiencing growing pains in order to become more proficient. Today it is hard to estimate their effectiveness, because we have no instrument to measure this, but we do know that since money was continually being put into propaganda, it must have been appreciated. The respective propaganda apparatuses played a salient role especially in the last year and a half of the war, mobilising their societies and soldiers, supporting the shared values and national unity, reinforcing the will to keep fighting "for the good cause," which was the moral duty of all the citizens.

Depending on the nature and aim of its operations, and its addressees, propaganda used a variety of instruments: leaflets, newspapers, posters. It also availed itself of films and theatre plays, puppet shows, and open-air performances. In the psychological war the crucial factors were the word and the image, and in America music and movement as well. The American supporters of the USA's entry into war against Germany often organised street events with jazz bands, singing and dancing, alongside slogan-chanting. Sometimes they were attended by stars like Charlie Chaplin.

Rumour was an important ingredient. The ban on information spawned favourable conditions for ubiquitous gossiping. Some of the stories were spontaneous, others nurtured by the authorities. Hungry for news, people were prepared to believe anything. Stories heard on the grapevine triggered strong emotions and impacted on the imagination, which made them the source of visions completely divorced from the realities of war. They made the world a product of the imagination. One of the tales that circulated said that at night the Gurkhas and Sikhs serving in the British forces crept into enemy trenches, slit German throats and drank the blood. The Senegalese were rather similar, supposedly: since they were said to be cannibals they devoured their victims' bodies. The Germans were no better, they were monsters and perverts, who apparently crushed the heads of French and Belgian babies with their heels and then turned the bodies into soap, grease, oil, or pigswill. Some swore they had seen Germans crucifying Canadian prisoners-of-war, the Kaiser personally torturing small children, and his son arrested and imprisoned in the Tower of London. Others had seen Russians who had sailed from Archangel in 1914 and arrived in Scotland, whence "in their snow-covered boots" they trudged to the Western front. This piece of blather got a place in the London papers, which made it look credible enough for German intelligence in London to send home information "from reliable sources" that there were Russian units in Scotland. News of Russians fighting on the Western front went round in France, too.

The British created the most effective propaganda machine. They were the first to establish a central office for psychological warfare featuring the editors-in-chief of the main British newspapers and illustrated magazines. It was in Britain that the first ministry of propaganda was set up, in 1918, headed by the press magnate Lord Northcliffe (Alfred Harmsworth, 1st Viscount Northcliffe). It was in London that the Allied command for psychological warfare was created, and the services hired of the most eminent men of letters like Sir Arthur Conan Doyle, John Galsworthy, Thomas Hardy, Rudyard Kipling. British propaganda also employed children's writers and academics. The other belligerents did not set up such a coherent, centrally managed system to wage the psychological war, although Germany had a propaganda agency already in 1914. Numerous institutions and associations took part in the creation of their propaganda, but at most they met to coordinate their activities only once in a while and it was hard to avoid the impression that their operations seemed chaotic and badly planned, despite efforts by the military to coordinate them.

The press, especially the tabloids or yellow press, played an important role, though its contribution was not as paramount as it would be in the Second World War, largely because research on manipulation and mass psychology were not so advanced yet and the techniques for the manoeuvring and fine adjustment of data to obtain the desired effect were not so well known. Nonetheless the experts believed that the Great War could be recognised as the first big media war in history. The demand for news grew prodigiously, burgeoning edition sizes of existing papers and triggering the emergence of new ones. By November 1918 editions of German newspapers had increased by 69.9%, while Northcliffe's *Daily Mail* rose from 800 thousand copies in 1914 to 1.5 million in 1916 and 1.8 million in 1918; and the Paris *Le Matin* rose from 1 million copies in 1914 to 1.6 million in 1918. But the press was not able to meet readers' expectations, as military censorship was impeding or actually stopping journalists' and photographers' access to battlefields and authentic news. German censorship was particularly pervasive. German journalists' movements on the front were rigorously limited and controlled, and the texts they wrote subjected to strict scrutiny. The military had little or no understanding of the way the modern media and manipulation worked. Journalists had to wait for strictly regulated news bulletins compiled by the German army's field news agency to be handed down to them.

As a result, there were no accredited journalists at all on the spot to report the German 8th Army's victory at Tannenberg in 1914. French journalists, too, had obstacles thrown in the way to military sources of information. The more insistent were told to consult the official bulletins and communiqués issued by high command, which one of them labelled "masterpieces of elusiveness." French journalists were not allowed access to the front unless they obtained a special permit. But even then they were not permitted to report the real number of casualties, types of weapons, names of the generals etc. As with the Japanese, the belief was that "war is to be conducted quietly and anonymously."

The British press had the most to say to its readers, as censorship in Britain was relatively mild. It wasn't even brought in officially until April 1916. Nonetheless journalists accustomed to the standards of a free press were irritated by the curbs on press freedom and accused the government of "keeping them on a starvation diet." In outcome of the criticism, as of May 1915 British journalists could freely travel to the front and write reports on the war. The traditions of a free press won. But apart from that there was also a different approach to information and propaganda on the part of the British military compared to their French or German counterparts. Thanks to this papers from neutral countries, including the USA, could be freely distributed in Britain, and therefore it was difficult to cover up British losses and setbacks.

The press in belligerent countries frequently took its cue from the government and military authorities and either hushed up defeats or reported them as if they were victories. The Russian press never mentioned the defeats of 1915 and 1916 as such, only described them as exemplary, Kutuzov-style retreats. On the other hand it amplified even small wins into spectacular victories, reducing Russian, and bumping up enemy losses. For the British press the economic blockade of Germany was honest, whereas the economic blockade imposed on Britain was absolutely unjustifiable. For Britons the bombardment of church towers was a sign of unparalleled barbarity, while for Germans it was a necessity dictated by the interest of their soldiers. For the Allies the deployment of poison gas was a mark of barbarity, but for Germans a chance to bring the war to an end sooner and save lives. And so on and so forth.

Propaganda pamphlets were treated as significant. In Britain large editions of "little red books" officially known as Oxford pamphlets were issued by well-known commercial publishers. The series numbered 87 items, on subjects like *Why We Are At War: Great Britain's Case* (Oxford: Clarendon Press, 1914). One of the contributors to the series was the historian Arnold J. Toynbee. German-language pamphlets on German and Austrian atrocities were distributed by the Russians among prisoners-of-war.

Cinematography emerged as a substantial medium for propaganda. Although owing to censorship and wartime legislature, not many films were made with direct reference to the war, nonetheless the cinematic repertoire was carefully sifted to make it politically relevant and functional in the service of the cause. In Britain only about 10% of the films shown in the cinemas addressed the subject of the war directly, and in France it was not much more. It was feared that too many war films would discourage filmgoers from watching them. The biggest event in the world of cinema at the time was the screening of the full-length documentary, *The Battle of the Somme*, which brought a 20 million-strong audience to 4,500 British cinemas within six weeks. It was a veritable sensation, and also made an impression on filmgoers in neutral and (understandably) other Allied countries. On the other hand, *Der magische Gürtel,* a German film on the successes of the U-35 submarine which sank 23 vessels, was given a bad reception in neutral countries, and boycotted in occupied Belgium, which had 1,500 cinemas. Film chronicles of the war turned out to be more important for propaganda and more popular than feature films. 600 film chronicles were emitted only in France. In Germany between 1 and 1.5 million viewers watched a film chronicle once a week; and so did 3–4 million viewers in Italy (particularly on the war in the Alps). Italians, whose national cinematography was one of the world's strongest at the time, made a lot of films. The best-known Italian war film was on the heroism and death of the British nurse

Edith Cavell. Film played a very special role in the USA in view of the impressive number of cinemas – 12 thousand picture-houses nationwide. Patriotic addresses were delivered during interludes between projections. In 1918 films on war subjects accounted for 20% of the American production, most of it made towards the end of the war. *Shoulder Arms*, the famous Charlie Chaplin comedy on the war, entered the cinemas a fortnight before the end of hostilities. However, by the end of the war attendance figures were dropping due to the risk of catching Spanish flu.

Posters and postcards also claimed a place in the propaganda effort. The best-known was the British recruiting poster showing Lord Kitchener with the inscription "Your Country Needs You!" which was modelled on a scouts poster. It was emulated by Germans, Italians, Bulgarians, Greeks, and Americans. The last-mentioned printed over a million Uncle Sam posters designed by James Montgomery which, along with its British counterpart, is still referred to in modern advertising campaigns. An Australian recruitment poster had the inscription "Will you fight now or wait for this?" (showing Prussian soldiers holding civilians at gunpoint); and an Irish poster showing a soldier wrapped in a question mark was inscribed "An enquiry from the front. When are the other boys coming?" The best known and most appreciated individual in the business was the Dutch cartoonist Louis Raemaekers, who worked for the British, publishing in *The Times* and in the American press. His cartoons of Kaiser Wilhelm as Satan and the Germans as barbarians gained global popularity. In Germany one of the most popular images was the postcard with the picture of the heir to the throne and an inscription reading "Only by relying on the sword will we acquire the place we deserve under the sun, for it will not be given us voluntarily." There were also the postcards commemorating the German Masurian Lakes victory. German postcards distributed among Russian soldiers recalled Bloody Sunday, the victims of the 1905 revolution, and encouraged Russians to desert. A favourite motif in German posters and postcards was the female avenger, a warrior woman with a sword or tornado. During the war the Germans published and distributed 9 million postcards, cartoons, and other graphic works, many of them on themes drawn from popular culture. Austro-Hungarian postcards eulogised soldiers and predicted victory by presenting images of a loyal and bellicose Tyrolese or a group of cavalrymen. The Russian propaganda made frequent use of religious subjects and promoted the dynasty. Postcards showing the tsar and inscribed "Rule so that enemies will fear you" were sold on a mass scale. Other prints which performed a propaganda function included postage stamps and leaflets dropped from balloons and aircraft. In June 1918 the Allies dropped 1.7 million leaflets from the sky on Germany and Austria-Hungary; in July it was 2.3 million; 4 million in August; and 5.4 million in October. However, there is controversy among the scholars as to their effectiveness. Soldiers' attitudes were affected more by hunger and the feeling that continuing the war was pointless than by leaflets or medals and decorations awarded on a mass scale. They were irritated by the sight of a general followed by his aides carrying baskets full of crosses of honour. Awards made on such a mass scale inevitably devalued the honours.

Industry produced, and shops or more often than not door-to-door salesmen sold, war gadgets, figures of soldiers made of metal, china, wood, or textile, iron swords, miniature rifles, war comics, and posters. And they did not forget about the children, for whom the psychological war industry manufactured board games and miniature uniforms, especially sailor suits.

Personalities from the world of the arts – writers, playwrights, painters, graphic artists, art photographers – were committed to the propaganda effort. Most of them supported the war. Those who didn't, were few in number and, like Paul Valéry or Marcel Proust in France, kept quiet about their dissent, in fear of being accused of treason. One of the best-known appeals in support of the German war effort was signed by 1,347 German intellectuals. It was the same in Austria-Hungary. The infamous *Haßgesang gegen England* (Song of Hatred against England) was written by the German Jewish poet Ernst Lissauer, who later moved to Vienna. At the beginning of the war Sigmund Freud expressed his support for Austria-Hungary, saying that he gave his entire libido for Austria, although later he distanced himself off from the war, like Rainer Maria Rilke. In Bulgaria as well the local writers and artists, like Ivan Vazov and Kiril Christov, voiced their support for the war. Alongside the writers and artists there were clergymen of various religions; religious iconography was one of the popular modes of visual propaganda. This was true even of countries as secular as France, where the churches had been separated off from the state since 1905. In all the belligerent countries priests and preachers attended the soldiers, from the open-air religious ceremony to the blessing of collective graves and the memorial service. All the countries claimed that God was "on their side." However, there were exceptions to the general rule. In Britain, for instance, the Archbishop of Canterbury, head of the Church of England, refused to allow the churches to be used to promote the war effort and army recruitment. Anglican churchmen who supported the war had to conduct such activities outside the churches.

Both sides applied tremendous zeal and commitment to the building up of a bad image of the enemy, attributing all the worst vices to him, presenting him in a malicious caricature, which was no surprise at all, for such are the standards of any war. The Allies were more effective in the psychological war of nerves: they came up with more examples of the barbarity, sadism, and singular cruelty of their enemy, whose soldiers – they wrote – were marked by the instinct of murderers, "new Huns." The razing and destruction of Belgian towns and villages and the slaughter of their inhabitants, the destruction of the university library of Leuven (Louvain) and Rheims Cathedral, the devastation of Ypres, the Zeppelin raids over London and Paris, the violation of international law, the sinking of the *Lusitania* with 94 children on board – these were all excellent opportunities for the devising and dissemination of an evil image. News of the execution of Edith Cavell, the nurse who helped British soldiers and Belgians who wanted to join the Belgian army escape from occupied Belgium (12th October 1915 in Brussels) shocked Allied and neutral countries. A British poster showing a wounded prisoner-of-war and a German nurse pouring water on the floor in front of him after he had asked for water had a similar effect. German propaganda materials could not rely on such good source documentation. They described the cruelty of the Russians to German prisoners-of-war and British brutality on the high seas; they recalled the Allied bombarding of German civilian targets; and they stressed the fact that the war was being fought on behalf of cultural values; but their propaganda effects were modest. In neutral countries the propaganda produced by the Central Powers was clearly losing to the Allied propaganda, not only in terms of information value, but also sophistication and visual impact.

The language of propaganda served to deepen or diminish the differences separating belligerents, as the needs required. For instance, British propaganda blackened the image of the Germans, since as the beginning of the war relations between the two nations were not so hostile; at the same time it upgraded the image of the French. The Germans did likewise with respect to the British: in the language of German propaganda the British were an exceptionally treacherous and deceitful nation. The typical German image of the Briton portrayed him with a cigar in his mouth, standing on a heap of skulls. The worst possible vices were attributed to the enemy, along with fundamental differences in what he ate, how he behaved, and even in how he performed the physiological functions. A French propaganda pamphlet claimed that the average German excreted more stool than the average Frenchman, and that it was more vile-smelling. For the Germans the English were a "villainous nation of shopkeepers," their foreign secretary was "a common mongrel," and King George V was "a traitor." Enemies were given derogatory nicknames or represented as animals. Germans presented Frenchmen as vain cockerels and Russians as clumsy bears. The stereotypes were dusted and given a new shine. In the German and Austrian propaganda the Russian was a primitive yokel, a red-nosed drunkard with his gun slung on a rope and bast shoes on his feet; while in the Russian propaganda the German was a dull flunky and a mindless glutton. The Austrians disseminated a suggestively repugnant image of Serbians and Montenegrans as contemptible, "worm-ridden barbarians" who never gave up since, as a cartoon put it, they could never find a scrap of clean linen for a white flag. Serbia was presented as "the canker of Europe," a threat of infection for the entire continent. This was a ubiquitous epithet encountered in the Balkan propaganda. The Australian and Canadian propaganda warned their citizens of the "insidious Germans," who were capable of "the worst villainy" and wanted to take over both of these British dominions. In Australia a map was put into circulation showing the country's new name, "New Germany." Adelaide was to be renamed Hindenburg, Perth Tirpitzburg, and Melbourne was to be called Zeppelinburg. The aim was to scare Australians into greater commitment to the Allied cause.

Battles, especially those which presented a clash of different traditions and systems of values, provided a good source of material for patriotic propaganda. The Battles of Tannenberg, Gallipoli, Verdun, and Prunaru offered the scope for smooth manipulation.

Tannenberg. In the German propaganda this battle was a fine example of the defence of the *Vaterland* and the successful avenging of the Battle of Tannenberg/Grunwald of 1410. For the makers of the myth it did not matter that there were no Russians at Grunwald, but Poles and Lithuanians; what was important was that Slavs were defeated in the 1914 battle, which enabled the propagandists to reiterate the myth of a perpetual war of German culture against barbarian Slavs. Paul von Hindenburg, its chief hero, basked in the cosy mythical creation of victory and grew into the champion of Germany overnight, eliciting anxiety even in the envious Kaiser. Medallions bearing his signature and postcards with his photograph were manufactured and sold in large quantities. Barbers styled Hindenburg moustaches; monuments were erected in his honour and used as venues for patriotic events; poetic tributes were paid to him. The German navy named a warship the *Hindenburg*, and the Silesian city of Zabrze had its name changed to Hindenburg. Tannenberg was associated with a second heroic figure, Erich Ludendorff. Journalists reported that there was boundless rejoicing throughout Germany over Tannenberg. The names of von Hindenburg and Ludendorff were on everyone's lips. Throughout the war no other military or political leader came anywhere near the popularity they won with just one stroke.

Gallipoli. In its mythology this battle had two victors: the Turks and the ANZAC forces. The latter transformed a military defeat into a moral victory, and the vanquished into victors, celebrating their debut in war beyond the borders of their respective countries. For the Turks a cult developed around Gallipoli (Galibolu): it served as the founding myth for the Republic of Turkey and its father, Mustafa Kemal Atatürk, the only Turkish general who vanquished the Allies. Turkish propaganda recalled that the Ottoman Turks had occupied Gallipoli already in the 14th century, hence it was the first sign of a Turkish presence in Europe.

Verdun. "The gate leading to Paradise on Earth is called Verdun," the French dramatist Jean Richepin wrote with a flourish of pathos. In Carolingian times a symbol of the rivalry and clash between Gauls and Germans, Verdun turned into an epithet for the strength and determination of both sides. The Germans emphasised that the sacrifice had not been wasted; and the French said the same – that a withdrawal would have meant moral defeat. Verdun was a subject of continuous debate and became the lynchpin of both sides' propaganda. The contention over Verdun continued in postwar times, and was intended to – and did – attract the attention of the world's media.

Prunaru. This battle turned into an outright symbol of the resistance, daring, and bravery of the Rumanian army and people. On 28th November 1916 the Rumanian Second Roşiori Cavalry Regiment charged on a combination of German and Bulgarian forces and although unsuccessful, gave Rumanians a reason for national pride and glory. In the aftermath Colonel Gheorghe Naumescu, their heroic commander, became a frequently invoked figure in the propaganda and is still honoured in Rumania today.

8. Arms and equipment

The ground forces of all the parties were made up chiefly of infantry divisions. Apart from infantrymen proper, there were also artillery units, engineers, telegraphy specialists, medics, cooks, and supply units. On both sides of the front the infantry had similar equipment. In August 1914 nearly all of the combat armies except for the French had camouflage uniforms, though not all the soldiers had been issued with them. The German army had withdrawn its navy blue uniform in 1910, replacing it with the *feldgrau* ("field grey") version, a greenish-grey which blended in well against a background of smoke, mud, and the dingy colours of spring. Following the Boer Wars, the British army had given up it red uniform in favour of khaki (the word itself was a loan from Hindi and Urdu). The Austrian army exchanged its white uniform for greyish-blue *hechtgrau* ("pike grey"). Only the French kept the traditional uniforms that they had worn in 1870, in the belief that a ban on the wearing of red army trousers would be contrary to the French sense of taste and their military destiny, as the *Echo de Paris* observed. Red trousers were regarded as epitomising French honour and military glory. "The armies of Europe are changing their uniforms; fortunately we in France have more important things to do," the Parisian *Le Temps* added. Frenchmen liked to refer to the words of their former minister of war: "Withdraw the red trousers? Never! The red trousers are France!" In 1914 1,000 graduates of the elite Saint-Cyr military academy had vowed they would go to war, but only in their white-feathered bonnets. Nonetheless the proponents of camouflage uniforms, including the Minister of War, Adolphe Messiny, were not sitting idle, thanks to which on 9th June 1914 the Assemblée nationale passed an act making it compulsory for the army to introduce *bleu horizon* camouflage uniforms. However, it was not until the bitter experience during the Great War that the French army actually donned *bleu horizon*.

The armies of the poorer belligerents did not introduce camouflage uniforms, either, due to shortage of funds. In any case many

Serbian and Montenegran soldiers had no uniform at all, unless it was war booty taken from an Austrian. Similarly, most of the men in the Turkish army had no uniforms. Turkey had only brought in an uniform in 1912 and had not fitted out all of its soldiers, unlike Bulgaria, whose infantrymen served in uniforms styled on a Russian prototype, and as of 1915 on the greyish-green German model. On the other hand, Bulgarian cavalry units were still decked out in brightly coloured, sometimes rather flamboyant field uniforms.

As a rule soldiers marched in leather boots. The British and French had ankle-length shoes with puttees, while the Germans had calf-length boots. Not all Russian soldiers, and fewer still Serbians and Turks, had leather footwear. Instead they wore homemade bast shoes, and often in combat they had the civvies in which they had been mobilised.

At the beginning of the war Russian, French, and Turkish soldiers had no helmets, and hence the huge casualties. The Russians, for instance, had flat peaked caps. The experience of the war enforced a change. The first to react were the French, who started off wearing the coloured *képis* – stunners during parades on the Champs Elysées, but a source of tragedy on the front. They soon began to manufacture helmets weighing 765 g and modelled on the Adrian plumed headgear of the Paris firemen. The Russians copied the French design, and slowly started issuing helmets even before the February Revolution. The Italians and Rumanians had their own models, but they harked back to the French shape. In 1915 the British started equipping their men with "tin hats" – the Brodie Mark 1, a shallow helmet with a large rim and weighing 980 g. The Australians and Canadians followed suit, and the Americans used a similar design. The Germans set off to war in leather helmets with a metal *pickelhaube* peak. Only their cuirassiers had metal helmets. But the *pickelhaube* helmets were heavy and not much use. They offered no protection against the sun and tended to slip down the soldier's face when he was shooting. So in 1916 the German army started issuing the Stahlhelm M 1916, a deep, massive helmet with a characteristic rim round the back to protect the neck. It weighed 1,200 g and is generally associated with the Second World War. The first to be equipped with these helmets in a camouflaging colour were the stormtroopers. As of 1917 the Austro-Hungarian army started issuing identical helmets.

Soldiers carried, or rather lugged gear weighing 30 kg or even 35 kg, consisting of a rifle, bayonet, hand grenades, an entrenching tool, a knife, grease-box for their weapons, and a rope to clean their rifles with, a food tin containing their iron ration – 1 or 2 tins of meat, 2 tins of vegetables, 2 packets of biscuits, ground coffee, a bottle of spirits and a bottle of water, chocolate, tobacco, a needle and thread, bandages and plasters, matches, postcards and writing paper, a sweater, shirts, socks, and a groundsheet/military cape nicknamed "the hero's coffin," because very often it was used to wrap the bodies of the fallen, and their identity disc. On the main belt of their braces they carried 3 to 6 pouches, each with 60 to 120 bullets. This was the gear of the soldiers of the best equipped armies. In 1917 the British brought in one of the best backpacks. Its maximum weight was 27 kg, and instead of heavy leather straps it had lighter and far handier fibre tapes.

The gear had to be arranged to distribute the weight a soldier had to carry on his back evenly, so as not to hamper his movement excessively. "Carrying your home on your back is no joke," soldiers commented. They were not allowed to use their iron ration without their commander's consent, on pain of court-martial. During the war they were issued with additional hand grenades, gas-masks, white bands for use during combat at night, while patrols of the foreground were given shields and armour. Some soldiers carried musket shells as well as a pickaxe, crowbar, or a shovel. So you can hardly deny they did look like Christmas trees.

Officers did not carry heavy backpacks. The essential components of their equipment were their field-glass, maps, notes, and documents carried in a leather bag. Instead of a rifle they had a pistol or a Nagant, Luger P.08 Parabellum, Colt, Smith & Wesson, or Mauser revolver. They had batons for signalling orders, and watches, necessary to synchronise attacks. Cavalrymen were equipped with smaller and lighter backpacks. Apart from guns for 15–25 bullets they had swords and steel lances, which turned out to be of not much use.

The semi-automatic infantry rifles had similar properties, weight, and range. All that they differed in was the name. They were manually operated, bolt-action and magazine-fed, with 5–10 rounds of ammunition in their magazine. They had ranges of 2,500–3,500 m, but were accurate up to 1,000 m. The most common calibres were 7.62 mm, 8 mm, or 7.92 mm. An experienced soldier could fire up to 12 shots a minute. Some rifles had a slightly longer range than others, but were more sensitive to contamination and bad maintenance. Some, like the 5-cartridge Mausers, could be loaded faster than others like Lebels. Some like the Lee-Enfield had an unfailing bolt-action system; others like the Mosin and Mannlicher were not so reliable. To shoot a soldier first had to unlock his rifle; next a round would be inserted in the chamber; then the soldier closed up the lock and the rifle was ready to fire. A soldier's shooting skills and the quality of his training turned out to be more important than the quality of his rifle. French and German soldiers were the best shots, the former using 1886/1893 Lebels, the latter the 1898 Mauser (Gewehr 98). British soldiers were armed with the 1895 Lee-Enfield Mark III with a 10-cartridge magazine. Russians had 1891 Mosins, always with a bayonet fitted on (it was impractical to keep it in its pouch). Americans used the Springfield (a modified Mauser); and Austrians and Bulgarians had lightweight Mannlichers (M1888/ 1890/ 1895), which only weighed 3.65 kg. Experts differ in their opinions as to which was the best rifle in the First World War, and the way they rank them depends on the criteria taken into account. In the course of the war manufacturers modernised their products, for instance the chamber on the 1916 model of the Lebel (M16 Berthier) changed from 8-round to 5-round, and it was faster-loading, shorter, lighter, and more convenient than previous models. Sniper rifles fitted with a telescopic sight were introduced for hidden marksmen.

Both infantry and cavalry divisions were armed with fast-firing machine guns – one of the most sinister types of weapons in the war. The machine gun had been invented by the American-born Hiram Maxim, and first used by the British in the late 1880s against the Mahdist Uprising in Sudan, and later during the Boer Wars. These conflicts confirmed the advantages of the machine gun both as a defensive and as an offensive weapon. The striking force of a single machine gun was comparable to that of a whole battalion during the Napoleonic Wars, and fired 400–600 rounds a minute. The British used M1915 Lewises; the Russians had 7.62 mm Maxims fed from a 250-round canvas belt, supported on a circular base and fitted with a protective shield. The Germans used similar machine guns – "devil's brushes" – mounted on a four-legged base. The French started with old St. Etiennes, which in 1915 they replaced with the much more efficient 8 mm calibre, air-cooled M1914 Hotchkisses. Water-cooled machine guns, such as the Russian and Austrian ones, produced clouds of water vapour, disclosing their location and helping the enemy to destroy them. Despite the cooling, they could get so hot that they would lose their calibre and soldiers would be burned. Their disadvantage was their weight, up to 50 or even 60 kg. The Austrian water-cooled M 07/12 Schwarzlose needed lubricated ammunition, and had an attached lubricator fitted with a pump, which was a considerable inconvenience. The Italians used the Fiat-Revelli, which was modelled on the Maxims; the Turks used German m-guns. The Americans used British and French models at first, and introduced their own Browning, which had an excellent quality, in late September 1918.

Light machine guns (LMGs) and hand-held machine guns came into service during the war. Not all of them proved successful, some like the French 20-round M1915 Chauchat were prone to frequent stoppages. The British Lewis (in use as of 1917), and the German Bergman (in service as of 1915) were slightly better, but designers continued to work on improvements. The outcome was the German MG 15, also known as the 08/15, which was simple to operate, fast-firing, lightweight (21 kg), and required only 1 soldier to handle it. In started to be issued as army equipment in 1917, chiefly to stormtrooper units. The Germans also manufactured the Parabellum LMG, which was used from aircraft and airships; as well as the fast-shooting, lightweight Mauser with a 10-round magazine. When a modifying butt was fitted it could be used like a rifle with a machine gun's hit rate.

The machine guns in service were not perfect yet. They often jammed due to overheating and poor cooling, the ammunition belts not being checked properly, the barrels being clogged up with impurities. Even thought they had the reputation of being deadly, they were not always effective and accurate enough. Infantrymen attacking zigzag fashion in a crouching posture could dodge machine gun fire fairly easily.

The infantry's firepower was supported by the artillery, the essential weapons of which were light, fast-shooting, grooved, breech-loading artillery guns characterised by a high resistance to wear and fitted with special butts. The French had the best guns, the renowned flat-trajectory 75 mm Schneiders. After being fired, they automatically returned to their initial position. They could shoot up to 12 rounds a minute to distances of up to 5–6 km, and only 9 men were needed to operate them. Their firepower was over tenfold the power of Napoleon's guns. They could keep up with marching infantry, and turned out to be excellent for manoeuvre war, but less so for trench war. They were the basic equipment in French, Polish, Czechoslovak, and Rumanian artillery units until the Second World War. The Italians purchased a licence for the 75s and gradually brought them in to replace their own, not very successful 65 mm guns. Other advantages of the 75s were their protective shield and fairly small size. The German equipment included 77 mm guns, which were not as good as their 76.2 mm French and Russian (Putilovsky) counterparts. The Germans were aware of this and worked hard to construct a new lightweight gun, which they started to employ in 1916. Artillery guns fired scatterable mines and shrapnel which disintegrated in flight into small pieces, but their effectiveness depended not only on the equipment and quality of the projectiles, but also on wind speed. Medium-calibre guns were also part of the artillery equipment, and the Germans had the best models, 105, 120, and 150 mm calibres, which were fast-firing relatively easy to operate. They also has a big 220 mm howitzer with a range of 9–10 km. The French did not have good long-barrelled, 155 mm artillery until 1916, and 105 mm calibres until the autumn of 1914. The Škoda 100 mm and 149 mm howitzers in the Austro-Hungarian equipment were not bad, but one of the drawbacks of the latter type was the weight. They had to be dismantled for transportation. The Russians had good but not very mobile howitzers, the Krupp 122 mm model, which they had started using in 1909. The British had 84 mm, 120 mm, and 127 mm guns, and 114 mm howitzers. The guns made a lot of noise when they were fired, so gunners had their ears stopped up with cotton-wool or special ear-stoppers, and as a safeguard they had their mouths open when a shell was fired.

There were also mortars, guns with a short, smooth barrel. They were muzzle-loaded and sent out projectiles on a steep parabolic path, usually over a short distance. The armies were equipped with mortars of various calibres: small, of the order of 60–80 mm, and large, 211mm, 220–320 mm and larger. The biggest were not very mobile due to weight and size. As of 1915 the French were producing good 240 mm, 260, 270 mm, and 370 mm mortars, which were later deployed by the American forces. The Italians used 280 mm mortars which were regarded as good. The armies of the Central Powers had 305 mm Škoda mortars. They had to be dismantled for transportation, and on reaching their destination the 9 parts were reassembled on a special base filled with rails. They weighed 32 tonnes, and had a maximum range of 11,800 m (effective range 8,000 m). They were pulled on the rails by special Austro-Daimler four-wheel drive vehicles, designed by the distinguished automotive engineer Ferdinand Porsche. The crews operating these systems wore goggles and thick protective covers over their eyes and mouths; gunners would lie down flat on the ground waiting for the mortar to be fired, which would give rise to a tremor felt a dozen kilometres or more away, shattering windows within a radius of several hundred metres. Mortars were fired using an electric wire ignition device at a distance of 300 m away from the gun. The Italians had mortars of this calibre, too, but needed a whole day to set them up. They were transported on carriers the height of a two-storey house pulled by huge lorries. They were not very mobile and if there was a need to retreat fell easy prey to victorious assailants.

The Germans used 420 mm mortars which the French called Big Bertha – a name which has entered history, after Bertha Krupp, the wife of Gustav Krupp. This mortar needed a crew of 200 men. "It was such a colossal gun that we just couldn't believe our eyes," a witness wrote, "This monster dismantled into two pieces was pulled by 36 horses… the road trembled." It weighed 90 tonnes and once an hour released a projectile 10 m long and weighing 800–930 kg, over a distance of 14.5 km. It took 6 hours to mount it on a special concrete platform several metres thick, and a crane was used to load the projectile. The shock wave that emerged when it was fired was powerful enough to topple buildings and smash windows within a radius of 5–6 km.

The Germans also had a huge, 128-tonne super-gun which they used in 1918 to bombard Paris from a distance of 120 km away. They had been working on its construction since 1916. They had 6 specimens, but used only 3 to bombard Paris. Every 15 minutes it shot a 1,000 kg projectile. It was transported by rail. Towards the end of the war these guns were destroyed. The French mistook it for Big Bertha, but in fact it was not identical with the mortar. It was not very effective, especially as its barrel had to be changed after about 20 shots.

When aircraft started to appear in the skies, the commands decided to have anti-aircraft guns constructed and produced. Some of these new weapons were transported on carriers. By the end of the war the equipment of the German army included small anti-tank guns. Mortars and special trench mortars were implemented to destroy trenches. The flamethrower which the Germans first used in 1915 turned out to be a formidable weapon despite its unreliability. The Allies lodged a protest against its application, claiming that it violated the Hague Convention of 1907 which prohibited the employment of "arms, projectiles, or material calculated to cause unnecessary suffering" (Art.23e). But the Germans were not in the slightest worried by this. The device consisted of a cylinder containing petrol and a steel tube through which compressed gaseous fuel was pumped in. It was usually employed for the destruction of concrete bunkers and defensive structures. However, it was only serviceable in the right weather conditions – a sunny day and wind blowing in the direction of the enemy. Soldiers were scared of having to handle it, as it frequently broke down, causing injury or even death. It was as dangerous as operating a mortar when a shell hit it. If that happened the soldier turned into a human torch. It is hardly surprising that people were terrified of them. Towards the end of the war the Germans deployed flamethrowers in combat in forests, as presented on film in the famous "Lost Battalion" (1919). The Allies had similar weapons, but they were used on a small scale, chiefly for the removal of dead bodies from battlefields.

Poison gas was another sinister symbol of the Great War. Signatories of the 1899 Hague Declaration had undertaken to "abstain from the use of projectiles the sole object of which is the diffusion of asphyxiating or deleterious gases." The Hague Convention of 1907 (Art. 23) expressly prohibited the use of "poison or poisoned weapons" in combat. But when war broke out, both the Allies and the Germans set about producing poison gas. The latter were the first to employ it. In the autumn of 1914 Fritz Haber, a German chemist of Jewish origin from Breslau (now Wrocław), who was awarded the Nobel prize for chemistry in 1918, came up with the idea of filling shells with chlorine gas. After the war he contributed to work on Zyklon B. German command gave the go-ahead for research on gas bombs and later argued that the Hague Convention did not apply to the *diffusion* of volatile substances. They (and certain historians following in their footsteps) claimed that poison gas was a humanitarian weapon, since it caused death without the loss of blood. In fact, poison gas was one of the most dreadful types of weapon. Even some German officers considered it "dishonourable" and "repugnant." "I must admit that the task of poisoning the enemy like rats disgusted me," wrote General Berthold von Deimling, commander of the XV Corps. Public opinion regarded poison gas as a violation of the rules of war. None of the means of warfare was as controversial and met with such widespread opposition as poison gas.

Soldiers were lying along the road, exhausted and gasping for breath. There was yellow mucus dribbling from their mouths, their faces were blue and full of despair. That's how a British officer described the effects of gas poisoning, having witnessed its first application at Ypres. He examined them and administered first aid. He wanted to go straight to the Germans and throttle them, pay them back for their devilish deed. Sudden death was better than that terrible suffering. German soldiers put 6,000 40-kg cans of gas produced by IG Farben in conduits dug at a fairly shallow depth into the ground along the trench line. The entire operation was carried out by a special poison gas unit, and the cans were manufactured by Bayer, the well-known company from Leverkusen. The date of the attack was put off several times to get the required wind direction. The Allies knew there would be a gas attack, but ignored it. At 6 p.m. on 22nd April 1915 the first poison gas was released from the pressure vessels along 6 km of the front and floated in the direction of the Allied lines. After a while a massive cloud of whitish-yellow chlorine gas hit them at a speed of 2–3 m per second. Since chlorine is two and a half times heavier than air it reached those who were in the trenches and those hidden in shelters. Suddenly people were running amok across the fields, as if they had completely lost their senses. The cloud of gas cut down everything in its path, including the vegetation. The men were blinded, they were coughing and panting, they were blue in the face. That's how witnesses remembered a sight that nearly made their hearts stop. Of the 15 thousand soldiers exposed to the poison gas, nearly a quarter died in long and terrible agony. The gas attacked and disintegrated the lungs, slowly leading to painful death. Another witness observed the blackened faces; coats and shirts torn at the throat in a last desperate attempt to catch a breath of air; some already lying motionless, others kicking madly in their death throes, dying the most terrible death the observer had ever seen. Other victims lost their sight, had trouble with breathing, their faces remained disfigured for the rest of their lives, permanent burn marks were left on their bodies. The Germans were elated; Haber was declared a national hero, but his wife Clara was so shocked by the effects of the gas that she committed suicide. But Haber was not very worried by that. The Chief of the German General Staff Erich von Falkenhayn, who had earlier had his misgivings as to the outcome Haber had predicted, was pleased.

On 31st May 1915 at Bolimów near Skierniewice in the Kingdom of Poland (the western part of the Russian partitional zone of Poland) the Germans conducted the biggest poison gas attack on the Eastern front. They used 264 tonnes of liquid chlorine, which they released from 12 thousand cans. About 11 thousand Russian soldiers were killed. Haber personally inspected the attack. In his opinion, in war science and technology should serve the fatherland, to minimise the casualties of its own soldiers, and maximise enemy casualties. "Men in their death throes crawled about on all fours, ripping up their clothes as if berserk. One lay with his fingers dug into the ground, another next to him with the irises of his eyes wide open. In his eyes lurked dread of the unknown. The wheezing, poisoned breath of the moribund spoke of the immense pain they were suffering," wrote Max Wild, a German officer. The injured, dying of asphyxiation, with eyes bleeding and lungs burned right through, were being taken to Warsaw. "What barbarity supported by science," Princess Lubomirska commented as it happened.

In subsequent years more and more pain-inducing and deadly poison gases were used many times on all the fronts, but they were not as effective as they had been originally because gas masks and other safeguards had been brought in. Gas attacks were used to create havoc in enemy defences. The last time gas was employed was by the British on the Western front in mid-October 1918. A gas attack made Adolf Hitler lose his sight for a time.

Production of the components needed to manufacture gas rose at a dramatic rate. By the end of the war the Germans were producing 1,000 tonnes of gas a month; the French over 500 tonnes; and the British nearly 3,000. Apart from chlorine more dangerous poisonous substances were produced, phosgene and phosphorus vapour, and the most lethal of all – mustard gas, also known as yperite because it was first deployed by the Germans in the Third Battle of Ypres in 1917. Mustard gas attacked all the moist tissues in the body and killed the careless, because it did not evaporate for weeks, causing wounds which did not heal and blindness. A total of 63 poison gases – causing irritation, paralysis, or burns – were deployed during the war. Nonetheless the introduction of poison gas did not mark a breakthrough, as the Allies were quick to follow suit. Moreover, a change in wind direction could make the gas cloud return and cause injuries in the despatching army. This was the fate of 2,000 British soldiers at Loos on 15th September 1915, killed by their own gas; and of German soldiers on 15th July 1918, when a gas cloud they had emitted turned back in their direction, breaking their attack and allowing the French to counter-attack. Thirdly gas masks and other protective devices mitigated the effects, although there still remained a residual toll of casualties. Before gas masks were introduced, there were spontaneous attempts to create protective devices, such as the Black Veil Respirator, a veil-like sack with eye slits and a chemically treated mouth-pad. British women responded to a press appeal by handing in 100 thousand wedding veils within a few days to make respirators, and thousands more in the following weeks. Later Hypo helmet respirators (the British Smoke Hood) were introduced. They contained a chemically treated cotton mouth-pad, soaked in a solution of sodium hyposulphite, washing soda, and glycerine, to absorb and neutralise pollutants, preventing their inhalation. However, the effect lasted for a few minutes until the absorbing substances were saturated and the chemical reaction subsided. Attackers utilised this fact and sent out a series of gas waves at intervals. The first masks were crude, made of a piece of rubber fitted with goggles and a mouthpiece with a filter for breathing. But they were inconvenient and so primitive that they could cause death by asphyxiation. As time went on developments were made, with impregnated textiles to cover the face and non-breakable glass for the eyepieces. Even horses were protected against gas attacks by having their fodder-bags put on.

Gas masks annoyed and irritated the soldiers. Many hated them. They made breathing difficult and hampered vision and mobility. They forced soldiers to learn to live in the gas environment (as the Canadian historian Tim Cook put it) and in the rhythm of the *danse macabre*. In outcome, despite the protective measures, throughout the whole of the war between 25 and 91 thousand soldiers died due to gas. The fatalities were not as great as those caused by artillery fire, but it was gas that determined the view of the Great War as a cultural phenomenon, the stamp of downfall for civilisation and of European barbarity. Stuck in a gas mask, a soldier was merely a puppet deprived of personality, a symbol of alienation. Stumbling about in their snout-ended, glass-eyed gas masks, soldiers had forfeited their human shape. Roland Dorgelès, a French novelist, dubbed the gas mask "the pig snout which represented the war's true face."

Both sides set up chemical units to conduct gas attacks. Laboratories were established in the rear to work on new types of lethal charges, as well as on preventive devices which would be more effective than existing ones. In 1917 the ingenious Germans besieging Riga fired gas-filled shells, which were independent of atmospheric conditions. The Russian defenders were blinded by the smoke and choked, and artillery fire did the rest. The Germans secured victory. Henceforth gas-filled shells were used more and more often on all fronts.

Another important symbol of the Great War was the tank. Machines protected life, and machine-power was standing in for humans. By applying human brainpower there would be less bloodshed and the extent of the carnage would be reduced. That was what Winston Churchill, a great enthusiast of armoured vehicles, said in the British parliament on 5th March 1917. No doubt his confidence in the tank, that it could be the breakthrough leading to the breach of the front, launched the ultimately successful project to design and construct tanks. The organiser of the tank corps was Major General Sir Ernest Swinton, originator of the idea to mount an armoured platform on a caterpillar undercarriage. Churchill broke the resistance of the officers and politicians who were against the idea of what they called "monstrosities," although the first appearance of tanks on the Somme in September 1916 did not endorse their proponents' optimism. Sir William Robertson, Chief of the Imperial General Staff, was diffident and called tanks a rather desperate invention.

The decision to start design studies for the tank was made in January 1915, once it was known that trench war and its barbed-wire front were a formidable challenge, and that the conflict would not be resolved soon. The term "tank" was derived from the name for a water cistern, and that's what the tank looked like. The British wanted to keep the work on it secret from enemy intelligence. The first model was called the Mark I. By 1917 the upgraded Mark IVs were in action at Cambrai. In 1918 the next generation, the Mark V, was introduced. It could carry 25 infantrymen apart from its crew of 9. A tank's weapons depended on whether it was male or female: the former had two 57 mm guns, and the latter had 6 machine guns. They weighed 20–30 tons and were 10 m long head to tail. Their shape was meant to facilitate negotiating craters, trenches, and barbed wire. They carried fascines, bundles of brushwood to fill up trenches. In compliance with the military doctrine behind them, tanks attacked in waves. Their operators expected them to be effective if used on a mass scale, hundreds of them in one sweep.

The first tanks had a speed of 1.5 kmph, the later models 6.5 and 7 kmph. They could only move forward. Their job was to destroy barbed wire and obstacles, and to provide cover against enemy fire for infantrymen moving forward. Their effectiveness was restricted by their imperfect motors and lack of radio communication. Tank crews used homing pigeons with messages to command. Tank components were transported by train to the battlefield and assembled near the front. They did not cover a long distance between successive fuel stops – they used up 6 litres of fuel for every kilometre! Crews could spend a maximum of 2–3 hours inside a tank due to the heat. Cases of fainting or carbon monoxide poisoning from the fumes were frequent. Smoke and fumes made communication between crew members difficult.

The French took to tanks and the Schneider-Creusot works set about their production. The first large-scale deployment of tanks by the French was on 6th April 1917, but they failed firstly because they were too heavy and not versatile enough, and secondly because their fuel tank, which was situated in the front, was easy to destroy. The

French military authorities turned to Renault, which made good use of the opportunity and produced the R-T 17, a slightly faster, more mobile, and safer vehicle than the original ones. R-T 17s weighed 5 tonnes and had a 37 mm gun. They became the basis of the French tank units. However, despite efforts, no joint Allied model was produced, owing to the continuing resentment and rivalry between London and Paris.

The Americans came to like tanks. General John Joseph Pershing was a tank enthusiast. The Americans set up a tank committee which they put on the Allied agenda for joint projects in late 1917. In the meantime, until 1918 US tank units were equipped with British and French vehicles. The officer appointed to organise the American tank units was Captain (subsequently Colonel) George P. Patton, renowned for his later victories during the Second World War.

On the other hand, tanks failed to win the approval of the Germans and Austrians. Although there was no dearth of German officers enthusiastic about tanks, the final decision was that in view of the shortage of manpower, raw materials, and steel Germany would not be able to produce enough tanks to make them viable in the field. The plan to put up 10 tank battalions by the end of April 1918 was halted. In fact the Germans did construct the A7 V, but they deemed it too clumsy, difficult to manoeuvre and, like the Allies' tanks, very slow. It was armed with a gun and 6 machine guns, and had a crew of 18. In March 1918 it made its debut at St. Quentin and took part in combat on 24th April, but was not successful. Instead the Germans concentrated on anti-tank defence. At first the tanks took them by surprise, but gradually they learned how to deal with them. They deployed guns against them, and later 37 mm anti-tank guns and anti-tank rifles.

Armoured cars appeared on the battlefields at the very start of the war, but they did not play a major role. The Belgians were the first to use armoured cars, which they equipped with machine guns and sent out against the German cavalry. Armoured cars proved useful in this application, but they were no good for breaching the front owing to their rubber wheels and insufficient armour and arms. They were used only for reconnaissance, and made just a modest contribution to the war. There were also armoured trains, equipped with cannon and machine guns. They were like mobile fortresses and were used to cover concentrations of forces, and occasionally to support attacks. When the need arose they were deployed to transport arms and ammunition, and to evacuate the wounded.

III. A Soldier's Lot

The thoughts on the mind of soldiers going off to the war were how to win, how to survive to the end, not to be wounded or taken prisoner. Most were not thinking of deserting, at least not in the initial phase of the war. But there were not many lucky enough not to be injured, fall ill, or be taken prisoner.

1. The wounded

The statistics for the wounded were far higher than for those who were killed. In the German army to the end of 1915 the figures for the dead (killed or dead of their wounds) were 628 thousand; while the figures for the wounded were 1,595 thousand. By November 1918 the numbers injured in all the armies exceeded 20 million. In Britain there were 27 thousand veterans receiving invalid pensions still in 1980. Medical staff tried to help soldiers recover as fast as possible, so that they could return to the front. The numbers serving in a division depended on the rate at which convalescents returned to the front, which in turn determined the outcome of combat. In the German forces 52% of injured officers, and 44.7% of injured men recovered enough to resume service; in the British army the figure for officers and men averaged about 45%. Many of those injured more than once returned to the front. The record-holder was Bernard Freyberg, a Briton resident in New Zealand, injured 9 times. He was a hero, too, and in 1917 became a general (a temporary brigadier-general) at the age of 27, the youngest in the rank in the Allied armies. Most injuries were sustained in outcome of artillery or infantry fire, with a certain contribution from air raids, poison gas, and flamethrowers. Only 1% of the wounds sustained on the Western and Alpine fronts were caused by combat with bayonets or knives. Injuries could also be, and were caused by attempts to cross obstacles in the field – mud, rivers, trenches, barbed wire, or in winter were due to low temperatures.

Grenades and shrapnel caused open head and body wounds, potentially leading to permanent disability. The injured included soldiers who had lost a leg, an arm, both legs and arms, soldiers who had developed psychiatric disorders, gone blind, had spinal injuries, and ones with mutilated faces, sometimes to such an extent that they did not have the courage to return home to their family and place of origin. In November 1918 the last-mentioned were estimated at 280 thousand, most of whom spent the rest of their lives in mirrorless welfare homes isolated off from the rest of society. In 1921 in France veterans with disfigured faces set up an association which had a membership of 10 thousand still in 1953. An orderly from London described one of them and the problems he had, writing that he was perfectly aware of his appearance. You knew that he knew you knew that a careless glance could make him suffer… Could any woman approach such a monster without showing repugnance? Wouldn't children run in fear? Societies were not prepared for such a number of disabled and war invalids. Alongside numerous instances of sympathy and assistance invalids met with aversion and even hatred for obliging others to maintain them. Sometimes hospitals turned them out into the street. The disabled were in the vanguard of the conscientious objectors. They were the ones who supported the anti-war movements – as far as their physical condition permitted – and united to defend their right to respect and a decent life. The first congress of the maimed and war invalids was held in the Grand Palais in Paris on 11th November 1917. Over 100 associations represented over 100 thousand members. It was a similar story in other countries. In Germany the first national discussion was held in Berlin in April 1915. The disabled elicited debate in the press and the parliaments on the means and manner of assistance they expected. They were staunchly backed by the churches and trade unions, thanks to which national organisations were created to aid invalids, financed by the state and from donations and public collections.

Doctors, especially surgeons and orthopaedic specialists, were able to help some of the disabled, providing those who had had amputations with artificial limbs. However, the prosthetic devices were not very operative and constantly reminded invalids of their pain and disability. Nonetheless, the joint efforts of doctors and designers advanced the quality and efficiency of artificial limbs, which improved with time. There was much slower progress in reconstructive surgery, which is more complex. On the whole the prospects of improvement for those with disfigured faces were bleak, although there were doctors who embarked on facial surgery. But such attempts were few and far between, with few specialists and few volunteers willing to submit to an experimental operation. Usually they were issued with a mask to conceal their disfigurement.

Progress was observed in the hospitals. The disinfection of surgical instruments became more regular, there was improvement in the prevention of gangrene, blood transfusions were carried out, skin was disinfected, and devices containing magnets were used to extract pieces of metal from the body. The treatment of the consequences of gas poisoning – ophthalmic disorders, skin diseases, burns, and blistered lungs – was a tremendous challenge. These conditions were previously unknown to the medical profession, a new experience both for patients and doctors, who were left helpless. Other challenges were posed by the effects of warfare in winter conditions, such as frostbite and photokeratitis (snow blindness).

The wounded were evacuated from the field by orderlies, but owing to the natural obstacles and the narrowness of the trenches this was not always possible. Witnesses of the Battle of the Somme wrote that for a few days cries for help could be heard from no-man's land, but no help was forthcoming. Finally the calls died down – the wounded had died of loss of blood, exhaustion, or dehydration. Similar observations were made at Verdun. "Anyone who hasn't seen the wounded deprived of assistance, emitting the shriek of death and drinking their urine to quench their thirst… has not seen war," a French soldier wrote.

On evacuation the wounded were taken to a medical dressing station, but they could not count on fast and good-quality aid due to the long queues waiting for attention. For many this was tantamount to a death sentence. After a gruesome clash nurses were extremely busy and sometimes fainted from being overworked. It was the same with doctors. Even though thousands of civilian doctors had been mobilised, there were never enough, and this applied to all the armies. In 1914 in Germany there had been 30,031 physicians (including 700 women doctors) in medical practice, and although 80% of them were called up, on the front the shortfall amounted to 20–30%. 1,819 German doctors died during the war from injuries or diseases, and 2,218 were wounded. There was a shortage of hospitals. The biggest shortages were in Serbia and Turkey, and the quality of the medical services there were far from perfect, despite assistance from wealthier, allied or other countries' medical staff. Out of all the combatants, Serbians and soldiers of the Turkish army had the least chance of recovery, and the prospects for wounded Bulgarians and Rumanians were not much better.

The plans commands had made before the war had taken neither the extent of the calamity nor the numbers in need into account. The scale and nature of the war caught the planners by surprise. In the first weeks of the war the commands of all the armies concentrated on enhancing the quality of medical services, improving management and staff training, and expanding the medical services, including the nursing and auxiliary medical corps. One of the first units of this type to be sent out was the British organisation Queen Alexandra's Imperial Military Nursing Service. The wives and daughters of kings and aristocrats set examples of self-sacrificing and dedicated service, to encourage other women from affluent homes to join them. This was nothing extraordinary – women from the wealthy classes had always been involved in charity work for those in need. What was special was the scale of the aid dispensed and the numbers dispensing it. Daisy Hochberg, Princess von Pless, wrote that she was glad and happy to be on a medical train, working as a nurse in charge of the carriage accommodating an operating theatre and 8 other carriages, and looking after the 80 patients hospitalised in them. The war and her endeavour to bring them relief from pain allowed her to forget her own problems. Another lady who thought of her service in a similar way was Eleonore Reuss zu Köstritz, the intrepid consort of King Ferdinand of Bulgaria, who was said to have "a special gift for relieving suffering." The Queen of the Belgians was yet another devoted carer, a paragon of fortitude, sensitivity, and responsibility; and so, too, was the Tsarina Alexandra Feodorovna. The Tsarina turned the royal palaces of Russia into hospitals and encouraged her older daughters to work in them, though not for long. When her perseverance ran out, she returned to her palaces.

For centuries European womenfolk had been perceived as considerate and valiant nurses, and this idea persisted during the Great War. Serving as a nurse with a Red Cross armband fitted the traditional image of femininity. The prevalent belief was that women should always be ready to help, treating wartime service in the hospitals as a laudable patriotic duty. That was their usual motive. In effect the brave and arduous service women rendered in the hospitals, and the death of many of them while on duty contributed to a rise in the status of women as such and of the nursing profession.

The Polish Nobel prizewinner Marie Curie-Skłodowska earned a special place for herself among the female volunteers dispensing medical services. In France Mme Curie organised a mobile X-ray station enabling medical staff to locate a bullet or shrapnel in a wounded soldier's body and to diagnose fractures. When the war broke out, the French army had only one X-ray ambulance, but thanks to the efforts of Mme Curie, by the end of the war there was a fleet of 20 ambulances and 200 sets of X-ray equipment. Sometimes she herself drove one of the ambulances, which were dubbed *les petites Curies* ("little Curies"). In 1917–1918 one million and a hundred thousand X-rays were taken in them. 150 women radiologists were trained in the Paris Radium Institute; however, they were not aware of the long-term effects of radiation and as a result their health suffered. Marie Curie also trained a group of American radiologists. She left a record of her wartime experiences in her book *La radiologie et la guerre* (*Radiology in War*). The other countries also had X-ray services.

Girls and young women were trained and sent to work in the hospitals, though not all of them were prepared mentally and emotionally for the tasks ahead of them. Some withdrew, terrified by what they saw and what was expected of them. Only the bravest and most resilient persisted. "I think you would faint overwhelmed by fear if you saw what the poor nurses have to do. They apply surgical drains and wash wounds that are so big and horrible that you tremble with fear, and you can only admire them for their perseverance. They dig out pieces of metal from the bodies of wounded soldiers. I assure you that the word 'responsibility' has acquired a new meaning here," one of them wrote. The first women doctors, including surgeons, worked in the war hospitals, arousing a stir and surprise. Only after some time were they admitted to these duties. "It's true! She's operating!" was the response to the surgical activities of Elsie Inglis, the "Lady with the Lamp," a woman doctor and surgeon from Edinburgh who left an admirable record in the annals of medicine working on the fronts in Serbia and Russia, where she died in 1917.

Private individuals, wealthy bankers, industrialists, and aristocrats helped to organise and finance military hospitals. Polish families – the Tyszkiewicz, Lubomirski, Sapieha, Sanguszko, and Kronenberg – were founders. Frenchmen and Britons organised hospitals in Serbia and Greece, and Germans set up hospitals in Turkey. There were also benefactors from neutral countries. Dutch and Swedish patrons tended to establish hospitals in the Central Power countries; and Americans in France and Britain. By April 1917 the Americans had set up 17 admirably equipped hospitals in France, with a thousand beds and a fleet of 200 ambulances. In Paris alone there were 110 young American doctors, surgeons, and senior medical students from Harvard working on a voluntary basis. Two British suffragettes, Flora Sandes and Evelina Haverfield, went to Serbia, where there was a dire shortage of medical staff, to work as nurses. They founded the Hon. Evelina Haverfield's and Sergeant-Major Flora Sandes' Fund for Promoting Comforts for Serbian Soldiers and Prisoners. There were 600 British doctors, nurses, and orderlies working in Serbian military and civilian hospitals (including 14 Scottish Women's Hospitals). Serbian soldiers and civilians recalled their highly professional services with the utmost gratitude. The French set up their own hospital network in Serbia and Greece, with 100 doctors working in them. Even more French doctors went to Rumania and set up hospitals there, equipping them with top-quality apparatus. The assistance provided by the Allies was disinterested to a certain extent, but they also wanted Serbian and Rumanian convalescents to recover as fast as possible and return to the trenches.

Usually the military authorities set up their hospitals in university buildings, schools, courthouses, warehouses, Nissen huts, and even in factories and palaces. The quality of their equipment varied over a broad range. Alongside those which were comfortable and had all the necessary apparatus there were also hospitals that were short on everything: heating, hot water, pain-killing drugs, medical staff, and goodwill, with wounded men in wards overcrowded to bursting point, where soiled dressings were collected up, sorted, washed, and recycled.

On receiving first aid the wounded were sent to a field hospital. Those who doctors decided were in need of hospitalisation and specialist operations were sent to hospital trains. However, often they had to wait days at the railway station before they could board, as the demand for transportation was growing all the time, trains and tracks more and more overexploited, while units being taken to the front, arms and ammunition took priority over everything else.

Hospital trains could carry 200–400 wounded men. During the intensive fighting at Verdun the wounded were taken to hospitals in Paris at a rate of about 2–3 thousand a day. In the fighting on the outskirts of Przemyśl in the autumn of 1914 seven long hospital trains passed through the city every day. But not all of these mobile hospitals had good sanitary conditions. Instead of having beds, the wounded were put into freight cars used for horses and cattle, and bedded on foetid, worm-infested straw. Many died on the way from infections, gangrene, contagious diseases, dysentery, typhus. The dead were removed from the train at the nearest station, but not before everything that was of any value was pilfered from their clothing. This was practised despite chaplains' appeals and warnings from the authorities that such behaviour would be severely punished. "Trains full of wounded men pass through Olkusz (near Kraków). When we hear them groaning and see blood dripping out over the steps of the railway cars we feel really sorry for them, for all that human misery," wrote a Polish witness. From the station the wounded were taken to hospital – in Vienna and Prague by tram, 8 men on stretchers to a carriage. In Prague 289 thousand were despatched to hospital in this way! But things weren't so good everywhere. Sometimes on arrival at their destination the wounded were left at the station for several days, waiting for transport. This happened in Warsaw in the autumn of 1914. Thousands of wounded soldiers who had received some treatment in the Russian field hospitals were left stranded at the terminal station of the Warsaw-to-Vienna railway, waiting to be taken to hospital. Many died there before the eyes of bystanders. There were not enough vehicles to take them to hospital, not enough beds in the hospitals, management was inefficient. "At the station there was a dreadful sight: the platforms were full of wounded lying on the ground with no straw, in dirt and excrement, in the cold and rain, rending the air with their heart-breaking cries or miserable pleas, 'For God's sake, tell them to dress our wounds,'" a witness wrote.

Wounded Allied soldiers were evacuated from Gallipoli in yet another way. They were first brought to medical dressing stations and clinics located on the beaches and in tunnels in the hills. Next they were taken by boats and barges up to ships, some of which were hospital ships. But the majority were brought by sea to British hospitals in Egypt and Cyprus.

Those who had a lot of luck and a strong constitution, walked out of the hospitals and went back to the front. Innumerable convalescence homes were set up to help them recuperate. Usually convalescents were fed well and entertained by singers and musicians. They had free theatre and music hall tickets. They could use libraries and reading rooms, attend talks on health and hygiene, and those who were illiterate could attend reading and writing classes. The fittest went sightseeing with volunteers. Educational societies collected books and magazines and sent them to hospitals and convalescence homes. Some of the convalescents were sent to holiday resorts, usually in the mountains. But there were others – the disabled, the blinded, those confined to a wheelchair – who never returned to the front. They were sent to training centres, where they were taught a new profession, and prepared to return to civilian life and earning a living. The authorities hoped that these men would be employed in factories producing goods for the army, which would prevent them from being a burden to society and the state. The scale of the aid dispensed to war invalids, and the methods used, were a completely new experience produced by the war.

2. Diseases and epidemics

The medical stations and hospitals to which sick soldiers were sent, received visits from senior officers and politicians, both of whom knew that one of the factors on which their army's success depended was the rate and effectiveness of hospitalisation. They also knew that the number of hospitalised soldiers depended on the efficiency of preventive measures. The better the prevention, the fewer would fall ill. Most attention was given to the prevention of epidemics of infectious diseases.

In trench conditions, with cold and permanent damp or waterlogging, it was easy to get rheumatism, trench foot, bladder disorders, inflammatory bowel disease, diarrhoea, pneumonia or tuberculosis, which only developed gradually. In the permanently cold and damp conditions of Flanders trench diseases sometimes claimed more victims than artillery fire. Soldiers were so debilitated and exhausted by the war that there was a particularly high sickness rate in 1918, albeit the figures must have included typical shirkers, malingerers feigning illness. From March to August 1918 there were over a million names on the German army's sick list. A high incidence of sickness, a consequence of difficulties with adapting to European climatic conditions, was observed in the British dominion forces. In 1917 the sickness rate in Australian forces was 144 for every thousand soldiers; the corresponding figure for Canadian forces was 158; and 34 in the British forces, with just a slightly higher figure in the French army. But according to estimates, the soldiers at the top of the table for sickness were the Turks. Malaria, cholera, and typhus wreaked immense havoc. Diseases caused seven times more fatalities in the Turkish army than combat. German and Allied soldiers were at particular risk from diseases prevalent in hot climates, in spite of adhering to the rules of hygiene, being vaccinated under medical supervision, and taking the antimalarial drug quinine. Cholera killed the German Field Marshal Colmar von der Goltz (19th April 1916) in Mesopotamia. The Russians fighting in the Caucasus and Middle East also encouraged their soldiers to be wary, and distributed leaflets in places where there was a risk, especially near wells, warning them not to drink water that had not been boiled because of cholera.

Typhus, a consequence of dirty hands and lack of hygiene, was a serious danger. Robert Koch's and Rudolf Virchow's research had proved the inverse correlation between hygiene and disease. The more dirt and insanitary conditions, the fewer preventive measures taken, the better the prospects for typhus. That is why the greatest number of cases was reported on the Eastern, Turkish, and Balkan fronts. Typhus made a salient contribution to the defeat of the Serbian army in 1915, depriving it of the potential to carry out the attack it had planned. Casualties due to disease exceeded those caused by enemy fire. In the Balkans and Near East typhus and other diseases such as malaria exerted a fundamental but unwanted impact on the progress of the war.

On all fronts typhus thrived thanks to lice. At the beginning of the war soldiers who became lice-ridden were embarrassed and kept quiet about it. But once they realised how dangerous lice were for their health, they demanded prophylaxis. On the Western front typhus did not develop into an epidemic thanks to a preventive campaign and the observance of the rules of hygiene. Chemicals were used for louse control, and the procedure was called "immunisation." Soldiers leaving the trenches for the rear passed through a delousing establishment and bath-house, where they learned the beneficial effects of soap, water, and a special chemical reagent. Their uniforms and personal belongings were disinfected or burned. Those going on leave received the same treatment, which was recorded in their paybooks. Lice-ridden Russian soldiers taken prisoner were quarantined, washed, scrubbed, and deloused before they were allowed into a POW camp.

Lice infestation became a problem for soldiers of the Central Powers on the Eastern front. It was serious enough for Prince Wilhelm von Hohenzollern to put a letter addressed to the public in the press, appealing for donations for the lice-infested. He wrote, "Our forces in the East are overwhelmed by a plague of worms, carriers of diseases, especially typhus. To overcome this threat, and particularly to stop the spread of disease we must have baths and disinfection for soldiers' clothing available, and that costs a lot of money." But the substance that turned out to be the best remedy for lice was the poison gas.

The belligerent countries introduced mass vaccination programmes for soldiers, prisoners-of-war, and civilians to stop infectious diseases. In 1914–1919 200 million vaccines were administered in Germany alone. The overall results of this gigantic effort by thousands were beneficial. No epidemics broke out on the Western front. Moreover, intensive research carried out on the sources of infectious diseases brought several important achievements. British scientists produced an effective vaccine against dysentery, and in 1915 the French produced an anti-typhoid vaccine, bringing down the mortality rate.

One of the biggest challenges the medical services had to face were psychiatric disorders. The figures for psychiatric complaints rose dramatically. Hundreds of thousands in all the armies put together – 80 thousand in Britain, 159 thousand Americans, and 270 thousand in Germany – are estimated to have come out of the war with severe psychiatric disorders. In fact, the German statistics should be even higher, since 600 thousand Germans had to be hospitalised owing to "diseases of the nervous system." Some were withdrawn from the front. Initially psychiatric patients were generally taken for malingerers, fakers, loafers, or even deserters and traitors, and even by the end of the war that's what many an officer thought of them. In addition, there was a tendency to regard homosexuals as slouches, cowards, and potential spies. It was widely held that punishment was what they deserved, not sympathy. Defined as "the crime of unnatural fornication," homosexual practices were usually punished by degradation and imprisonment.

Misdiagnosed psychiatric cases sometimes led to a tragic finale, when the patient was court-martialled for treason and executed in the full majesty of the law. Doctors' limited knowledge of psychiatric disorders could not be of much help to military courts. The problem had still not been resolved when the war finished. Usually the symptoms of psychiatric disorders evoked by the experience of war, although highly diverse, were lumped together and labelled "war neurosis," "névrose de guerre," or "Kriegsneurose." British psychiatrists adopted the term "shell shock" after an article published in the prestigious medical journal *The Lancet* in February 1915. One of the psychiatric disorders given a name of its own was "barbed wire psychosis." Soldiers suffering from it could not be induced, even by punishments, to leave the trenches and attack across the barbed wire.

The heated debate on the origins of psychiatric disorders did not bring a conclusive answer. Sigmund Freud and the psychoanalysts associated neurosis with sexuality, while the clinical psychiatrists saw it as connected with neurological disorders. The psychiatrists tended to support the theory that "war neurosis" was the result of a permanent state of stress due to the experience of the war and its atrocities, risk of death, injury, and helplessness. Others, including Austrian psychiatrists, saw a connection between neurotic disposition and low social status, or "inferior" nationality, and they tried to show that it occurred chiefly in non-Germans and the uneducated. Nonetheless proof that it was the war that was the chief source of psychiatric disorders was at hand on all the fronts. After combat soldiers were observed to have faces that were "scared stiff." "They lost their senses." Some went torpid, others sank into depression, still others into profound anxiety states caused by extreme horror. Others got diarrhoea at the sight of a battlefield. Many of those who could not cope with their distress took their lives. One of them was the Austrian Expressionist poet Georg Trakl, who committed suicide in 1914 in Kraków, and was buried there.

The most common symptoms of "war neurosis" were hallucinations, an unusually neurotic condition, aggressiveness or apathy, paralysis, amnesia, loss of bowel and bladder control, nervous tics, insomnia, chronic headaches, and nightmares. No-one really knew how and where to treat psychiatric patients. Nonetheless the authorities decided to establish psychiatric wards. The therapy administered was hypnosis, tranquillisers and narcotic drugs, as well as ECT (electroconvulsive therapy), which often led to cruelty and abuse. Some patients subjected to ECT died, and after the war there were legal proceedings in several countries concerning such cases.

Venereal diseases were among the most common ailments, as in any war. They were embarrassing, hence prevention and treatment was problematic. They were referred to as the "war diseases," albeit some conscripts and volunteers were already infected with VD when they enlisted. For the young French, English, German, or Czech workers who were called up visits to a brothel were commonplace. It was estimated that about 50% of the British soldiers who were diagnosed with VD had caught it while still in Britain. The rest got it in France, even though they were warned about excessive drinking and women. Apparently half of the 3,907 registered prostitutes in Paris were suffering from VD. Access to them was easy: the French gutter press advertised their addresses for soldiers looking for a "godmother." As a result in 1916 about 19.2% of the patients admitted to British military hospitals in France were suffering from VD. The corresponding figure for the entire period of the war was 27%. A total of 416,891 cases were diagnosed. In 1915 VD was confirmed in 22% of the Canadian soldiers. But some British conscripts got themselves infected deliberately to avoid being sent to the front, as medical examinations revealed. This was a common practice in all the armies. Some who caught VD lost their sight because of it.

A widespread opinion shared by soldiers of diverse armies was that they deserved life's pleasures, even though they might be hazardous. For this reason military bases were surrounded by a ring of cheap joints, palaces of pleasure, and brothels. Popular music hall songs claimed that there was a girl for every soldier: let them enjoy life while they can, for who knows which of them will return home. And that was the clinching argument – they might never return home, so why deny themselves the pleasures of Life?

Both the Allies and their adversaries keenly observed the growing number of infections. The commands introduced prevention campaigns. Army doctors warned soldiers of the dangers of casual intercourse, and of sexual intercourse in general. They conjured up scary stories of soldiers who caught VD and the consequences they suffered. "I dread looking at the symptoms of gonorrhoea," one soldier confided, "I think that if that ever happened to me, I'd probably kill myself." Army commands inspected the brothels and set up licensed bawdy houses for soldiers only. The men queued up for them, just as to the latrines, the only difference being that in the brothels there were military police on guard. By 1917 there were 137 soldiers' houses of pleasure in 35 French towns. In March 1917 the British authorities prohibited the use of public brothels for soldiers and set up licensed ones. They also imposed severe penalties for girls who infected soldiers. The Austro-Hungarian authorities did likewise. In the winter of 1916 on the initiative of General Karl Bardoff, chief-of-staff of the Second Army stationed in Russia, they set up licensed houses of pleasure, which brought down the incidence of sexually transmitted diseases. Sometimes condoms were issued to soldiers going on leave. The Empress Zita protested against the "soldiers' houses of pleasure," but that did not make military command change their mind. There were protests, not only in Austria, from clergymen and moralists, too, who saw this as moral and religious decline. The German military authorities followed suit, treating the matter as a necessary evil. The army recruited and registered the girls, who were regularly examined by army doctors. The army also regulated the price of sexual services. By the second half of the war all the armies had appointed military police and sanitary officers to oversee their soldiers' "houses of licence." The increasingly restrictive policy was due to the more and more aggravating consequences of sexually transmitted diseases, but it turned out to be effective. In all the armies the rigours were not relaxed until the autumn of 1918, which made the contracting of VD easier. American soldiers on their way to France were warned not to indulge in intercourse and discouraged from visiting the houses of pleasure. But the ones who were the main victims of VD were not the soldiers, but civilians who availed themselves of the services of infected women.

3. The killed

I have described the tragedy of the thousands of wounded who died before help arrived. While this is true, we must bear in mind that thanks to progress in medicine only 8% of the American soldiers who were wounded died, whereas the figure was 44% still in the Civil War. There was an improvement in the proportion of the dead to the sick. During the Napoleonic Wars for every soldier killed there were usually 5–7 fatalities due to disease; whereas in 1914–1917 on the Western front the ratio was reversed: 1 death due to disease to 15 killed in battle. Only in the Middle and Near East and in the Salonica area was the ratio the inverse.

The large numbers of soldiers killed every day was a consequence of the new technologies of killing and the strategy of attrition both sides had implemented. The lives of a whole generation were sacrificed in the battle for a few kilometres along the front; every metre cost hundreds of lives. "The front rotted with corpses," "death factory," "the slaughterhouse of Europe," "the lunatic asylum," "bloodbath" were the comments. The worst was that the determination of the units engaged in combat and the commitment of their soldiers started to be measured in terms of the numbers killed, and officers whose companies or battalions sustained relatively few casualties were suspected of malingering. The death of thousands ceased to be a cause for anguish. People soon got accustomed to it. Winston Churchill wrote to his wife Clementine that death was no longer shocking nor surprising, it was just natural, ordinary, something that could happen to anyone any time. The sight of mangled bodies hanging on barbed wire, the stench of decomposing corpses, the stink of the trenches became everyday experiences. In any case soldiers needed to adapt to such a war and be reconciled with it if they were to keep their sanity. A French soldier described the gory details of the death of his friend. His face was burned off, one piece of shrapnel entered the skull behind the ear, another ripped up the belly and broke the spine. You could see the spinal cord floating in a red mass. The right leg was shattered to above knee level. The worst was that the victim was still alive for a few minutes. There were thousands of similar, or even more drastic descriptions. The battlefields were not venues for the duels of heroes but sites of atrocity and suffering. No wonder that many years later veterans were still being haunted by nightmares of the war.

Understandably, the death of their loved one was extremely distressful for families. They were informed by telegram with the same wording that read that their relative was a valiant and good soldier, that he was loved by his comrades, that he had done his duty well, that he had died like a hero on the field of glory, that he had fought "for King and Country," "für Gott, Kaiser, und Vaterland," "pour la République." The texts were what the families expected. The words about heroism were theatrical clichés. In reality soldiers were killed by shellfire. They never saw their killers, who never knew their victims. Death would often come "like a hurricane," they wrote, for it was death wreaked by the ritual of artillery fire and snipers on the prowl. Still in the Franco-Prussian War of 1870 a soldier could see enemy guns pointed straight at him, but no longer in the Great War. Before he could experience the presence of the enemy in his own trenches –

if he ever got the chance – he experienced the consequences of shellfire, poison gas, the whizz and barrage of bullets, the groans of the wounded. An anonymous cog in a great army, he was just a manhandled tool. Technology had triumphed over human ingenuity on the battlefield, making for a depersonalised war. The rifleman and the artilleryman did not consider the person they were to shoot, but the accuracy of the shot.

Death notices were sent out within 10–14 days, while information that a soldier was missing was despatched much later, sometimes several months later. The correspondence was handled by the unit's officers or the regimental office. The names of those who were killed or had died of wounds were published in the press, which secured a high level of readership. The Germans published lists of the dead every day except Mondays. Sometimes a deceased man's personal belongings were returned to the family, but this never became the rule. The items which were returned most often included photographs, crosses, holy pictures and scapulars. Sometimes soldiers took the personal belongings of enemy soldiers who had been killed, treating them as a sort of trophy which they sent home to show that they were making a significant contribution to the war. Germans found watches on dead Englishmen, and gold and iron crosses which had been taken from German soldiers. They admired the British mid-calf lace-up boots, while British soldiers liked the German rubber galoshes for protection against mud and water. It was natural to consider enemy equipment, uniforms, coats, and shoes better. Some families lost two, or even three sons. One Frenchwoman died heartbroken on losing three sons. General Edouard de Castelnau, the hero of Verdun, also lost three sons.

The dead included those who were killed, those who died of their wounds, and those declared missing. In the several battles at Ypres, in which about a million lives were lost, 42 thousand British men could not be identified. Only one-third of those who fell in the fighting for Fort Douaumont were identified. Artillery shells ripped up bodies literally in pieces, so it was hard to identify the fallen. It was hard to tell whether a given soldier had been killed, had deserted, or was missing. The dead fell into the pits and craters made by the shells and were covered with mud, hence bodies could not be found. French and Belgian farmers still come across the bones of soldiers from the Great War in their fields. In 2004 the frozen bodies of three Austro-Hungarian soldiers were discovered at an altitude of 3,400 m in the Alps, at the foot of Punta San Matteo, and were given a funeral with military honours.

The colossal number of dead meant that not all of them could be buried. Often soldiers had to bury their mates or remnants of their mates near, or sometimes in the trenches, or put the bodies into sandbags and inter them in local graveyards. Not much could be done to preserve a fallen soldier's identity, which made identification difficult or impossible later. Rarely were soldiers buried with military honours. The custom was most frequently observed in the British army, where soldiers organised funeral cortèges, carrying their guns upside down. Those who died in hospital were buried in mass graves or in their family graveyard. A custom developed, especially in France and Germany, for a standard text or occasional verse to be inscribed on soldiers' gravestones instead of an individual epitaph.

Sometimes the dead would be laid in provisional roadside graves near crosses or holy statues, which were regarded as hallowed ground. Later they were exhumed and reinterred in military cemeteries. To prevent epidemics quicklime was put in the graves. Families claimed the right to bury their relatives where they thought most suitable and protested against the exhumations. Even while the war was still on families journeyed to the front in search of their son's, husband's, or brother's grave, despite the prohibition on such travel. It was an old tradition going back at least to the Napoleonic Wars. After the war a civic campaign was organised in France and Belgium by the families of the fallen, who demanded the right to have their relatives returned for burial in the hallowed ground of local graveyards and next to their kindred.

Usually in the European military cemeteries burials were conducted with no segregation according to nationality into "them" and "us," in line with the tradition of European culture. Death and burial reconciled the antagonists. There was no spatial segregation, either, so as not to spoil the aesthetics. Only members of the Judaic religion were buried in the nearest Jewish graveyard. Similarly, in Russia and the Balkans Moslems were buried in Islamic graveyards, though this was not a hard and fast rule. The exception was France, where all the fallen were buried in one plot, regardless of race or creed. In 1915 the French government decided to establish an archipelago of cemeteries, which would include burial places for British soldiers, but a year later the authorities in London decided to set up separate cemeteries for their own. At first the British founded the National Committee for the Care of Soldiers' Graves with the Prince of Wales as its president, changing its name in 1917 to the Imperial War Graves Commission (and much later to the Commonwealth War Graves Commission), since soldiers from the Dominions were buried there as well. The Committee decided that soldiers should be buried as near as possible to the place where they died. Gravestones were being transported from Britain to France already during the war, and at a rate of 4 thousand a week in 1920–1923. No information was inscribed on the headstones on decorations, race, or religion: all were equal in the face of death. Other countries adopted the same principles.

The Italians built beautiful cemeteries, some in the form of mausoleums. They, too, established a state institution to organise and construct places of last repose for their fallen soldiers. The Americans did not want their boys to lie far away from home and made arrangements for transport to America. Nonetheless, about 30% of the Americans who fell stayed in the European cemeteries. In the interwar period the US authorities financed the travel of families to pay their respects at their relatives' graveside. The Belgians decided to exhume all their dead from small and circumstantial places of burial and reinter them in a central cemetery at Langermarck, specially built on a scale comparable to the cemetery at Verdun. In December 1915 the Ninth Department for War Graves started its operations in the Austro-Hungarian Ministry of War. A special group was set up under its auspices to look for suitable locations for military cemeteries, design their layouts and arrange them. First-rate artists, painters, graphic artists, sculptors, photographers, architects and landscape planners, such as the Slovak architect Dušan Jurkovič and the Polish painter Wojciech Kossak, were commissioned. Many of these cemeteries are a veritable work of art, a picturesque if sad landmark on the cultural horizon. In Western Galicia alone, which is now part of Poland, 378 war cemeteries and burial plots were established while the war was still going on, and more were created after 1919. There are now 403 of these graveyards, meticulously looked after and conserved. On the fence of one of them there is an inscription which says, "Our names have been extinguished, but our deeds continue to shine." A special unit in the Department for War Graves (the *Evidenz-Gruppe*) was created to keep records of the fallen, search for those declared missing, and identify bodies.

The Russians, too, were involved in the organisation of war graves, though not as assiduously as the others. The Alexandrian Committee conducted its operations from the very beginning of the war, identifying the fallen, designing and organising cemeteries. The Germans had a central war graves commission (*Volksbund Deutsche Kriegsgräberfürsorge*, founded in 1919), as well as separate organisations in the various regions and cities of Germany. They had an efficient identification system, thanks to which the overwhelming majority of the German dead could be identified. Every German soldier had a metal dog-tag or one with his personal data on parchment enclosed in a special box.

In Europe the creation of war cemeteries was financed by the state with additional funds coming from private individuals and institutions. They were designed in a similar way. The guidelines issued by the Allies as well as Germany and Austria-Hungary recommended simple landscape design. There were wooden, metal or stone crosses. Sometimes the names of the fallen would be inscribed in a golden mosaic script. There would be an earthwork and stone wall around a war cemetery, with a ring of oaks and birches for additional fencing, particularly where there were collective graves in the shape of a mound or tumulus. Some war cemeteries had chapels or, in Alpine areas, churches erected on them, with memorial tablets inside.

There was also the question of commemorating and honouring the unidentified fallen. This was done by the creation of tombs of the unknown soldier – a new phenomenon in European culture. The first of these monuments went up in Paris under the Arc de Triomphe, and in Westminster Abbey in London – places which signified the highest tribute. Only the Germans, Austrians, and Hungarians – the losers – had problems with commemorating their unknown. War graves and cemeteries offered a means of commemoration, just as special ceremonies did, to mark the anniversary of a battle, the beginning or end of the war. The poem "In Flanders Fields," written by the Canadian John McCrae to commemorate a friend's funeral made the poppy a symbol of the war and those who fell in it. In Britain Remembrance Sunday, popularly known as Poppy Day, has been held every year since 1921 on the Sunday nearest to 11th November, with the custom of laying wreaths of red poppies on the graves of the fallen.

4. Prisoners-of-war

On all the fronts a total of 8.4 million soldiers became prisoners-of-war, 3.9 million in Allied POW camps, and 4.5 million held by the Central Powers. The Hague Convention gave a definition, though in very broad terms, of how POWs were to be treated. They were to be isolated off to prevent them from returning to the battlefield. Officers were to be separated off from the men. Officers were given better conditions than rank-and-file. The predicament of POWs was shown in a true-to-life manner in the once famous French film "La Grande Illusion" (1937). Belligerent states conferred with each other on the territory of neutral countries on the exchange of prisoners-of-war. As of March 1917 POWs who had gone blind, had amputations or disfigured faces were exchanged. Holding them only meant costs, as there was no risk of them returning to the field due to their disability. As of May 1917 POWs with psychiatric disorders, and from July those with "barbed wire syndrome" were exchanged on the same grounds. As of December 1917, on the grounds of the Berne agreements, those over 48 and those in detention for 18 months or over were exchanged – a total of about 1 million POWs to the end of the war.

Tens of thousands are estimated to have escaped from captivity. To make escape more difficult, detaining authorities gave orders for POWs' trouser buttons to be removed. Nonetheless, by April 1916 12,440 POWs including General Lavr Kornilov had escaped from Austro-Hungarian detention camps. One of those who tried to escape from German captivity was Captain Charles de Gaulle. He made 5 unsuccessful attempts. In the camp at Ingolstadt he met the young Russian officer Mikhail Tukhachevsky, future Marshal of the Soviet Union, and the French air force ace Roland Garros.

The largest number of POWs, 3.0–3.6 million, came from the Russian army. Until January 1917 for every 100 Russian soldiers who were killed, there were 200 who surrendered. The ratio for the British army was 20 to 100; 24 to 100 for the French army; and 26 to 100 for the German army. POW camps were inspected by the International Prisoners of War Agency (established by the International Red Cross) and the plenipotentiaries of the governments of neutral countries, the USA (until April 1917), Spain, and Sweden. However, the inspectors were not always admitted. In any case their critical remarks did not have to be respected. The inspectors observed the quality of the food, the sanitary conditions, and in the Turkish camps the brutality of the guards and the violence they exercised, especially on Indian prisoners. Indian soldiers had a notorious reputation for killing Turkish POWs. Arabian insurgents were infamous for robbing POWs and letting them loose naked in the scorching hot desert. In general POWs received parcels from home with food, warm clothing, and medicine, and had money sent to them and paid out by a bank, thanks to which they could buy extra food. Austrian, Hungarian, and German POWs detained in Russia could go to Sweden to convalesce, on a doctor's recommendation. But the biggest problem was the shortage of food. In 1917 one of the Polish POWs (former soldiers of the Russian army) detained in Hungary complained,

"We have been starving for three weeks. We have been told to join the Polish Legions, a Polish army. No-one has been allowed to go home, and we don't know how it will all end, except that we are dying of hunger." As regards food and sanitary conditions, the POWs in France and Germany were best off; conditions were not so good in the Russian, Hungarian, and Italian camps; and the worst were in the Turkish camps. 70% of the British and Indian POWs in Turkish captivity died from thirst, hunger, disease, the heat, and sandstorms on the way from Mesopotamia to camps in Central Turkey, in what became known as the March of Death. The graveyards in the vicinity of POW camps testified to the scale of the problems: POWs emaciated by malnutrition were easy prey to diseases. Only 60% of those who reached a camp in Central Turkey survived to the end of the war. 750 thousand POWs are estimated to have died in camps in various countries. Apart from Turkey, the mortality rate was highest in Serbia (25%), Rumania (23%), and Russia (17.5%). In France and Germany it was no more than a few per cent, and most POWs held in those countries were liberated at the end of the war.

POWs were forced to work, doing a variety of jobs on the principle of food for work. They were employed in mines and munitions factories; building fortifications and digging trenches, corridors and tunnels; they transported food and ammunition; repaired electricity and railway lines, roads and bridges; they built cemeteries. In Germany 65 thousand French forced labourers built the Hindenburg Line. Earlier 15 thousand Russian POWs had constructed German fortifications near Verdun. In February 1917 POWs accounted for 60% of the workforce in the Russian iron ore mines and 30% in the steelworks. In 1915–1916 about 25–40 thousand POWs died on the construction of the Murmansk railway. There were many deaths among the Turkish POWs working for the British in the Near East. Russian POWs in Austria-Hungary were employed on the construction of roads and tunnels in the Alps. Many of them died as evidenced by numerous Orthodox Christian roadside crosses and icons.

Many of those digging trenches or building shelters died from friendly (their compatriots') fire. POWs sent letters to the International Red Cross to protest at their treatment; Allied soldiers held in Germany even tried to stage strikes, which were brutally put down. POWs complained that their country had forgotten them. A growing sense of alienation and camp claustrophobia vexed them. The predicament of POWs never became part of their nation's collective memory of the war, perhaps because there were no spectacular escapes of the kind which could excite journalists, writers, or film-makers. The way they spent their afternoons and evenings – playing cards, chess, draughts, or basketball, attending lectures given by their learned colleagues, or reading newspapers – was not particularly exciting.

Sometimes certain groups of POWs enjoyed privileges, for example captive Serbs and Czechs held in Russian camps; likewise Poles and Czechs in French and Italian detention. Some were offered their freedom, if they joined the armies of their captors. In January 1915 an Adriatic legion was set up of Serbian soldiers held in Russia, alongside a Czech company (*Česká družina*; later reorganised into the Czechoslovak Rifle Brigade, and then the Czechoslovak Corps in Russia). A division of Czech POWs and deserters was established in Italy, and a Czechoslovak legion was created in France. Polish POWs in France enlisted in a Polish army under the command of General Józef Haller; and after the February Revolution Poles held in Russia created Polish corps and regiments.

5. Deserters and mutinies

There were also camps – different ones – for deserters and mutineers. Both groups were severely punished, in some cases with the death penalty. The military authorities realised what a bad effect deserters and mutineers would have on the morale of the rest of their soldiers. Punishments were particularly severe in Italy because of the scale of the phenomenon. In 1915 66 Italian deserters faced the firing squad, 167 in 1916, and 359 in 1917. In that year the Italian authorities introduced draconian measures to restore discipline, such as the execution of every tenth soldier in units which mutinied. By the end of the war they had executed over 1,000 soldiers. But these measures were not effective. On the contrary, it turned thousands of Italians against their country and army. Deserters and mutineers deemed less culpable were placed in detention camps and set to hard labour in overalls with the word "deserter" printed on them. In the British army there were 361 executions, and 48 in the German army. Many more were convicted in those countries, but usually the death sentence was commuted to long-term imprisonment. Some sentenced to life imprisonment in Germany were liberated by the Allies… in 1945.

In the first two years of the war the number of deserters in the various armies was not so large, and only marginal on the Western front, where the soldiers were motivated to fight for their nation and country. Not surprisingly, the propaganda campaigns encouraging desertion were not very effective. Desertion crops up in the plot of *Pădurea spânzuraților*, (Gallows Bird Forest), a novel by the Rumanian writer Liviu Rebreanu. Nonetheless desertion did occur. In 1915 soldiers from two French battalions marched out of the trenches singing the *Internationale*. Similar incidents happened in the Austro-Hungarian army.

A higher rate of desertion was observed in the Russian and Turkish army. According to estimates around 450–500 thousand had deserted from the Turkish army by November 1918, and 1.5 million from the Russian army by the end of 1916. The desertion rate rose in Russia after the February Revolution. Russian soldiers did not have a strong sense of identity with their country, and still less with their nation, but they did feel a bond with their monarch and fought well as long as they were watched and punished for insubordination. Once the father figure – the tsar – had been removed and discipline became lax, Russian soldiers no longer saw the need to fight. The well-disciplined army dwindled down into a bunch of marauders and deserters. Not surprisingly, about 900 thousand deserted in the course of 1917, before November. Bolshevik agitators encouraged them to desert, and many a deserter joined the Bolshevik Party.

The revolutions in Russia and the protracted war stimulated desertion and mutiny in all the armies. Courts-martial had plenty of work on their hands. There were mass desertions from the Bulgarian and Rumanian armies. In the second half of 1918 desertion became a serious problem in the Austro-Hungarian forces. Some deserted in search of food, others because they could no longer see any sense in fighting. In August 1918 the number that had deserted from the Austro-Hungarian army was estimated at 100 thousand; by the end of September it had risen to 250 thousand; to reach 400 thousand in late October – 5%–8% of the Austro-Hungarian forces. Usually the deserters were soldiers who never returned from leave, hence measures were taken to curtail leave. Fairly large numbers of deserters got to Switzerland, where they even set up a deserters' union. Preventive measures failed in view of the scale of desertion; the severe regulations were effectively suspended. Those who were convicted had their sentences suspended or mitigated. Courts handed down sentences of hard labour instead of the death penalty. Some malingered as soon as they were called up. Whenever that happened, gendarmes would visit the malingerer's parents with a warning that if their son did not report to barracks the father would be called up. Usually deserters would hide in the woods and set up dangerous criminal groups known as "green bands." They earned their living by robbing civilians. There were also numerous gangs of this type on the prowl in Italy, Rumania, and Bulgaria. In the summer and autumn of 1918 the high rate of desertion had an effect on deteriorating conditions in the German army. 10% of the German soldiers absconded while being repatriated from Russia. Many of those who stayed in the army joined covert strikes, in other words carried out orders in a lazy manner. Their numbers are estimated to have risen to a million by the autumn of 1918.

The history of the First World War also has organised or spontaneous mutinies of whole units on record, such as the mutiny in the Austro-Hungarian navy at Kotor in January 1918, although they were not as widespread as desertion. One of the more serious mutinies as regards scale occurred in France in the spring of 1917. The one in

Russia in 1917 led to the February Revolution. Similarly in Germany the naval mutinies in early November 1918 precipitated the uprising known as the November Revolution. The mutinies that occurred in the other armies were not so large.

In late April and May 1917 some battalions, regiments, and divisions in France refused to carry out orders. The incident coincided with the breakdown of the Nivelle Offensive, which had been badly planned, and conducted even worse. "We've had enough killed," the mutineers chanted. One of the units marched through several towns baaing like sheep led to slaughter. Mutinies did not have a decisively political undercurrent, although the February Revolution in Russia and the emergence of soldiers' councils left its impression on the imagination. With certain exceptions mutineers did not call for peace immediately, although they wanted peace on French terms. Signs of insubordination were recorded in nearly half the divisions of the French army, but the soldiers who defied and were ready to fight against the authorities are estimated to have numbered 25–30 thousand. They intended to seize control of a number of trains, attack Paris, and overthrow the government. But they had no leaders, and were in the minority. They spent too much time arguing and drinking wine to take effective action. When they sobered up they found themselves in jail.

To deal with the mutineers Marshal Philippe Pétain, the new French Commander-in-Chief, applied the traditional carrot-and-stick method. He extended soldiers' leave and gave them a pay rise, improved the quality of their meals, increased war widows' and orphans' pensions, made military administration more efficient, and won the soldiers' trust. He ordered officers to organise regular conferences for the men to tell them why France was fighting. On the other hand, he had no qualms about imposing reprisals. He ordered the arrest of 5 ringleaders out of every company that had engaged in the mutiny. In the course of 1917 the courts handed down 554 death sentences, but only 48 were carried out. It was decided that excessively severe measures would be counter-productive since, as Pétain said, "all the soldiers are ours." Reprieves were granted to the leaders of the Senegalese division. French socialists stood up staunchly to defend the mutineers, whom they saw as apostles of democracy and freedom. Left-wingers called for the setting up of revolutionary councils based on the Russian model. "Soldiers are in a permanent state of agitation which is being exacerbated by the press, full of reports on the events in Russia," General Louis Franchet d'Espèrey assessed the situation.

By mid-June the excitement had started to subside, and Pétain assessed that in October 1917 the crisis was over. There was a return to discipline and military order, which lasted to the end of the war, for the French war machine, including provisions, the war economy, the political system, and the communications infrastructure, worked well. What had happened in the spring of 1917 were incidents of mutiny, but not of revolution, unlike the situation in Russia, and later in Germany and Austria-Hungary. The French had once again confirmed their commitment to their republican country, their state, and their proud nation.

IV. The Civilians' War

1. The war economy

The belligerents were not planning to introduce major changes in their economy, as they expected the war to end soon. However, after a few weeks the state authorities decided that a switch to a wartime economy was the order of the day. Some civilians were to don uniforms and march off to the front, while others were to transform into "soldiers behind the front" or "soldiers on the home front." A supporting base had to be created and geared to work for the front, providing it with human and material resources on a hitherto unimaginable scale.

In the First World War the boundary between the front and its hinterland, as it was known from earlier wars, was completely obscured due to the colossal scale on which belligerent countries mobilised their resources, which called for an absolutely co-ordinated effort on the part of the military and the civilians. This was achieved sooner in France than in Britain; much faster in Germany than in Austria-Hungary; and at the slowest rate in Turkey. In the Allied countries the mobilisation of civilians worked well until the very end; but in the Central Powers by the summer of 1918 it was encountering formidable obstacles which foretold the impending disaster.

To introduce the rules of a wartime economy and make them viable, the authorities had to put civilian administration and civilians under military control and military courts, which handed down summary sentences with no right of appeal. Internment laws and regulations were introduced, and on their grounds individuals suspected of sympathising with the enemy and citizens of foreign states were interned. Suspected persons were put under surveillance, or they could be arrested, interned, or even executed. Drastic instances occurred chiefly on occupied territories and areas bordering on the front. Restrictions were put on rights and freedoms such as the freedom to travel, the right to privacy in the home and its inviolability, the right to assemble, organise strikes and protests, and set up trade unions; or they could even be suspended for the duration of the war. Other restrictive measures which were introduced included censorship, the control of correspondence, and phone tapping. Publication in "enemy languages" was banned. The scale of these restrictions varied from country to country and changed with time; it was bigger in Austria-Hungary than in France, and bigger in Germany than in Britain. Parliaments conferred special powers on their respective governments for the duration of the war. The purpose of all these measures was to increase the state's domestic security and the efficiency of its war economy, and thanks to them the state was able to extend the level of its interference in production, the supply of raw materials, and the food and agricultural market.

In Britain, Germany, and other countries the state subsidised farmers and supervised imports. Even in the USA with its reputation for economic freedom in 1917 a war economy was imposed for food. A fundamental input to this decision came from the lively and ingenious Herbert Hoover, serving as head of U.S. Food Administration. It was presumably on his initiative that a campaign was launched to make Americans realise that their "food was fighting," with slogans like "Food will win the war" and "Food is ammunition – don't waste it." But despite such special efforts food production fell, not only in the USA but in all the countries. In Europe this was due to the scale of requisitioning, the slaughter of animals due to lack of fodder, the devastation of crops and pastures in areas along the front, shortage of agricultural labourers, a cessation in the use of artificial fertilisers due to the application of the chemicals in the war industries, and the mobilisation of horses – a fact which was particularly vexing and regrettable, for most of the animals mobilised never returned to their owners and work on the land. 8 million horses died! In outcome, 41% of the prewar cereal yield was harvested in Austria in 1918, and 56.8% in Hungary.

State interference went even further in industry. Industrial plants changed their product range as fast as possible, from civilian to military goods. Many private businesses were taken over by the state or put under state control. The extent of this phenomenon was relatively small in Italy, where industrial mobilisation was left to the private sector; but larger in Germany. In Turkey the few factories engaged in military production were effectively controlled by German military consultants and managers. In Russia state interference in industrial production was extensive enough to warrant the opinion that a "wartime socialism" had been established. In 1916 the famous Putilov and Obukhov works were nationalised, and the fuel and energy market was put under control.

The centralisation of power, and the prioritisation of military over civilian authorities, and of the executive over the legislative authorities was an inevitable step. New government institutions, or joint government and private institutions had to be created to carry out wartime objectives. The imperial powers had to find the means to mobilise their colonial manpower and material resources. In Italy the number of ministries went up from 12 to 22. 75 special committees with a membership chiefly of businessmen were set up in the British Ministry of Munitions, where Winston Churchill was minister as of 1917. The situation was similar in the USA and the other countries: everywhere special committees and commissions were appointed to plan production and manage orders.

The state imposed its production plan on private, co-operative, and state-owned companies, compelling them to produce specific goods at a fixed price. Popular politicians, including Socialists such as the French Minister of Armaments Albert Thomas, who enjoyed the confidence of the working class, were appointed to the national committees and commissions. Thomas raised the level of workers' participation in factory management. As a result the volume of arms production rose dramatically in all the countries, while civilian production diminished, or even in some sectors disappeared altogether. Despite the increase in arms production, the overall level of industrial production fell. The causes of this were wartime devastation, requisitions, embargoes, shortages of capital, and – most importantly – shortages of raw materials and labour. In Germany industrial production in 1918 fell to 57% of its level in 1913; in Bulgaria the corresponding figure (for January 1918) was 65%; and in Turkey 53% (for July 1918). In Hungary the extraction of coal fell to 79.8% of its prewar level, and steel production dropped to half its prewar level.

The state had to be powerful enough to monitor and control transport. The army had the categorical priority on the railways. Passenger services were reduced to a minimum, and a permit had to be obtained for travel. The state supervised the production, repair and maintenance of rolling stock. Nevertheless it was unable to guarantee the replaceability of damaged stock. In the summer of 1918 in Austria-Hungary one-third out of a total 14 thousand engines was being repaired. The transportation of infantry divisions from Galicia to Italy, which used to take 4 days in 1915, rose to 14 days in 1918. The state was the initiator and constructor of railway lines, especially in the area around the front, bridges, and macadamised roads. The British built a railway line from Egypt to Jerusalem. The Germans built bridges, railway lines, and roads in the Kingdom of Poland, Lithuania, and Ukraine for more efficient management of the land they had occupied and faster transportation of troops across it.

State interventionism meant that the authorities controlled about 30–40% of the gross national product, and this was true even of Britain, with its free market conditions. The state represented by its officials soon came to love this. The omnipotence of the state, defended on the grounds of the needs of the war, did not always guarantee efficient management.

The role of the state rose in the neutral countries of Europe, too, which took the opportunity to quickly develop and modernise their armies and transform at least part of their economies from civilian to wartime. They were worried they might be attacked by one of the belligerent coalitions. The state authorities of neutral countries had to handle the problem of reconciling political neutrality with lucrative trade with both blocs.

An astronomical sum of money was needed for the war, which cost far more that the planners had foreseen. The war of 1870/1871 had cost Germany 7 million marks a day. In the autumn of 1914 Germany's daily war expenditure was 36 million marks; and by 1918 it had risen to 146 million. War funds were collected relentlessly; a larger and larger portion of the national budget was set aside for the war, and the parliaments of the various belligerent countries passed the requisite legislation already in the first days of the war. The percentage of the German budget assigned to the war was 25% in 1914, 33% in 1916, and 53% in 1918. Britain's war budget rose from £91 million in 1913 to £1.956 billion in 1918, making up 80% of the national budget at 52% of its GDP. Some of this money came directly from the pockets of the people. Belligerent states introduced war loans, issued war bonds, printed more banknotes, and issued special stamps and postcards with the portrait of George V, Bismarck or von Hindenburg. Germany practically did not raise taxes, unlike Britain and the USA, which brought in a tax on luxury goods, high stock market profits, and extraordinary income. People trusted their countries, and so war loan campaigns such as the ones in France, the United States, and Germany, which offered a good return in interest, were usually successful, but they soon made the state the debtor of its citizens. The national debt rose several times – most of all in Germany, which did not have easy access to international loans. In 1913 Germany's national debt amounted to 5.4 billion marks, but by 1918 it had risen to 156.1 billion marks. People treated the purchase of war bonds as a sign of their civic solidarity with the troops, so they did not protest and paid up, in accordance with the press slogan, "Lend your money to your nation." A country's citizens made up a nation that was aware of its national objectives and capable of heroic effort and self-sacrifice. Germany issued 9 war loans; Austria-Hungary issued 8; Russia 6; Italy and the USA 5 each; France 4: and Britain 3. Russia did the least well, for the people of Russia did not trust their government and dragged their feet over buying war bonds and loans. The Russian authorities decided to print more banknotes, which were not backed by any assets whatsoever. As a result prices soared and there was high inflation.

By February 1917 the number of banknotes in circulation in Russia had risen by 600%. The corresponding figures for France and Germany were 100% and 200% respectively. In August 1914 Britain left the gold standard and the Treasury issued £300 million of paper banknotes, without the backing of gold. In late July 1914 the Russian government suspended the exchangeability of the rouble for gold. By January 1917 only 16.2% of the Russian banknotes were backed in gold. The corresponding figure for France in 1918 was 21.5%. The other countries did likewise, calling their citizens to exchange their gold for paper money. In point of fact they had no option. In March 1917 the Reichsbank appealed to the people of Germany to deposit their gold to reduce the gold deficit. There was a fairly good response, at least much better than the one elicited by the disastrous Russian issue of "liberty bonds" following the February Revolution. Russians were distrustful of the revolutionary government and were afraid to buy, fearing they would never see their money again, or if they did it would be next to worthless because of inflation.

All the belligerent countries found themselves in a difficult situation. The value of their currency was falling; their revenues, gold reserves, and the currency reserves in their central banks had fallen, too. Russia was in the worst situation, with a serious deficit only partially covered by foreign and domestic loans. In addition it lost more revenue when a prohibition was imposed on the production and sale of alcohol, which had supplied one-quarter of Russia's revenues in 1913. Despite the prohibition Russians were drinking twice as much as before the war. Bootlegging was a common practice; various raw materials including fermented bread were used to produce moonshine. On the other hand, in America the consumption of alcohol dropped when prohibition was imposed. Americans were disciplined citizens and could show solidarity with their country: being a teetotaller was tantamount to being a good patriot.

Foreign loans were an important source of finance. In the first years of the war Britain was the biggest creditor, becoming the coalition's banker. By 1st April 1917 the war loans, which the Allies had advanced to one another, amounted to a total of $4.3 billion, of which 88% came from Britain. However, the needs were so great that even the resourceful Britons had to solicit loans from the American banks. Earlier France had tried to secure an American loan, but this proved difficult, as the agreement between the French government and J.P. Morgan's Bank was quashed by President Woodrow Wilson and his Secretary of the Treasury, who protested that money was the worst form of contraband. By refusing the loan Wilson had hoped that the belligerents would sit down to negotiate a peace treaty sooner, ending what he considered senseless slaughter. However, the French and their American partners did not leave the matter at that, and a few months later came up with a new legal interpretation, claiming that the loan could be advanced through private American banks without infringing the United States' neutrality. In October 1915 Morgan's advanced a loan of $500 million to the French government, regardless of protests by Germany and the pro-German press in America. For Paris it was a tremendous success. Morgan's didn't grumble, either: the commission on the transaction was 1–2%. The French paid in gold, foreign currency, and shares and bonds. By the end of March 1917 they had been advanced a loan of $1.071 billion. America loaned a total of $2.3 billion to all the Allies, serving as their banker, arsenal, and bread-basket. The American loans enhanced the status of the USA, making it a financial superpower, and turning Wall Street into the world's second financial centre alongside the City of London. The Allies became America's debtors, and in the autumn of 1918 found themselves on the brink of financial disaster, encumbered by a huge public debt.

Formally the American banks did not grant loans to the Central Powers, who did not apply for American loans. Instead they had loans through the Swiss, Swedish, and Dutch banks, some of which were in fact transfers from American banks.

Notwithstanding the various measures to secure funds, the belligerent states were unavoidably heading for a currency crisis. Not only states and their citizens suffered, but also cities and regions which issued surrogate money to meet their liabilities. Private businessmen and agriculturalists did the same to pay their employees' wages. Surrogate money often carried the issuer's promise to redeem the bill after the war. Usually surrogate money was a paper bill, but occasionally it took the form of counters made of tin, iron, or pottery.

The growth of wartime production was determined by the transfer of the labour force from civilian to military production, which meant that the proportion of the workforce employed in military production was growing all the time. In August 1914 only 24% of the total industrial workforce in Russia was in military production, but by 1917 it had risen to 76%. In Italy it rose from 20% in 1915 to 64% in 1918. In Germany the war industry employed 1.5 million workers in 1914, and 3.5 million in 1918. Only in Britain and the USA less than 50% of the workforce was engaged in the war industry, chiefly because the soldiers of these two countries were supplied with French equipment.

Another challenge was how to manage the labour force to make production rise due to increasing productivity, not numbers employed. For this reason the authorities militarised the job market. Some of the workers employed in the munitions industry were put under military rule and barracked. Strikes and other forms of workers' protests were banned. The German authorities went the furthest in such restrictions on labour relations, which was taken as a sign that the war had become "total," a clash between nations and their economies. Walther Rathenau, the chairman of AEG, was put in charge of the mobilisation of the workforce and war production, an office he held until March 1915, establishing wartime companies. The following year the German authorities went even further to facilitate the implementation of von Hindenburg's breakneck plan of 31st August 1916, which envisaged an increase in equipment for the war by one-third, and in ammunition by a half, alongside an increase in the number of divisions, all in the space of a few months. To achieve it, some of the German workers were sent back to the factories from the front. In addition, on the grounds of the Auxiliary Service Act (*Hilfsdienstgesetz*) of 5th December 1916 all men between the ages of

16 and 60, as well as childless married women, and women and girls engaged in "useless activities" were obliged to work for the front and perform auxiliary military service. In effect it meant mandatory employment, accompanied by longer working hours and shorter holidays. In the following year those who had not been called up for military service were assigned to specific factories where they had to stay, just like serfs obliged to till their lord's land. They could not change their job without the consent of the authorities. Not only in Germany was there ready employment for the young and for old-age pensioners. The arrangements in other countries were similar, though perhaps not as far-reaching. Militarisation improved productivity very substantially, especially as it was accompanied with improvements in the organisation of labour.

The numbers of female employees rose as well. Posters appeared on the walls of towns and villages urging women to take up a job in a munitions factory and "be doing their bit." Another poster rallying British women to work said "On her their lives depend. Women munition workers. Enrol at once." Women's organisations demanded the right to work for women as well, though the women who took up a job probably did so more out of material exigencies and poverty at home than due to the fine propaganda slogans, and despite the fact that their pay was 50–60% of the pay men on the same job took home. At any rate the men were not pleased with the feminisation of what had been men's jobs hitherto. In some factories men's trade unions adopted resolutions banning women from employment. They did so not out of male chauvinism, the belief that only a man could support a family, but out of fear that women would take their jobs and then they would be sent to the front. Working men argued that the employment of women reduced their capacity for procreation, while of course the country needed new citizens. American trade unionists were none too friendly to their female colleagues at work, either. They accused working women of immorality and taking up a job for dishonest or trivial reasons, such as wanting to buy trinkets or useless items. In effect working women were more discriminated against than coloured (male) workers.

The winner in the tussle between men and women was the state, which cut production costs by reducing women's pay and denying them social security, treating them as cheaper and less demanding workers. The prospect of mass female employment was a threat in the hands of the state and industrialists against recalcitrant male workers liable to stage protests and strikes.

Although female employment rose very substantially in terms of numbers, it would not be true to say that women took all or almost all of the men's jobs. In Australia the percentage of female labour in industry rose from 24% in 1914 to 37% in the autumn of 1918; in Britain the respective figures were 26.1% to 36.1%, in Germany 22% to 35%, in France 27% to 40%, and in Russia 27% to 43%. The largest increment was in services, though it was also considerable in industry. Before the war 2.5 thousand women were employed in Krupp's munitions plants; by 1918 the figure had risen to 28 thousand. In the French Renault car works there had been 190 women employees in 1914; by 1918 there were 6,770. All countries witnessed a considerable feminisation in occupations such as secretaries, shop assistants, teachers, and nurses, but women lawyers or engineers were rare. In April 1916 the Germans compelled 20 thousand Frenchwomen from occupied Lille to take up employment. By employing Frenchwomen the German authorities wanted to convey the message to German women that they were being spared.

Prisoners-of-war and deserters were also sent to work in the war industries. The colonial empires made use of the resources in their colonies and dominions, setting up auxiliary corps consisting of native Africans, who were deployed directly on the front or in the rear lines. Workers for labour corps were contracted from semi-dependent countries such as Siam, Egypt, China, or neighbouring states. The French contracted 200 thousand Spaniards, 190 thousand Chinese, 100 thousand Algerians, and 50 thousand workers from Indo-China. On their days off the Asians and Africans appeared in the streets, arousing understandable curiosity with their different culture, and sometimes there were incidents of racial tension. The press devoted a considerable amount of attention to this issue. The most irritating situations occurred when African workers and soldiers visited brothels. There were voices in the press that Africans should not be admitted, as it was "a contamination of the white race." Fights broke out, and there were even murders. Despite the unsatisfactory experience of relations with French people, some of the Chinese and Vietnamese stayed in France illegally after 1918. Similarly in Britain, some of the workers recruited from India and the African colonies never returned home and settled in Britain. And that is how the arduous growth and development of multiracial and multicultural societies started in Western Europe. The tradition of migration from the colonies to Western Europe dates back to the Great War.

The inhabitants of occupied territories were forced to work. There were even street round-ups, and the Germans specialised in this. So street round-ups were not a Second World War invention. Their victims were Belgians, Poles, and Frenchmen. The Germans deported them for work in their factories and farms, and on the construction of the Hindenburg Line. A total of 120 thousand Belgians, 600 thousand Poles, and 100 thousand Frenchmen were rounded up for forced labour on behalf of Germany. They were employed in civilian workforces, and were issued with distinctive uniforms.

Once a source of financing and a workforce had been procured, the belligerent states had to obtain the raw materials necessary for the production of armaments. To make the process efficient they established government committees and departments, endowing them with a broad range of prerogatives. The needs were so huge that it was extremely difficult, and sometimes impossible, to keep producers supplied. Prohibitions were imposed on the export of raw materials needed for the war. Raw materials were to be used economically, and the production of surrogate industrial commodities was introduced. Industrial laboratories worked at their full capacity, and the scientists and engineers employed in them searched for new types and kinds of raw materials. In many cases the experimentation and research led to invaluable discoveries and inventions, thereby prolonging the war. The greatest achievers in this respect were the Germans, who were affected by an import blockade. They developed a technology to obtain nitrogen from the atmosphere, which relieved them of the need to import saltpetre for the production of ammunition. They also developed methods to obtain sulphur from gypsum, and glycerine from sugar. Synthetic oils, lubricants, and rubber were produced. Flax and hemp replaced cotton; fibre and textiles were also obtained from nettles, reeds, hops, willow-bark and human hair. Artificial cotton, artificial silk, and paper yarn were manufactured.

There was large-scale requisitioning on occupied territories. The goods and commodities subject to requisitioning included church bells, copper roofing, kitchen utensils, tin and brass objects, underwear and warm clothing. Campaigns were organised to collect raw materials, scrapyards were set up to collect metal. There were collections of old clothes and fabric remnants, a task usually done by women. In 1916 the German Women's Self-Assistance Union appealed to women not to waste any commodity – not to burn paper, not to throw away pieces of rope, sack, or empty tins. These materials were to be collected and recycled, as were rubber, scraps of leather, used pen-nibs and stamps, bottles, jugs, cigar butts, stearin, bottle corks and tops, and fruit pips. All these materials could be recycled for industrial production, German women were told. Another poster urged them to collect women's hair: every school ran a collection centre. The campaign did not forget about children, either; schools took part in it.

The Allied countries were not obliged to resort to such campaigns, at least not on such a scale, as they were in a better position over raw materials. They could buy as much as they needed of raw materials, semi-manufactured and readymade goods overseas, from the USA, Latin America, Australia, South Africa, or Indo-China. The countries which were least developed industrially such as Turkey and Bulgaria experienced the greatest problems. In the latter part of 1918 Bulgarian industry was working only at 20% of its capacity due to shortages of raw materials, and the situation in Turkey was not much better. But manufacturers in neutral countries complained about the shortage of raw materials as well: they had to pay a heavy price for the naval blockade and war at sea.

2. Military occupation and resistance

The first countries to be occupied by the German Reich were Luxemburg and Belgium. The former did not experience many unpleasant consequences of occupation; the government of Luxemburg was allowed to stay in power and the only sign of occupation was discreet German control of the railway lines. Belgium fared much worse. In the first few weeks the invaders applied a policy of intimidation, repression, and collective responsibility. They took hostages and in a few places conducted public executions of prominent members of society such as priests and representatives of the educated class. By the end of 1914 they had killed over 5,200 persons. From the very first days the Belgians put up active and passive resistance. In 1914 there were armed resistance groups (*franc-tireurs*, or *vrijschutter*) who made sudden attacks against the Germans and if caught were treated as war criminals. The invaders retaliated by burning towns and villages. In 1914 Helmuth von Moltke, the German Chief of the General Staff, wrote to his Austrian colleague General Franz Conrad von Hötzendorf admitting that the Germans were certainly being brutal in their march across Belgium, but that they were fighting for their life. The war forced hundreds of thousands of Belgian refugees to flee, to Holland, France, and England. To prevent their escape the Germans put up live wires on the border between Belgium and Holland. Belgium was left totally devastated by the war and requisitioning, economic exploitation, and acts of sabotage. In 1919 85% of its industrial plants remained shut down. Still in 1929 Belgium's gross national income was lower than it had been in 1913. To subdue Belgium, the Germans incited the ethnic tension between the Flemings and the Walloons. On 21st March 1917 the Germans set about separating off the Flemish-speaking administrative authorities from the French-speaking (Walloon) authorities, and in January 1918 declared the Flemish part of the country an independent entity with its capital in Brussels. On 22nd June the Flemish Council lodged a petition for the recognition of a free Flanders as an allied state of

Germany. However, the Germans did not take any further decisions on the future of Belgium before the end of the war, but one thing was certain: if the Central Powers had won, there would have been no room on the map of Europe for an independent Belgium within its historical borders.

The Germans were only slightly milder in occupied France, although there, too, they burned down villages and executed hostages on pretexts such as Frenchmen killing Germans from Alsace and Lorraine in 1914. As in Belgium, they imposed a military and an economic (civilian) command on the French territories they occupied. They exploited French steelworks and mines, taking over coalfields and industrial plants which in 1913 had produced 50% of France's coal, 64% of its iron, and 58% of its steel. A rule imposing mandatory labour on French and Belgian workers was introduced; and under German occupation industrial plants were forced to produce whatever the German authorities specified at prices fixed by the Germans: it was a form of compulsory duty or tribute to be paid to the invader. A change of time to "German time," which differed by 1 hour from French time, was symbolic of the occupation. Incidentally, the Germans also imposed "German time" in the Kingdom of Poland (the western part of the Russian partition of Poland) when they occupied it. Another symbol of German occupation in France was the enforced barracking of French labourers in work camps, from which every day they were made to march to work.

German occupation of territories in Eastern and Western Europe effectively continued until the end of hostilities. On the other hand, Russian occupation of Habsburg lands was comparatively short-lived. By the end of 1914 almost all of two of the Austrian crown lands, Galicia and Bucovina, were under Russian occupation. This situation lasted for about 8–12 months. The Russian authorities declared the eastern part of Galicia and Bucovina Russian territories and incorporated them into the Romanov empire. Repressive measures were imposed against the patriotic Ukrainian and Polish communities, and Austrian administrative units were abolished one by one. Some of the Ukrainian politicians, such as Mykhailo Hrushevsky and Archbishop Andrey Sheptytsky, head of the Ukrainian Uniate (Greek Catholic) Church, were deported to Russia. On 22nd September 1914 Count Georgiy Bobrinsky, the wartime governor-general of these territories, took over the administration in Lemberg (Russian Lvov; Polish Lwów; now Lviv, Ukraine), ordered the replacement of Polish with Russian as the official language, and the introduction of Russian law and constitutional order. Three Russian-style gubernyas were established with regional capitals in Lwów, Stanisławów (now Ivano-Frankivsk, Ukraine), and Tarnopol (now Ternopil, Ukraine). The Russian occupying authorities treated pro-Russian Ruthenian communities as a privileged group. Galician Russophiles were led by the Carpatho-Russian Liberation Committee presided over by Vladimir (Volodymyr) Dudykevych, which endeavoured to convert the Uniates (Greek Catholics, viz. Eastern-rite Christians in communion with Rome) to the "true Russian Orthodox religion." In effect over 100 parishes converted. Russian Orthodox priests arrived in Galicia, now known as Galichina, to convert the Uniates. The Russian generals did not find this clerical invasion a welcome development at all. The brutal conversion drive and religious persecution was a boon for the propaganda of the Central Powers, and an embarrassment for London and Paris.

However, on the recovery of East Galicia in 1915, the Habsburg authorities pursued an even crueller and more remorseless policy with respect to the Ukrainian/Ruthenian and Polish population than the Russians, sniffing out treason and collaboration, meting out punishment to suspects, imposing a harsh military regime and suspending political rights. They brought in an oppressive level of taxation; confiscated church bells and other metal items, especially copper, brass, and tin; and impounded foodstuffs from the peasants. They dismissed many of the administrative officers, and imprisoned those suspected of being pro-Russian. Polish and Ukrainian politicians lodged protests in Vienna. The local authorities of some towns in Galicia resigned in protest. The first to suffer from the severe repressive measures were the Russophile groups. Thousands were sent to concentration camps. The Thalerhof camp in Styria earned a notorious reputation. A reign of terror was the Austrian way of ensuring that the local population would remain loyal if the Russians tried to return.

For a few weeks Russian forces occupied East Prussia. The Germans evacuated the German, Masurian, and Polish population. On 27th August 1914 the Russians took Allenstein (now Olsztyn, Poland). Initially they were commendably disciplined. There was not much looting or damage, they did not burn villages and towns, and paid for food. Officers warned their men they would be executed for molesting women or for pillaging and violence. There were instances of punishment – soldiers being publicly flogged with 50 or 100 strokes of the whip, which of course showed that there were some infringements of the rules and instructions. On the other hand, severe punishments were imposed on local Germans and Masurians suspected of spying for Germany. There were summary executions without trial of forest rangers. The Russians put to death a total of 1,620 civilians. The local Jews left a bad impression on German memories; some of them were alleged to have encouraged the Russians to loot German homes, whereupon they would buy up the stolen goods. Russian policy changed during the retreat: they no longer spared anyone or anything, so as not to allow any resources to fall into the hands of the enemy, leaving the pursuing Germans with a stretch of scorched earth. They destroyed 34 thousand buildings, looted 100 thousand homes, stole 135 thousand horses, 250 thousand cattle, 200 thousand pigs, and deported 13 thousand Germans to Siberia. Taking into account the short period of occupation of a fairly small territory, the losses were quite considerable.

The local population also had their part in the pillaging. Germans took the opportunity to rob their German neighbours. The inhabitants of Galicia, Bucovina, Rumania, Serbia, and the Italian and Slovenian Alps did likewise – it was standard practice under wartime occupation. Of course not all civilians used violence against their fellows; there were also thousands of examples of admirable behaviour and attitudes of solidarity.

The Austrians, Hungarians, Germans, and Bulgarians imposed extremely severe regulations in occupied Serbia and Montenegro, and at the same time started an unrelenting process of economic exploitation. Especially the Austro-Hungarian authorities became notorious for their severity. At the very outset they imprisoned 1,200 Serbian political leaders. In the course of the following years they barracked 150 thousand Serbs in prisons and concentration camps. 20 thousand inmates died of the exhausting, mercilessly exacted labour they were forced to do. The Bulgarians were not so harsh on the territories they occupied, which they considered ancient Bulgarian lands. They stopped at arresting Serbs known for anti-Bulgarian views. A large proportion of the population regarded Bulgarian rule as friendly. The Serbs and Montenegrans in areas under Austro-Hungarian rule never reconciled themselves to occupation and put up staunch resistance, forming armed resistance groups which were particularly active in Montenegro in what is sometimes referred to as the secret uprising. Resistance groups attacked and assassinated Austro-Hungarian agents, policemen, gendarmes, and officers. In no other occupied country was resistance so strong. The Serbs and Montenegrans were determined to recover their independence. Towards the end of the war Montenegran insurgents ousted the Austro-Hungarians from the capital Cetinje.

The German occupation of the Kingdom of Poland left a dreadful impression in the memories of millions of Poles. It could hardly be called anything else but the most extreme, unrelenting, and efficiently carried out economic exploitation. In their over three years of occupation the Germans and Austrians carried off 12.3 million quintals (100 kg, approximately a hundredweight) of cereals and 5.5 quintals of potatoes, partly under the guise of enforced wartime contributions. But at the same time the Austro-Hungarian and German regimes were predictable, albeit harsh; the laws they introduced were generally observed, within the bounds of wartime conditions. To start with the Germans established a *Passamt* – a passport office which issued passports and travel permits to civilians allowing them to travel within designated areas. Russian passports were exchanged for German and Austro-Hungarian numbered documents with the holder's photograph. Both occupying forces rounded up civilians in the streets and imprisoned them in detention camps behind barbed wire. But at the same time they tolerated Polish cultural, educational, and economic associations and institutions.

Stalwart military and civilian resistance would become a hallmark of the Second World War. During the First World War the scale of resistance was modest, and effectively limited to Belgium, Serbia, and Montenegro. The fact that the Central Powers allowed the nations of East-Central Europe to exercise the political freedoms and dropped hints on the prospect of independence within a German *Mitteleuropa* was an obstacle to the growth of clandestine resistance movements. Nonetheless, such movements did arise, for instance in Poland, but they had to wait until the end of the war for their time to come for political activity.

3. Everyday life

During the war you could observe two different pictures of everyday life. Contemporary photographs give a good record of this. On some photos you see people leading the same affluent life they had before the war; on others there are poor, forsaken people, dying of disease or starvation, standing in endless bread queues. Which of these pictures is true? Well, both are. Many inhabitants of Rome or Paris were serenely having coffee in the cafés as they had been doing for years, chatting over ice-cream, flirting, and orchestras were playing merry music-hall songs. The only tell-tale sign that a war was going on was that alcoholic drinks, which were prohibited during the war, were served in coffee cups. In London and Berlin there were full houses in the theatres, music halls, opera houses, cinemas, and night clubs; spectators watched sports events. Gambling continued to go on in the casinos, and the fashionable foxtrot continued to be danced in the dance-halls. Crowds of visitors were milling around in the spas and holiday resorts, and their memories of the war were quite unlike those that the poor remembered. State authorities launched appeals for temperance and moderation, and in Vienna from July to November 1916 there was a "seriousness campaign" intended to curtail entertainment.

But this was just one side of everyday life during the war. There was another. For of course the war economy could not fail to make a negative impact on consumer goods and the quality of life. Although rationing was brought in for food and manufactured goods, some products were not available in the shops, and queues became symptomatic of the war. In Germany ration cards were brought in at the beginning of 1915, initially for bread, fats, milk, and meat. Rationing became an everyday reality pretty soon in Austria-Hungary, too. However, in Britain there was no rationing until 1918, when coupons were introduced for meat, butter, vegetable oil, and sugar, on a surge of panic on the market, but in general the British authorities eschewed food rationing, which they regarded as an infringement of the free market. In Paris bread rationing was introduced in February 1918, and four months later in the whole of France. The supply of foodstuffs and consumer goods was better in the Allied countries than in the Central Powers, who were hard pressed by the effects of the sea blockade. In Germany and Austria food and butchers' shops were closed for several days a month by order of the local authorities. Scuffles and fighting were a common occurrence outside shops. The worst supplied were the shops in northern Germany. There were also queues for articles of personal hygiene. Soap was in short supply. People washed their bodies, and laundered their clothes less frequently, which inevitably led to a lower level of hygiene and hence diminished resistance to bacteria and viruses. The worst off were the poor. The well-off had their servants queue up for them, and could afford to top up their provisions on the black market. However, rising prices made the biggest difference (in relative terms) to the budgets of the rich, who really had to pay much more than before to get expensive goods. Queues and rationing were the order of the day even in neutral countries like Switzerland, where ration coupons were introduced for meat, bread, sugar, and flour, and no meat was sold on two days in the week. Neutral countries were spared the direct effects of the war, but they did feel its consequences, particularly as a result of the sea blockade.

The worst time was the winter of 1916 to 1917, when official rations in Germany, Austria-Hungary, and the countries they occupied fell to half the nutritional value needed by the human body. The poor fed on pigweed and turnips, which earned the nickname "Hindenburg's delicacy" or "Prussian pineapples," and the period was called "the turnip winter" (*Kohlrüberwinter*). In the spring of 1917 the German potato ration was cut to one-quarter of the average consumed in 1913. Butter disappeared altogether, and the heavy wartime bran (or in fact chaff) bread was eaten with a substance called jam but with a flavour not very reminiscent of real jam. In the last six months of 1918 things were even worse. Meat rations in Germany fell to 12% of the average consumed in 1913; butter went down to 28%; vegetable fats and oils dropped to 17%; lard to 7%; and potato rations were 94% of the average consumed before the war. However, there were hardly any signs of starvation in the streets; the German authorities were systematic, meticulous, and effective in their interventions in food provision. For example, on 25th March 1917 the municipal authorities of Berlin issued a regulation imposing limits on cake-baking, banning the use of yeast and baking powder, and ruled that flour could not make up more than 10% of the ingredients by weight. For a few weeks there was a complete ban on cake-baking.

The situation was catastrophic in the cities of Russia. Owing to chaos, corruption, and inefficient administrative authorities the harvest was being left to rot in the fields, or devoured by rodents in the granaries, but not reaching the towns, especially the cities, the inhabitants of which were the worst affected by the war. City dwellers were the segment of Russian society most dissatisfied with the war and the way it was being managed. The worst off were the cities in the north, where the sight of paupers standing for hours in bread queues in subzero temperatures was common already by the winter of 1916. In October 1915 Petrograd was being supplied a daily quota of 116 train carriages of food instead of the prewar average of 405. And it only got worse as time went on. There was a shortage of rolling stock, and the freight trains purchased from the USA were left to rust in the rail depot at Vladivostok. In effect, in cities like Petrograd and Moscow gigantic queues were ubiquitous. People queued up for everything. In 1917 housewives in Petrograd spent an average of 40 hours a week in queues, and not always managed to buy something. The people of Russia could not understand how it had happened that their country – known prior to 1914 as Europe's bread basket – was now starving.

What measures were taken to deal with the shortages? First and foremost, substitute goods were put on the consumer market. Germany devised the greatest number of ersatz goods: the very name came from German and was assimilated by many languages. Germany put 11 thousand ersatz goods on the market, including 837 kinds of meatless sausages and 511 ersatz coffees. "Tea" was brewed from dried fruit; leather shoes were replaced by wooden clogs; carbide lamps took over from paraffin (kerosene) lamps; and soap-making became a cottage industry. When bread started to be in short supply in Scandinavia and Switzerland, bakers and housewives produced rice cakes, which would be eaten with jam. The reason why so many ersatz products could emerge was that the chemical industry, particularly in the production of foodstuffs, had been briskly developing before the war, especially in Germany. During the war research continued, leading to even faster growth in the natural sciences. Secondly, people grew their own produce in their gardens, vegetable patches, and allotments. One British lord could not understand why he should convert his tennis court into a vegetable garden, as the official appeal had urged. In their gardens or yards people kept domestic animals – chickens, goats, rabbits – to supplement the food allowance. The slump in alcohol consumption meant that more money from family budgets could be spent on more urgent needs.

Thirdly, the black market softened the effects of the shortfall, although heavy fines were imposed on black marketeers. In January 1917 a "pillory decree" was issued in Austria, whereby the names of illegal traders were made public. The First World War was a veritable breeding ground for the black market. If they were to survive people were forced to sidestep the official allowances and resort to unofficial food supplies from the countryside, of goods not available in the shops. As time went on, black market prices soared, at least in some countries like Russia or Bulgaria. In Serbia, Turkey, Bulgaria, Greece, and Rumania the black market did not cause such a stir thanks to the long tradition of law evasion, but it was a shock in law-abiding Germany and Austria. The black market was not so important in France, and still less in Britain, where the shops were better supplied. Black markets also sprouted in neutral countries which were doing well on the war, but were not always able to satisfy the demand for goods in short supply. The war disrupted Europe's economic network, hence neutral countries, economically linked up with belligerents, could not help feeling these effects of the war.

To afford the black market, those on more modest incomes had to sell their valuables and household goods. The market was flooded with offers of watches, irons, kitchen utensils, china, furniture, jewellery, pictures, cooking pots, clothes, underwear, and shoes for sale. The large supply caused a reduction in their value, which made people sell more stuff. Who bought these things? Those who had done well on the war, especially a broad assortment of racketeers and wide boys. Sometimes these things went for a song; food was highly valued, not luxury goods. Farmers, who made money by providing the produce in short supply, were among the buyers. Wartime exigencies brought about a transfer of goods from the towns to the country.

Another worry for thousands was heating fuel, or rather shortage of fuel. Most countries had considerable problems with fuel supply, which aggravated with time. The worst were the winters of 1916–1917 and 1917–1918. The inhabitants of Germany, Austria-Hungary, and the lands in the east they occupied had the biggest problems. Buying coal from a coal depot was next to impossible, as many miners were out on the front instead of at their jobs. Although in Belgium, Germany, and Austria there was still quite a lot of coal on the spoil tips from prewar times, no rolling stock was at hand to transport it. Another serious obstacle to rail transport was caused by the winters. The severe cold damaged tracks and rolling stock, and blizzards prevented movement. The waterways could not be used for inland transport, either, as they were frozen over. During the last two winters of the war deaths due to the cold weather were fairly common in Germany, Bohemia, Austria, Bulgaria, and Turkey. To make up for fuel shortages, people resorted to the forests for firewood. Whole families would set off on such expeditions, even though forest rangers tried to prevent illegal lumbering. In towns desperate inhabitants cut down the trees in parks and squares. In winter, owing to the fuel shortage the authorities ordered the heating systems to be switched off in schools and factories, which gave workers unexpected days off, and children enjoyed extra-long winter holidays. The drive to save fuel and energy resources, as well as wartime regulations meant that towns were not lit up at night, cars had headlights switched off, and windows were blacked out.

Inflation – a new phenomenon, completely unknown before the war, now emerged. People anxiously wondered about the limit to the continual rise in prices. But it was impossible to establish such a limit. The nearer the end of the war, the more aggravating the galloping prices. The costs of the war were bigger and bigger, and it was hard to balance income and expenditure, for private households as well as for the state. During the war the global price index rose only by 227% in Britain thanks to rigorous price control; in France it jumped by 340%; in Germany by 415%; in Italy by 409%. In Russia it went up to 238% by June 1916, 398% by December of that year, and to 600% by June 1918. Hungary finished the war with inflation at a staggering 977%, whereas in June 1918 it had only been 382%. In Paris a kilogramme loaf of bread had cost 40 centimes in 1913, and 1 franc and 25 centimes in 1918; while the corresponding prices for a kilo of sugar were 75 centimes, and 3 francs and 25 centimes.

Under wartime conditions a fall in the standard of living was inevitable, but some professions did not feel the pinch, and some even benefited. In Britain the winners were the unskilled labourers, who took over jobs and wages hitherto held by skilled workers. They also gained because the introduction of tax reductions forced factory owners to establish staff canteens. Likewise in France blue-collar wages did not go down very much, or in fact rose in real terms. There was a general shortage of workers on the job market, thus employees were in a good position to demand and obtain pay rises. In outcome incomes in working-class families increased. But they increased also thanks to the fact that there were jobs for the unemployed and for women. The groups which gained the most were the miners, steelworkers, and employees of munitions factories. Wages and the standard of living were subject to the constant attention of the trade unions, which negotiated the conditions of employment and pay, and participated in arbitration.

The working class of Italy fared worse: on the whole its standard of living went down, and wage rises did not keep up with inflation. In Italy blue-collar workers bore the brunt of the war. The situation was even worse in Germany. Millions experienced a fall in their standard of living, especially under the gruelling Hindenburg plan, which nearly led to famine. To the end of the war real wages fell by 73% compared to 1913. People said that young civilians starved to death before they could be called up to the front. 300 thousand "unnecessary deaths" of young people between 15 and 19 were recorded from November 1916 to October 1918. These figures were for young recruits who were incapable of carrying out orders on the front due to malnutrition. In Russia workers' pay doubled in the period up to the Bolshevik upheaval, but prices went up four times or more in the same time. On the other hand, peasant farmers gained on inflation, selling their produce for much more than in 1913. Some could afford to buy land and goods regarded as luxury items. In France and Britain, too, farmers' incomes improved thanks to rising food prices, enhanced efficiency, and an increase in areas under cultivation. Thanks to this they could invest more in their farms, repair and improve their facilities etc. In all the countries the most affected by the war were the middle and upper classes. Admittedly, their standard of living was still high, but not as high as before the war. Real income fell for senior administrative and bank staff – in Germany, Austria, and Bohemia by 47–70%. The drop was not so high in the Allied countries. In addition, the richer and more patriotic lost out on buying up government bonds.

The crime rate and violations of the stringent wartime regulations went up. Counterfeit food coupons were put into circulation;

stolen goods included food, heating fuel and food coupons; prices were pushed up beyond the statutory limits. By the end of the war in Greece the number of fake ration cards was several times more than of authentic ones, which inevitably led to a depreciation in their value and did not solve any problems. The Greeks were outright winners in the art of forgery, although in the Balkans they had stiff competition. But even in Germany the crime rate rose, and this included counterfeiting ration cards. For instance in Breslau (now Wrocław) the crime rate trebled by 1916 (albeit from a low initial level). Although the perpetrators were mostly boys and young men, there was also an alarming increase in female crime by girls under 18 and women in the 19–21 age group. In some regions it was up by 50%, or even 90%. On the other hand, the number of reported crimes committed by women over 30 fell. Many demoralised young people faced prosecution – for forgery, vandalism, wilful damage of property, aggressive vagrancy and begging. Restrictions were put on their admission to taverns and bars. In many countries the authorities appealed to home owners to lock up, padlock, or even bolt their properties if they were going away.

During the war far fewer people travelled, especially abroad. At the border travellers were controlled fastidiously and in a humiliating way, the aim being to discourage them from going on a voyage again. Domestic travel was not much better, though. Those who wanted to go on a journey by rail needed a valid ticket and a travel permit, and by the end of the war also a large sum of money, as ticket prices had spiralled. Only in Britain were there no restrictions on travel and fares went up only moderately. In 1918 it was no longer safe to travel by rail, and still less to venture on the roads. There were groups of armed criminals everywhere, ready to attack road users and even to stop trains. The worst situation was in Russia and the Balkans. With a slump in morale and falling religious standards, housebreaking and rising violence on the roads and streets were inevitable, especially as the power of the state, police, and army had fallen. Soldiers no longer wanted to fight, and were even less inclined to run around the woods and fields chasing bands of thieves made up of deserters.

4. In sickness and in health. Charity

Wartime conditions, malnutrition, and devastation could not but have resulted in a lower level of hygiene, a decline in wellness, loss of weight and resistance to disease. There was a fall in birth rate and total fertility rate due to the fact that the men were away on the front, but also because of the women's inherently stressful lifestyle, the queues, the food shortage, and their employment in the factories. The drop in fertility rate was larger in Germany than in Britain. In 1917, the worst year of the war, doctors in Germany, Italy, Austria, and Hungary observed that due to stress, poverty, and weight loss some women ceased to menstruate. Research carried out in many cities showed that their inhabitants had lost from a few percent to over 20% in weight. Weight loss was lowest in Britain. The calorific value of meals went down by 20–30%. In many cities in the Central Powers the malnutrition rate went up, unlike the situation in Britain, where there was a fall in malnutrition thanks to the introduction of successful social schemes. In effect, the rise in the mortality rate was higher in Germany than in Britain.

What central and local government authorities feared most was the outbreak of epidemics, which could bring down the battle-worthiness of their armies. Hence they made a special effort to introduce preventive measures, with educational and poster campaigns, talks and lectures on the dangers of infectious diseases. Schools, churches, and academics were invited to join such campaigns. Information was disseminated on infectious diseases and what precautions to take to avoid catching them. The list of dangerous diseases was long: typhus, typhoid, paratyphoid fever, cholera, dysentery, scarlet fever, diphtheria, whooping cough, tuberculosis, scabies, venereal diseases.

The most dangerous disease was an influenza known as "Spanish flu," which affected the civilian population most of all. It appeared in Europe in 1918. As the First World War was drawing to a close the war against Spanish flu was beginning. It most probably came to Europe from the United States. The papers of neutral Spain were the first in

Europe to report news of it, and hence its name. In the Walloon part of Belgium it was called "Flemish flu;" in Russia it was known as "Chinese fever;" in Poland as "the Bolshevik disease" or "the Ukrainian disease;" and in Ceylon it was dubbed "Bombay fever." Spanish flu turned out to be the world's biggest killer, causing more deaths than the war. For instance, 1,000 soldiers from North Carolina were killed during the war, while 13,000 people in that state died of Spanish flu. In Germany the mortality rate for boys in the 5–10 age group rose by over 50% from 1913 to 1917, but in 1918 it went up to over 90%. The corresponding figures for boys in the 10–15 age group were 55% and 115% respectively. The rise in the mortality rate for girls, who are stronger and better programmed genetically, was much lower: 40% in 1917, and 50% in 1918.

Spanish flu was a pandemic. It ran round the world, from country to country with no regard for political borders. In India the rivers were full of corpses; there was not enough wood to cremate them. In the USA morgues were full, cadavers were piled on top of one another, gravediggers worked day and night. According to estimates about 500 million were ill with Spanish flu in 1918–1921, and 20 million to 50 million, or even 100 million died of it. The symptoms were a high fever, diarrhoea, rapid dehydration, and pneumonia. It attacked the young and strong rather than the elderly and feeble; and the rich to the same extent as the poor. It evoked terror and overwhelming dread; it disrupted the normal course of public life. The peace negotiations at the end of the war were conducted in the shadow of Spanish flu. Its first wave came in 1918 and was marked by a large morbidity rate, but not as many fatalities as in the next year, which turned out to be the most tragic. There had been no human pandemic like it since the cholera. No treatment was found for it. The medications which were suggested failed. Preventive measures failed. The gauze masks recommended for policemen, doctors, postmen, and nurses were of no avail. Alcohol, large amounts of which were recommended and administered even to children, was no help, either. It is thought that other precautions, such as limiting contact with other people, drinking water that had been boiled, washing hands, airing buildings, refraining from spitting in the street (for which there were fines), chewing tobacco, taking baths in ice-cold water, burning incense in the home (as practised in Africa), wearing amulets (a Polynesian remedy), and casting sheets of paper with passages from the Koran downstream on the River Niger (practised in Nigeria) – did not help much, either. For a long time scientists searched for the virus causing the disease. It was not found until 1997, and allocated in the Influenza A (H1N1) virus subtype, but there is still no agreement as to what triggered the outbreak of the pandemic.

Typhus was a dangerous disease. It reaped the largest harvest of victims in Serbia and Montenegro, owing to the disastrously low sense of hygiene and the poor medical service. Within just over a year more than a quarter of the doctors in Serbia died or were killed. About half a million Serbs went down with the disease, and 150 thousand died. The American pacifist journalist John Reed called Serbia "the country of death." In the spring of 1915 there were up to 9–10 thousand new cases a day. The typhus epidemic started in the Serbian trenches and was brought into civilian settlements. On Belgrade's appeal for assistance Allied and American medical staff arrived to help. In March 1915 they set up an international sanitary commission to fight against the typhus epidemic. In 1916–1917 the disease wreaked havoc in Rumania, claiming almost as many victims as in Serbia. In 1917 in Russia things were even worse, especially in areas ravaged by war. According to estimates, in 1916–1918 more soldiers died due to typhus and other contagious diseases than in the hostilities. Typhus and malaria combined with famine menaced the Levant and Mesopotamia. 80 thousand are believed to have died of disease and starvation in the Levant alone.

Typhus and Spanish flu killed victims within a short time of the emergence of the first symptoms, while the consequences of tuberculosis could be observed developing gradually over a long period from the time of infection, so this disease did not engender such anxiety. In all the countries the incidence of tuberculosis rose during the war: by 20% in France, 25% in Britain, and over 50% in Germany in relation to 1913.

In view of the risk of disease, treatment and preventive measures were indispensable everywhere. Social committees and national sanitary commissions were set up to help those in need. Mobile sanitary corps were established which went out into the country towns and villages. They entailed field hospitals and laboratories staffed by nurses and medical students. The sanitary corps administered smallpox vaccinations, set up disinfection units, and established treatment centres including tuberculosis hospitals, and even conducted delousing campaigns and ran bath-houses.

Scabies was the most common ailment attributable to dirty hands, and it was an embarrassing condition, like the venereal diseases. Warnings about the dangers of VD from sex with prostitutes were given in thousands of talks and lectures, distributed on leaflets, and even delivered from the pulpit in the churches of France and Austria-Hungary.

During the war charity and social welfare had to change their form. Although the scale of the social problems caught society by surprise, nonetheless the spirit of civic solidarity and readiness to help was very strong and on the whole people rose to the occasion. In effect, the war gave rise to a socially widespread civic movement on an unprecedented mass scale. For example, there were over 400 relief institutions in Scotland alone, and some of them were founded during the war. Some dispensed material and moral support to war widows, orphans and invalids; others provided aid for the poor and distressed; still others cared for refugees and political émigrés. There were about 3 million war widows, some of whom married a second time, but not straightaway. 40% of the German war widows had remarried by 1926. Some, especially from the working class, were not in such a hurry to wed again; having tasted the sweetness of freedom they were loath to forfeit it. The problem of how to help the orphans in bereaved families was a major challenge. Over half of these children were under three when they lost their fathers in the war.

To encourage people to be generous, charity organisations ran appeals and campaigns on a mass scale, such as Russia Day, Serbia Day, Bulgaria Day, the Belgian Refugee Appeal, the Prisoners-of-War Appeal, the Wounded Horses appeal etc. Collections were made in the churches, lotteries were organised, and charity concerts, opera and theatrical performances were held. Propaganda activities were successfully blended with charity work, for instance the sale of the Remember the Lusitania medal, the proceeds of which were to go to aid war victims. In Austria-Hungary there was a sales drive for stamps showing the new Emperor and Empress, promoting the Emperor Karl's charity fund. All the countries issued postage stamps to support charities dispensing aid to war widows, orphans, and invalids.

Charity funds helped to organise war kitchens which served meals for women and children from soldiers' families; established welfare centres and orphanages; and set up the Save the Children Fund to alleviate malnutrition. Social funds were used to found homes for soldiers' children, organise holidays for orphans and children from poor families, help adults including war invalids find employment or set up in self-employment.

The largest international relief organisations (mostly American-based) in terms of available funds and number of volunteers had considerable financial assets at their disposal. They dispensed aid firstly to the Belgian and French inhabitants of occupied territories, and secondly to the Serbians and people of the Kingdom of Poland. The organisation which played the fundamental role was the American Relief Administration (ARA), established on 6th August 1914 on the initiative of and headed by Herbert Hoover. Thousands of volunteers, chiefly Americans, worked for Hoover's committee. Its representatives went to Europe to determine where the greatest needs were, and what kind of relief the war's civilian victims wanted. On 4th October 1914 the Commission for Relief in Belgium initiated operations under the auspices of the ARA. Its French counterpart was the Comité d'alimentation du Nord de la France. Hoover became deeply committed to the campaign, as befitted a Quaker, and worked indefatigably and very efficiently on behalf of others. Thanks to an ingenious promotion drive the Commission for Relief in Belgium collected \$52 million, \$35 million of which were donated by Americans, and \$17 million by the British. Other associations and foundations, particularly the Rockefeller Foundation, provided aid for Belgium, and in outcome Belgium, which is a small country, received substantial aid. The German repressive measures and Belgian heroism made the Belgians the favourite beneficiaries for international aid, turning their story into a subject for many publications including fiction, and films. To the end of the war they received over 3 million tons of supplies. Hoover's committee also dispensed aid to Serbia, and as of the spring of 1915 to the Kingdom of Poland. However, distant Serbia was not the darling of the Allies, and effectively only received assistance in the battle against typhus, which was a threat to the Allied armies as well. In Hoover's publicity materials the Serbs and the Poles were definitely treated as second-best to France and Belgium. The Poles did not stir the world's conscience, because they were not widely known. Poland was an unknown entity, since it was not on the world map. Poland did not evoke much sympathy even in the United States, which was inhabited by millions with Polish roots. When President Wilson announced that 1st January 1916 would be Polish Relief Day, at the instigation of the famous composer and virtuoso Ignace Paderewski, the result was a fairly meagre collection. However, thanks to the efforts of Polish intellectuals and politicians in the West (including the USA), gradually aid started reaching the Poles in need. Unfortunately, they did not manage to persuade the British to join the campaign, who saw no interest in helping Central Europe and were worried the aid might fall into the hands of the occupying German authorities.

Substantial aid reached the Jews of Central and Eastern Europe, dispensed by Jewish organisations including the American Jewish Joint Distribution Committee, which not only supplied relief but also drew the world's attention to the plight of Jewish communities, the pogroms and the growing wave of anti-Semitism. It was hardest for them to conduct activities in Russia, especially during the Revolution and chaos of 1917–1918. At any rate Polish and Russian charity organisations met with the same problems, and many of their volunteers ended up in front of a Bolshevik firing squad.

5. Material damage. Migrations

The greatest amount of material damage occurred in places where hostilities were conducted on the land or from the air, and that is where civilians suffered the most. On Polish territories the city of Kalisz was burned, the cities of Gorlice and Żyrardów were devastated, and Wiślica Collegiate Church was badly damaged. In Belgium the city of Leuven (Louvain) was gutted in a fire, and its library dating back to 1426, along with a collection numbering 280 thousand items including manuscripts and 15th-century printed works, was razed. The cities of Ypres, Malines, and Namur were devastated, and the renowned town houses, including Rubens' house, on the market-place of Antwerp, were destroyed. Historic buildings in Venice sustained damage. The Hague Convention was violated when Rheims Cathedral, the coronation church of the kings of France, was seriously damaged. In 1917 Salonica was gutted by a fire probably accidentally set alight by soldiers. During their retreat from the Western front in 1918 the Germans destroyed churches, including Noyon Cathedral, and castles. The towers of churches and cathedrals fell victim to wartime destruction because they were convenient observation points and potential machine-gun sites. Roads and bridges, railway lines, houses and homes and public buildings were damaged or demolished. A full enumeration of all the material damage would not do justice to the suffering and anguish of the people in the lands afflicted by the war. Not all the devastation was directly connected with the carrying out of wartime objectives. Wherever hostilities erupted villages and towns disappeared into thin air; the people camped out in the forests or fled to safer areas. Some of the villages around Verdun were razed to the ground and never rebuilt. Nothing remained of the village in the vicinity of Fort Vaux. It was never rebuilt but its ruins were left as a grim memorial of the barbarity of war. The Polish territories were a tragic sight after the departure of the Russians in 1915. They employed a scorched earth policy, annihilating everything that could be destroyed so that nothing should fall into the hands of the pursuing armies of the Central Powers. They burned down all that was combustible, and blew up what couldn't be burned – country houses and mansions, public amenities, railway stations. They looted and made off with whatever had any value. They drove herds of thousands of cattle and horses off with them, they carted away food and metal, they pillaged factories taking away machinery and electrical equipment. Sometimes due to the haste of their retreat, they did not have enough time to carry out their schedule of destruction to the full, so in places such as Lemberg (Lwów/Lviv) many sites listed for explosion were saved. On many occasions a bountiful gratification offered to a corrupt Russian officer sufficed to save a building from destruction.

The Germans were no better than the Russians and Austrians in terms of the scale of destruction. "Whole units pulled down walls, and sat on roofs throwing down the tiles. Trees were cut down and window-shutters broken. Smoke and clouds of dust rose up from piles of rubbish. A frenzy of destruction was afoot. Soldiers ran around in obsessive excitement, dressed up in women's gowns and… top hats… They set mines on the roads, they poisoned or filled up wells, blew up houses, set up death-traps, vandalised railway tracks, telephone lines, and burned down literally everything that could be burned down," Ernst Jünger observed during the German retreat from the Western front in February 1917. The overall results of the destruction were over 100 thousand homes devastated in Belgium, over 850 thousand in France (the largest number in the department of Meuse), and one and a half million buildings on the Polish territories, 10% of which were historic.

The war was also a time of forced migration, or rather of mass displacement – a word which now earned itself a permanent place in the European languages and awareness. The mass evacuations opened up a dismal chapter in the social history of Europe, a time of suffering and tragedy for the civilian population shifted from place to place, not at all expected or made welcome in their place of resettlement, quite on the contrary – given a hostile reception and treated as the cause of misfortune, bringers of disease and deterioration in the standard of living for the local community. Evacuees were effectively made to live and work in new, usually inhuman conditions. Those who fled or were forced to move were mostly inhabitants of areas where hostilities were being conducted or where there was an impending risk of hostilities. A total of over 10 million changed their place of residence during the war. The largest groups fled or were forcibly removed from the western territories of Russia and the Kingdom of Poland, moving into the Russian interior. In mid-February 1917 over 3 million refugees were reported there, and by the autumn of 1918 the figure had risen to 5 million. Londoners fled London during the air raids, and in September 1914 700 thousand Parisians fled Paris in the atmosphere of panic in anticipation of a German attack. In July 1915 350 thousand fled Warsaw. In 1914 800 thousand refugees left East Prussia – 30% of its population – and 400 thousand of them arrived in the western regions of Germany. Thousands of refugees left Serbia and Montenegro ahead of the invading forces of the Central Powers, and thousands more were forced to evacuate areas neighbouring on forts and strongholds. Tens of thousands of Belgians from Liège, Namur, and Antwerp, and Frenchmen from Maubeuge and Verdun were ordered to leave their homes. The Austrians likewise forcibly evacuated part of the inhabitants of cities like Przemyśl and Kraków which they had turned into defensible fortresses. Over 10 thousand were expelled from Przemyśl, and over 63 thousand from Kraków – one-third of the city's population – in three waves of evacuation. In all in rural and urban Galicia 700 thousand to 1 million fled or were forcibly driven out of their homes, over half of whom were Jews. Some Jews were voluntary refugees, fleeing south-west to Austria and the Czech territories with the Austrian authorities; others were forcibly resettled; and still others were deported to Russia by the Russians, who suspected them of sympathising with their enemies. On the way they were harassed, albeit in general the Russian authorities did not treat refugees too kindly, in contravention of the Hague Conventions. Some of the Ruthenians of East Galicia, who considered themselves kindred of the Russians, followed them into Russia.

The authorities of the Central Powers and Russia sent refugees and evacuees to interim camps, where the food and sanitary conditions tended to be bad, and worst in Russia. Many refugees and evacuees died; many returned home ill. A large part of their belongings was lost or destroyed during the evacuation. The victims of hostilities, those whose homes were destroyed in the fighting, were evacuated as well, and sent to interim camps. Hundreds of thousands of Italians fled to southern and western Italy in the aftermath of the Battle of Caporetto. When the Rumanians attacked Austria-Hungary the Hungarians evacuated 200 thousand of the inhabitants of Transylvania west. When the tables turned for the Rumanians, they evacuated thousands of their own citizens east, to prevent them from working or fighting for the enemy. In their places of resettlement evacuees were to work for their own side in the war.

6. The plight of women

The broad spectrum of women's social and public activity gave rise to changes which they welcomed in their status in the family, in national and local affairs and government, and in their political and civic status. The war witnessed a rise in feminist movements, and feminist literature expanded its readership, which has sometimes been interpreted as the origin of the women's revolution. It had been heralded in by Gertrude Atherton, an American woman who lived for years in Germany and in 1918 wrote *The White Morning: a Novel of the Power of the German Women in Wartime*, which was translated into many languages. She claimed that the menfolk had made a mistake deciding on war, and that they could not control their emotions and psychological reactions. Under Atherton's leadership, feminists appealed to women to become active in political affairs and urged them to take over power in the state, as only women would be able to save humankind by assuming power. The sooner they did so, the better for everybody. There were more feminist manifestos of this kind.

The best-known came from the pens of British suffragettes, who were full of reproach for male violence, which they called "Prussianism." Their books were a sign of a women's awakening and an expression of their authors' belief that politics was certainly not a male domain. During the war the feminist vanguard earned the support of at least a segment of the working women, which was a genuinely new development. They no longer wanted to play the same role in society as they had done hitherto. In 1915 the women of Denmark were granted the constitutional right to vote, and in Russia women were given the vote in 1917. On 12th November 1918 in Germany the Council of People's Deputies (*Rat der Volksbeauftragten*) declared that all women over 20 would be given the vote in parliamentary elections. On 10th January 1918 the US House of Representatives granted women full voting rights in presidential and congressional elections. The Senate stalled over ratification and did not sign the 20th Amendment to the Constitution until 26th August 1920. Until that time the women of several individual states had the right to vote. In Britain the vote was granted to women of 30, who were declared "settled and mature." Women under 30 were regarded as "unstable and wilful" and had to wait. The parliamentarians of France declared their admiration of women, but did not grant them the right to vote until almost the end of the Second World War, considering them politically immature, susceptible to what priests told them, and liable to listen to the opinions of men rather than follow their own mind. There was no possibility of a general European victory for women, as women's activists were divided. Some staunchly fought for women's political rights while at the same time voicing their opposition to the war. Others were committed to the war and did not have much time left to support the campaign for women's rights. Still others supported government campaigns and urged their followers to "have as many children as possible to fill the vacancies caused by the war," and engaged in government undertakings such as "Baby's Week" to improve the social and material status of women and children.

Some women's activists demanded the right to serve in the military for women. This was new. In Britain the Women's Army Auxiliary Corps (the WAAC) was founded in 1917, followed by the Women's Royal Naval Service (the Wrens) at the end of that year, and the Women's Royal Air Force (the WRAAF) in 1918. In Russia women's fighting units were established after the February Revolution; they included the 1st Russian Women's Battalion of Death, created by Maria Bochkareva (Yashka), a peasant's daughter remembered for her bravery. Women served in the Polish Legions; and a British woman in a man's uniform served in the Serbian army. Women's auxiliary units were established in some armies, where they served as nurses, cooks, Samaritans, instructors, and secretaries, but basically they did not enjoy a very good opinion with the soldiers. They tended to be regarded as prostitutes. A good example of patriotism and women's civic involvement was set by Ecaterina Teodoroiu, a platoon commander in the Rumanian army.

In outcome of the changes which ensued during the war some women freed themselves from the protective shield or straitjacket imposed on them by their homes, fathers, and families, and their self-confidence grew. Ideas on women's social roles started to change; women's view on their rights and potential grew stronger; and their activity in organising their own lives increased. The freedom born of necessity was best visible in women's clothes. Dress and skirt lengths became shorter and women's wear was looser, more comfortable and more practical, although this was a trend that had started before the war. Wartime impoverishment and insecurity did not favour the purchase of expensive and elaborate apparel, and hence the fashion for simpler, cheaper, and more convenient clothes made of softer fabrics – a development welcomed especially by younger and middle-class women. Lace-up and whalebone corsets, which had reigned supreme in women's fashion for decades, were discarded, and the jackets and trousers women now sported more and more often had pockets. Shorter skirt lengths, which had allowed women to show their ankles even before the war and somewhat later their calves, went down to just below knee level by the end of the war. Dresses with hip-level bodices came in. Apparel which before the war had been regarded as shocking or even immoral now became normal and taken for granted. The so-called American fashion disseminated by the movies made a significant impact. Already by the end of the war in Paris, London, Berlin, and Stockholm there were women who stood out in the crowd with their short hairstyles, make-up, lower neckline, wearing trousers instead of a skirt and holding a cigarette. Cigarettes became a fetish for the liberated avant-garde women. At first there were only a few of them, but they were pioneers staking out the trend that said women were allowed to do the same as men. For why should it be any otherwise? – they said. Before the war decent women could not appear in public on their own, without a male or female chaperone. Only women from the lower classes or prostitutes could be out in the streets. Now all this started to change. In Britain women entered the male territory of the pubs and ordered beer, causing a sensation and giving the papers something to write about. "Thousands of bonds which have tied women to men have been broken," the Belgian feminists wrote somewhat optimistically, and their British sisters added, "independent management of their homes as head of the household during the war has given many married women a new sense of security." Evidence for this was the rising divorce rate. While in 1913 in Germany there had been 27 divorces for every 100 thousand inhabitants, by 1920 the figure had risen to 59. But these statistics showed that the institution of marriage was effectively still indissoluble.

These changes affected the avant-garde. Millions of women were still in the dark about them, and continued to live and work just as their mothers and grandmothers had done. Some of the changes were only a transient wartime episode. A lasting change in women's status and behaviour was possible only by means of evolution, not revolution. The power of the patriarchal structures and traditions sanctioned by the churches and religions was strong. Men continued to be considered the head of the family and responsible for it, while women were still "maintained."

7. Revolutions

In August 1914 the socialists, anarchists, and pacifists went quiet. Some relished saying that pacifists protested against war only in times of peace. Not only pacifists, but also the majority of socialists accepted their country's and government's war policy. But as the war drew on, more and more people asked what was the sense of continuing it, more and more people protested against its high social and material costs. The number of the generally illegal strikes and anti-war demonstrations, growing year by year, was a measure of the dissatisfaction. Perhaps surprisingly, the largest number of strikes were staged in Britain. But they were short-lived, and died down as fast as they erupted, since employers and employees quickly managed to reach an agreement without waiting for state mediation. Often women turned out to be the more determined and active, since they were not afraid of consequences such as being barracked up in the event of their protest being forcibly brought to an end. Some of the demands women called for were shorter working hours and more pay, so that they could reconcile employment with the duties of motherhood. In 1915 a total of 401 thousand went on strike in Britain; whereas only 14 thousand came out in Germany in the same year. In 1918 923 thousand were on strike in Britain, while the corresponding figure for Germany was 391 thousand. According to estimates there were 3,227 strikes in Britain in 1915–1918, in which 2.6 million participated. The corresponding figures for France were 1,608 strikes and 520 thousand strikers; and respectively 1,801 strikes and 575 thousand strikers for Italy. In Russia 2,306 strikes erupted in 1916, but the figure for January and February 1917 was 751.

Most strikes broke out spontaneously, especially in the first phase of the war. Strikers demanded better working conditions and pay, and returned to work when their demands were met. Similar strikes erupted in neutral countries such as Switzerland and Spain, and Asian countries such as China and Japan. In India and Indo-China strikes often took a violent form, since the metropolitan states were burdening the colonies with the costs of the war. Some had a national undercurrent and were essentially a demonstration of the right of nations like the Khmer or the Vietnamese to their own way of life.

With time more and more strikes were organised by trade unions and social democratic groups. Their aims were a combination of social claims with anti-war demands and they often ended in mass demonstrations. Their numbers rose as the war neared its turning point, and under the impact of the Russian Revolution. Despite prohibitions, the number of strikers often went over 100 thousand, for example in Paris in May and June 1917, or in Berlin, Hamburg, Munich, Vienna, and Budapest in January 1918. On that occasion a total of 700 thousand came out on strike in Austria, 500 thousand in Hungary, and even more in Italy, which was one of the European hotpots for strikes. In June 1918 there was an attempt to stage a general strike in Hungary, but it was thwarted and the strikers were conscripted. Mass strikes tended to fail; they were broken either by a lock-out, or by the militarisation of the workforce, which meant that any who refused to work could be treated as refusing to do national service. These methods turned out to be very effective for breaking strikes.

A form of protest characteristic of the First World War were the women's hunger strikes. The protesters demanded better pay and called for the improvement of provisions, price reductions, and an end to the war. It would be hard to enumerate all the places where hunger strikes occurred, and perhaps easier to name those which did not have hunger strikes. Often such protests ended in shop window-smashing and looting, which led to police and army intervention. Some demonstrations turned into pitched battles between demonstrators and police and soldiers – for example, the "women's uprising" in Bulgaria in February 1918, or the violent clashes in Milan and Turin. Casualties and deaths occurred. Widows and orphans marched, supported by war invalids in a joint moral anti-war front.

The pacifists came out of hibernation already in 1915, although their slogans carried weight only insofar as they accorded with the voices of the dissatisfied masses. Nonetheless, it would be hard to ignore the activities of pacifists like Bertrand Russell, who was arrested and convicted, or Henri Barbusse, author of the anti-war novel *Le Feu* (translated into English by William Fitzwater Wray as *Under Fire*). Pacifists from 10 countries, most of them holding left-wing views, met in The Hague, to which the Second Socialist International had moved its headquarters following the occupation of Brussels, and set up an international pacifist organisation to prepare the foundations for a perpetual peace. But it was not the pacifists who determined the attitudes and views of the masses, but instead the nationalists and militarists, who organised mass demonstrations in favour of greater involvement in the war effort. Pro-war attitudes were predominant almost until the end of hostilities, although as of the spring of 1917 peace was being spoken and written about more and more often. The word "peace," which in the first years of the war had been regarded as virtually synonymous with "treason," returned from exile.

Alongside the pacifist intellectuals there were also the socialist pacifists on the left wing of the socialist movement. They were more vociferous and called for immediate peace. Their ranks included Bolshevik-oriented revolutionists who wanted to transform the war, which they called an "imperialist war," in to a "revolutionary war" to wipe out the capitalist world and build up a communist order. Bolshevik revolutionists appealed to the soldier-workers to turn their weapons against the capitalists in their home countries and the officials of the capitalist states. They denounced imperialism as the source of the war and encouraged Socialist and Social Democrat parliamentarians to leave bourgeois governments and vote against the assignment of more money for the war. They wanted soldiers to fraternise with their counterparts in enemy armies. Their best known representative and ideological leader was Lenin, who was followed by others, at first few in number but determined and hungry for success.

One of the first of conferences organised by the Socialist pacifists was held in September 1915 at Zimmerwald near Berne in Switzerland. During their debates they adopted a resolution calling for immediate peace, no annexations, and the right of nations to self-determination. The conference was attended by Bolsheviks. However, Lenin failed to persuade most of the socialist pacifists to adopt the Bolshevik postulates. The same happened at the next conference, which was held in Switzerland again, at Kienthal near Berne, in April 1916. The socialist pacifists passed a resolution criticising the pro-war attitude of the social democrats, who continued to support the military policies pursued by their countries. The socialist pacifists deplored the Second Socialist International for having followed a policy of submission on the war waged by the imperialist states. A Bolshevik resolution calling for revolution was adopted as a minority opinion. At subsequent conferences, including the 1917 Stockholm Conference, the socialist pacifist view continued to predominate over the Bolshevik view. Nevertheless the working masses in all the belligerent countries lent their support to moderate social democratic movements which were in favour of the policy pursued by their country, viz. in favour of the war, and which Lenin dubbed "socialist chauvinists," traitors to the workers' cause.

Thus, by the end of 1917 there were three main groups of socialists: 1) social democrats, who enjoyed the support of the majority of working-class people; their representatives were members of governments and voted in favour of the war; 2) socialist pacifists; their representatives were against the war and also against the idea of revolution; and 3) the Bolsheviks; their representatives were against the war but enthusiastic about the revolution and wanted to take over power by force of arms. In 1917–1918 the split between the diverse factions of socialists deepened and their mutual polarisation came to be seen as the normal situation, particularly in Germany, where socialist views were most prevalent. Alongside the predominant German Social Democrats (SPD), who supported the German state and its war policy, there were the German Bolshevik-oriented activists, the most esteemed of whom was Karl Liebknecht, who adopted an anti-war attitude in 1914 and persisted in it, and Rosa Luxemburg. Liebknecht, Luxemburg and their associates set up secret Bolshevik structures in opposition to the SPD, and as of 1916 were known as the Spartacus League (*Spartakusbund*). In May 1916 Liebknecht was arrested and imprisoned. In June 1917 the same befell Luxemburg.

They were liberated by the November Revolution in 1918. The Socialist Pacifists were a larger and better organised group, and established the USPD (the Independent Social Democratic Party of Germany, *Die Unabhängige Sozialdemokratische Partei Deutschlands*) led by Hugo Haase, a Reichstag deputy, and Karl Kautsky. Haase built up a reputation for voting against war credits in 1915, whereupon he was dubbed a renegade and along with a few colleagues expelled from the SPD, after which he founded the USPD. The left wing of the USPD was the Spartacus League, though in point of fact they were an entirely separate group. Unlike the Spartacus League, the USPD did not want to destroy the capitalist state.

The end of the war and defeat for the Central Powers radicalised German society. The signal for anti-war protest was given by men of the German navy. The mutiny which erupted on the night of $4^{th}/5^{th}$ November 1918 at Kiel led to the establishment of a sailors' council. It started on news that German warships were to sail out for a final showdown with the Royal Navy. Sailors took control of the ships, arrested the officers, and put up red flags. During the next few days the same happened in other ports such as Hamburg and Bremen. In early November, when the German command announced that Germany had lost the war, millions of Germans were infuriated. They had been fed lies to the very end by the propaganda machine, which had forecast imminent victory. Their anger turned against the Kaiser and his political entourage. The soldiers' war was drawing to a close, and the war of the civilians was beginning. Throughout Germany soldiers' and workers' councils were formed. In some the SPD predominated; in others the USPD or the Spartacus League was the leading force, and they quarrelled vehemently with each other. On 7th November the Munich USPD supported by a crowd of many thousands of demonstrators under the leadership of Kurt Eisner forced Ludwig III, the Wittelsbach King of Bavaria, to flee. "The Wittelsbach dynasty ruled Bavaria for seven centuries, and I chased them out in seven hours with the help of seven people," Eisner boasted. The Social Democrats acting through the Workers' and Soldiers' Council assumed power. Eisner was declared prime minister and minister of foreign affairs of the Free State of Bavaria, in compliance with the will of the assembled people of Munich. The events in Munich speeded up developments. On the following days demonstrators in Berlin and other cities called for the Kaiser's abdication. They were supported by right-wing politicians and generals, who hoped that it would make the armistice conditions less severe. They expected Germany would lose Alsace and Lorraine at the most, but keep its army and the rest of the territories including most of its colonies. On 9th November thousands of demonstrators marched along Unter den Linden in Berlin shouting, "Hang the Kaiser!" On the same day the Chancellor, Prince Maximilian of Baden, telephoned the Kaiser, who was at Spa (Belgium), to inform him that he had publicly announced his abdication, and that the Social Democrat Philipp Scheidemann, the future Chancellor of the Weimar Republic, had made an announcement on the stairway of the Reichstag declaring Germany a republic. The change of Germany's political system had been accomplished in a very short time. Only a fortnight before the Kaiser had declared that a descendant of Frederick the Great would never abdicate, and on 2nd November he had turned down the Chancellor's suggestion that he should abdicate, saying he had no intention of leaving the throne because of a few hundred Jews and a thousand workers. However, on 10th November, on learning that German revolutionary units were on their way to Spa to arrest him, he fled to Holland. Queen Wilhelmina of the Netherlands granted him asylum, though not without hesitation. He boarded a train for the Dutch border, where he got into a car, as the revolutionaries had taken control of the railway lines. Thus 504 years of Hohenzollern rule came to an end. The dynasty's last representative could not and did not want to be reconciled to the fact, and like a medieval monarch believed God had invested him with the divine right of kings. A fortnight later he signed his act of abdication. Many European politicians wanted the "blood-bespattered monster who deserved to hang" to be tried. Ultimately he managed to save his neck.

Soldiers' and workers' councils took power in Germany, and policing was done by the defence units of the soldiers' councils. Central and local government, and municipal authorities hitherto in power resigned. However, unlike the situation in Russia, the majority of the members of the new councils did not want to embark on a Bolshevik revolution, despite Liebknecht's call, and were satisfied with the declaration of a republic, a broad scope of democratisation, and social rights for the workers. A revolution of the Bolshevik type was out of the question due to opposition from a strong middle class, the influential "workers' aristocracy" and the farmers of Germany. The leaders of most councils were either Social Democrats or Independent Socialists, whom the Communist Spartacists called "Socialist Traitors." Council leaders did their best to make the state structures work properly to prevent anarchy. Sometimes representatives of the centre of the political spectrum, Christian Democrats, assumed power. For instance in Cologne the Christian Democrat Konrad Adenauer stayed in office as the city's mayor (*Oberbürgermeister*).

Revolution broke out in Austria as well, but was limited to Vienna and Linz and did not reach rural areas. Workers' councils were established in Vienna and the largest cities, while elsewhere people's councils or parish councils dominated by Christian Democrats were set up to manage security and food provisions, and protect the people against criminals. The anti-war and revolutionary movement was not as strong in Austria, nevertheless Russian-style revolutionary campaigning could be observed, as police informers reported. Following a demonstration in Vienna on 30th October 1918 the Social Democrat Friedrich Adler, who had assassinated the unpopular reactionary prime minister Karl von Stürghk (21st October 1916), was released from prison and became a member of the new government. He was one of two Social Democratic ministers in the new cabinet, which held power only in the German-speaking territories, as the non-German regions of Austria had seceded and were setting up their own national states. Due to war weariness and problems with food supplies the revolution in Austria was not so violent nor so widespread. Austrian soldiers returning home were physically exhausted, spiritually drained, and completely demoralised. They went on only thanks to the need to find food and tranquillity – such were the observations and comments.

On 11th November the Emperor Karl signed a document in which he insisted that he was neither abdicating nor renouncing his dynastic right, but merely "withdrawing from state affairs," whereupon he and his family left Vienna for Eckartsau Castle, and from there went to Switzerland. On the following day the Austrians represented in a provisional national assembly declared a German Austrian republic (*Republik Deutschösterreich*), which they wanted to be part of the German Republic. However, the Allies decided that Austria would be an independent state.

Revolution reached Hungary, too. It was led by Mihály Károlyi, a Hungarian aristocrat who was in favour of Hungary's secession from the Habsburg dual monarchy, Hungarian independence, and social reform. On 25th October 1918 he created the Hungarian National Council, a body which was independent of the Habsburg government. The revolution won the support of the army and police (though after some hesitation in the latter case). During the revolution Prime Minister István Tisza, who was regarded as responsible and the most to blame for Hungary's misfortunes, was assassinated. Károlyi assumed power on 31st October. His coalition government included Social Democrats. On 1st November Hungary proclaimed neutrality, but General Franchet d'Espérey, Allied Commander-in-Chief in the Balkans, treated it as a defeated state. Meanwhile the historical Kingdom of Hungary disintegrated as the territories inhabited by non-Magyar national and ethnic groups seceded, forming their own national states.

Further developments in the revolutions in Germany, Austria, and Hungary belong to the history of the postwar period. Revolutionary trends on the Czech territories, in Croatia, Slovakia, Serbia, and Poland, albeit present, were much feebler and lost out to the patriotic intentions of the masses to set up their own national states.

Revolutionary trends could be observed in the neutral countries of Europe, too, especially in Spain, where numerous soldiers' councils and juntas sprang up, and 1917/1918 is referred to as "the two Bolshevik years." In point of fact it was not the Bolsheviks that had a large following in Spain, but Anarchists, who were anti-Bolshevik, proponents of terror, and Syndicalists. The black flag of the Anarchists was hoisted more often than the red flag of the Socialists. In 1916 and 1917 Spain experienced a series of general strikes which paralysed the country and the government had to introduce martial law.

Even in the normally quiet countries of Scandinavia strikes and demonstrations were the order of the day. Strikers called for democratisation, pay rises, and fewer working hours. They did not want all the profit and gains which had accrued from the auspicious wartime trading to fall into the hands of the rich. They wanted those who had got rich on wartime trading and the black market taxed. They set up councils controlled by moderate Social Democrats to act as their authorities. Soldiers' and workers' councils were established even in France and Britain, but they were not very significant and were relatively free of Bolshevik influence.

There was a revolutionary trend in Latin America, too, under the impact of either the Mexican Revolution, which came to an end in 1917, or the Russian Revolution. The workers' councils established in Latin America were left-wing, nationalist, and anti-USA in character, but not Bolshevik. 1917–1918, the turbulent days of revolution, triggered the emergence of national movements in India, Indo-China, and an Islamic independence movement in Indonesia.

V. The War of the Nations

Some of the belligerent states were multi-ethnic like Russia, Austria-Hungary, and the Ottoman Empire. However, on the whole the ethnic communities inhabiting them did not voice any aspirations to gain independence, stopping at a demand of the right to autonomy within the existing state. The desire to set up their own nation-state could be observed only in some ethno-national groups (such as the Poles), or merely their upper strata, and even there it was certainly not a hard-and-fast rule. None of the ethno-national groups in the imperial states contemplated wide-scale clandestine military action in a liberation movement against the state they were in. At any rate none of them had the forces needed for such action. The nature of the 1914 mobilisation and of the war, at least in its initial phase, ruled out irredentist activities of any kind whatsoever. Soldiers from the various ethnic communities making up the multi-ethnic states marched off to war without asking questions to do their soldier's duty. If the governments of the multi-ethnic states had been seriously worried by the risk of irredentism, they would never have decided to go to war. In the first phase of the global conflict the so-called national question (viz. national aspirations) had absolutely no impact whatsoever on the progress of the war. The multi-ethnic armies were loyal to their monarchs and dynasties, and there were bonds of solidarity binding the ethno-nationalities to their state, despite the repressions or discrimination against them. This was so for historical reasons and the traditions of loyalty reinforced by the churches and state authorities, as well as for pragmatic reasons: people were in sympathy with the army in which their brothers, sons, and cousins served. Austria-Hungary was not let down by the Transylvanian Rumanians, who bravely fought to defend their state against the Rumanian army in 1917. Germany was not disappointed by the French-speaking inhabitants of Alsace and Lorraine, as evidenced by the low rate of desertion until the autumn of 1918. In effect on many of the fronts there was fratricidal bloodshed. Poles fought against other Poles; Ukrainians met other Ukrainians in combat; and likewise Rumanians clashed with Rumanians, Italians with other Italians, and Frenchmen battled against other Frenchmen. Rumanians served in the armies of Rumania, Russia, and Austria-Hungary. Poles served in the Russian, Austro-Hungarian, and German army. There were Ukrainians fighting for the Russians, Austro-Hungarians, and under the Hungarian Honvéd colours. Notwithstanding the general sense of loyalty, there were instances of desertion for ethno-national or religious reasons, soldiers joining the ranks of the enemy or spreading enemy propaganda, but the scale of the phenomenon was small and had no effect on the progress of the war. The authorities in Berlin, Petrograd, Istanbul, Budapest, and Vienna were more anxious over the possibility of national irredentism in the "nationally foreign elements" in their ranks than they needed to be. Not until the final phase of the war, when the belligerents were exhausted and soldiers' bonds of solidarity with "their" army, dynasty, and state had worn out, did the national elites come to the fore, calling for their own national states, in compliance with the right of nations to self-determination President Woodrow Wilson had outlined.

1. The Czechs and the Yugoslavs

Let's take a look at those nations which saw the war as a chance to go their own way, in accordance with their national interest. This means first and foremost the national groups in Austria-Hungary. We'll start with the Czechs. Nonetheless, the Czechs did not have a unified idea of how to behave during the war and how to put forward their national postulates. Some banked on a continuing union with Vienna. Others wanted a special status for the lands of the Bohemian Crown within Cisleithania (the Austrian part of the Habsburg monarchy), and this was the most popular idea. Still others, a minority, looked to Russia and were thinking of full independence. The majority of the upper and educated classes were at loggerheads with Vienna, as their postulate of special status for the Czech lands had not been met. They switched their option, pinning their hopes on Austria's arch-enemy, Russia. Some Czech politicians were active members of the Pan-Slavic movement even before 1914. When war broke out they hoped Russia and her allies would win. However, it would have been dangerous to express such opinions openly – they would have faced arrest and prosecution. Knowing that they would have to keep their mouths shut, Czech anti-Habsburg politicians left the country for the West, not for Russia, for they had an intuition that it would be the Allies who would be making the decisions on the map of Europe and the fate of the Habsburg empire.

This was the option chosen by Professor Tomáš Garrigue Masaryk, who turned out to be a first-rate, far-sighted politician with a fine sense of political intuition. For him Austria was "the tool of European reactionism." He had a small group of skilful collaborators, the main one was his student, Edvard Beneš. Masaryk and Beneš embarked on a publicity campaign for the creation of a free and independent Czech state after the war, thereby rejecting the continuation of the Czech people under Habsburg auspices. There were few Czechs who shared this opinion at the time. Originally Masaryk envisaged the future independent Czech state as a monarchy with a Romanov for its king. But soon he abandoned this idea in favour of a pro-Western Czech republic in federation with Slovakia – as Czechoslovakia. In 1916 in France Masaryk founded the Czechoslovak National Council, with the Slovak Milan Štefánik as a member. They launched a publicity campaign in French and English, starting with the most basic issues – informing the decision-makers and opinion-shapers in the Western countries and their societies that there was a Czech nation, of which not many had heard, and that it had aspirations. At the same time they kept up the spirits of the anti-Austrian groups at home. They smuggled in publications from the West, hiding them in children's toys, soap, or boxes of soiled linen. They supported the Czech Panslavists led by Karel Kramář, who was arrested in May 1917 for making public statements which were declared seditious, subversive to the Habsburg war effort, and, along with three companions, was sentenced to death on a charge of treason. However, the clement Kaiser Karl commuted the sentence to long-term imprisonment, to avoid creating a hero and martyr for the Czech cause. However, apart from the group of the most radical activists, the rest of the Czech politicians, including the Agrarian and National Social parties, and most of the Catholic groups, all remained loyal to the Habsburg empire, at least in their public activities, seeing Masaryk as a Russian and Serbian agent. On 31st January 1917 the presidium of the Czech club in the Council of State at Vienna wrote to Foreign Minister Ottokar Czernin that "the Czech nation did not envisage its future in any other manner but in continuance under Habsburg rule, just as it had always done in the past."

Despite the servile enunciations the authorities in Vienna did not trust the Czechs, especially as it was precisely the Czechs who masterminded the most spectacular desertions. There was a lot of talk about the 28th infantry regiment, which in April 1915 absconded for the service of the Russians. But the pragmatic Czechs saw no point in combat that was useless from their point of view, and even less sense in dying for a cause they could neither comprehend nor espouse. The Russians sent the Czech deserters and prisoners-of-war to an already existing unit called the Czech Company (*Česká družina*), which consisted of Czech volunteers, immigrants living on the territory of the Romanov Empire. Later the Czech units were reorganised as the 1st Czechoslovak (Hussite) Rifle Regiment and afterwards renamed the Czechoslovak Corps, now generally known as the Czechoslovak Legion. The Corps/Legion continued to grow after the February Revolution. The men serving in its were trained and armed well, and they knew what they were fighting for. They were the apple of Masaryk's eye. Not surprisingly, the Czech regiments fought bravely in the Battle of Zborov (Zborów, now Zboriv, Ukraine) on 2nd June 1917 and were the best fighting units in the Kerensky Offensive. After the Bolshevik Revolution the Allies pinned their hopes on the Czechoslovak Legion, which was formally put under their command. When the Germans occupied Ukraine in March 1918 the Allied Supreme Command ordered the Legion, which was 40,000-strong by then, to move east for Vladivostok and north, for evacuation from Russia and reinforcement of the Western front. An earlier concept put forward by the military authorities in Paris to deploy the Czechs and White Russians wishing to continue in Allied service for the reactivation of the Eastern front turned out to be impracticable. The first of the Legion's units, numbering 14,000 men, reached Vladivostok in late April, but there were no ships to transport them to Europe. In May there was a skirmish at Chelyabinsk between the Czechs and the Bolsheviks. In retaliation Lev Trotsky gave the order for the Czechs to be disarmed and arrested: any armed Czech caught near the main railway line was to be shot on sight. Pressing on in an eastward direction, the Czechs had to defend themselves in a constant series of battles against the Bolsheviks. They availed themselves of the Trans-Siberian railway, which they came to control. Their heroic passage marked by combat and death made a good impression on the West and raised the Czech standing on the world emporium of national interests very substantially. Eventually most of the legionnaires managed to reach Vladivostok, which was then in Allied hands. A few thousand of them, including the committed Communist Jaroslav Hašek, author of *The Good Soldier Švejk*, stayed with the Bolsheviks.

The legionnaires were the trump card in Masaryk's policy. He played the Czech hand adroitly and made good use of the auspicious international situation. He became the most popular politician of the "new" Central and Eastern Europe that was coming into being – far more popular than any of the Polish or Yugoslav politicians. Although not as numerous as the Poles, the Czechs had more soldiers serving with the Allies. Apart from the renowned Legion, the Czechs also had a division fighting on the Italian front and units fighting in France. On 16th December 1917 the French President published a decree on the establishment of a Czechoslovak army subject to the political authority of the Czechoslovak National Council in Paris.

Meanwhile in 1918 history took a fast turn, which could only have pleased the Czechs. In May of that year the government of Austria-Hungary announced the division of the Czech territories into districts according to ethnic criteria, to separate the Czechs off from the Germans. The Sudeten Germans were delighted; the Czechs were annoyed. Even those Czech politicians who had been pro-Austrian hitherto, now came out in opposition to Vienna, with the overriding support of the people. Owing to the tension the government in Vienna withdrew from its plan. In the autumn of 1918 the Czechs and Slovaks reached an agreement on the need to create a joint state, and the potential to accomplish this. Incidentally, their first agreement was concluded on 30th May 1918 in Pittsburgh. There were nearly one million Slovaks in the USA, and they were better educated and aware of their national identity than their compatriots in Transleithania (the Kingdom of Hungary). It was easier for them to enter an agreement with the Czechs on US territory.

President Wilson supported the ambitions and efforts of the ethno-nations to set up their own national states, in accordance with the principle of self-determination, and for defence against the Red Revolution. The top echelons of the subjugated nations living in the Habsburg empire interpreted this as meaning that he did not rule out the possibility of its collapse. On the other hand, Britain and France did not see the need to dismantle Austria-Hungary as a necessary objective of the war, chiefly because they were counting on a separate peace treaty with Vienna. Moreover, they were not at all pleased by the prospect of several new national states emerging on the ruins of Austria-Hungary. A relic of the 19th-century way of thinking appears to have lingered in their attitude. They were used to the notion of the Concert of Powers as the decisive factor in Europe, and the presence of Austria-Hungary in it seemed self-evident. After the war the Powers were to negotiate with the other Powers, just as they had done before, and they feared that the new multi-ethnic and multicultural states would be a source of future conflicts, thereby destabilising the continent. They were apprehensive both of the rise of Slavic states, which they called "semi-literate," and of the separating off from the Czech lands of the German areas, which wanted to join a Greater Germany (consisting of both prewar Austria and the Reich). Even Clemenceau's famous statement made on 17th September 1917, that the Habsburg empire was "a land of counter-revolution, the habitat of Jesuits, and the torturer of the nations" was not a declaration of support for irredentism, but should rather be read as pressure on Vienna to quit the war as soon as possible. Likewise the Allies' declaration of 10th January 1918 on the need to liberate the Czechoslovaks from foreign rule can hardly be seen as the undertaking of an obligation. Wilson was even more cautious. His 14 Points of January 1918 did not envisage any new national states in place of Austria-Hungary – a big disappointment for the Czechs, Serbs, Croats, Slovenes, and Slovaks. Only the Poles were taken into consideration. The disintegration of the Habsburg empire was not acknowledged as a viable project until the middle of 1918. In August of that year the Allies recognised the right of the Czechoslovaks and of the Yugoslavs to establish their own independent states.

On 28th October, after a series of pro-independence demonstrations and a general strike, the Czechoslovak National Committee declared the foundation of a sovereign Czechoslovak state. On 30th October at a meeting in Turčianský Svätý Martin (now Martin, Slovakia) the Slovak National Council adopted a declaration on the foundation of a new state jointly with the Czechs. Its western and northern frontiers were to run along the historical borders of the Bohemian Crown, which made for an inevitable clash with the Poles over the Těšín (Cieszyn) region of Silesia, and even more ominous conflict with the Sudeten Germans. Already on 23rd October the Germans living on Czech lands announced that they wanted to be incorporated in German Austria – in other words that they did not want to be with the Czechs. Similarly the Hungarians could not imagine being with the Slovaks in a new Czechoslovak state, reduced to the status of a boarder after a thousand years as landlord.

The war roused the Southern Slavs and their national elites to action. However, they did not share a unified view on friends and foes. The lands of the Southern Slavs had a population of Catholic Croatians and Slovenes, Orthodox Serbs and Montenegrans, and Muslim Bosniaks. The Serbs wanted a Serbian state – a Great Serbia encompassing all the territories of the Southern Slavs, including the lands of the Croats, whom they regarded as Roman Catholic Serbians, and the Adriatic seaboard. The Croats in turn wanted a Great Croatia, a state encompassing both Croats and Serbs, whom they regarded as Croats belonging to the Eastern Orthodox Church. The foundation of this state would be the autonomous Kingdom of Croatia-Slavonia hitherto belonging to Hungary. Some Croatians wanted to establish a Great Croatia in co-operation with Vienna and Budapest; others imagined a new state set up in defiance of Austria-Hungary. Neither the Slovenes nor the Muslims of Bosnia entertained such ambitious plans. During the war the Yugoslav option started to gain ground. Its staunchest propagators were the anti-Habsburg Serbs and Croats living in exile. On 20th July 1917 they met on the Island of Corfu. The leader of the Croats was Ante Trumbić, and the leader of the Serbs was Nikola Pašić. With the support of the Slovenes, they made an agreement that after the war and the disintegration of Austria-Hungary they would jointly establish a new kingdom with a monarch from the Serbian Karađorđević dynasty. They adopted a declaration to this effect and won the support of the deputies to the Habsburg Council of State who were members of the joint Yugoslav Club. However, the nationalistic politicians who wanted a Great Serbia, and their Croatian counterparts who opted for a Great Croatia, continued to enjoy a large following.

Nonetheless the Yugoslav idea became more and more popular as the Southern Slavs realised that unity was strength and that they would not manage to resist their neighbours' imperial plans unless they were united. The Slovenes and Croats counted on Serbian support in their imminent tussle with Italy, which wanted to incorporate disputed territories like Istria, Gorizia, and Dalmatia. In fact, the conflict with Italy made some Croats and Slovenes opt for the establishment of an autonomous Yugoslavia within a Habsburg state. The Serbs in favour of the Yugoslavia concept wanted a joint state because of their prospective conflict with Hungary over Vojvodina, and over Kosovo with the Albanians, who were being favoured by Austria. The Serbs were not sure of the loyalty of the Macedonians, some of whom wanted to join Bulgaria, and some were thinking of a separate state of their own, with only a minority wanting to join Serbia.

The Allies encouraged Italy and the Southern Slavs to reach an agreement, and thanks to their mediation the Italians agreed to convene in Rome on 8th April 1918 for the Congress of Oppressed Nationalities, in other words those who inhabited Austria-Hungary. This included the Poles. At the Congress the Italians expressed their consent to the establishment of an independent Southern Slavic state and promised to hold negotiations on the question of borders, but made no binding commitments. The outcome of the debates and backstage discussions was the initiation of good working relations between the antagonists of Vienna and Budapest – the Czechs, Slovaks, Yugoslavs, and Transylvanian Rumanians, which could be read as a forecast of their future anti-Hungarian alliance.

The Congress outlined the prospects for a new European and world order, and the role in this of an international organisation about to enter history under the name of the League of Nations. That was the first thing the Congress achieved. The second was that it acknowledged the national state as the best institution to organise a nation. And thirdly it recognised the right of the "oppressed nationalities" to self-determination, provided that they respected the interests and aspirations of other nations. These were important declarations opening up the road to freedom and independence for the hitherto dependent nationalities.

In the spring and summer of 1918 the Southern Slavic nations started to set up their own national councils. On 5th October 1918 the National Council of the three nations was founded in Zagreb. It was to be the supreme authority of the new State of Slovenes, Croats, and Serbs (SHS). The Slovene Dr. Anton Korošec was appointed its leader. On 29th October the National Council declared the independence of the SHS State, and on the 31st issued an address to the coalition expressing its hope that they would confirm the sovereignty and territorial integrity of the Yugoslav state. However, the Italians dragged their feet and the coalition withheld its decision. Serbia, Montenegro, and Vojvodina did not join the new state. In outcome of further negotiations, on 1st December 1918 the Kingdom of Serbs, Croats, and Slovenes was founded.

2. From Poland to Finland

In the second phase of the war there was a rise in the activities of national movements in East-Central Europe, which was gradually occupied by Germany and Austria-Hungary in 1915–1918. Victorious in the East, these two states abolished the Russian administration and established their own occupying military administration and a supreme eastern command known as the Ober Ost. However, it was a provisional arrangement, which Austria-Hungary was ready to accept as satisfactory, but Germany wanted something more and came up with the *Mitteleuropa* concept, in other words a German Central Europe. The original idea was put forward in 1915 in a famous book by Friedrich Naumann, a Lutheran pastor and Liberal deputy to the Reichstag since 1907. In 1914 a fairly similar concept of arrangements in the East, which could be described as an economic union of the countries of East-Central Europe, had been represented to the Kaiser by Chancellor Theobald von Bethmann-Hollweg, and the two concepts were implemented in the autumn of 1916. The occupying powers set about creating new state entities on the territories taken from Russia. They were to be associated politically, economically, and militarily with the Central Powers and subjected to a "mission of German civilisation and culture," as Berlin put it, to create a common economic zone east of Germany. The German authorities believed that the modernisation of these territories would facilitate their exploitation, bringing them a bigger return, since impoverished, backward, and badly organised areas were harder to exploit. The *Mitteleuropa* scheme was to secure a more efficient management of the former Russian territories as a contribution to the war effort. This was to be its first and most important purpose from the point of view of Berlin. Secondly, it was to facilitate the disciplining of the local peoples, turning them into a guarantee of peace and stability. And thirdly, it was to bring Germany and Austria-Hungary new adherents. The three aims were coherent and mutually complementary. The Central Powers did not rule out the possibility of recruiting local inhabitants for police and military forces working in co-operation with them, and this prospect became more and more important as the war dragged on, making the human resources of Central and Eastern Europe an asset of increasing consequence. *Mitteleuropa* was an experiment to test the potential for the establishment of a German Europe, envisaged as an outcome of victory for the Central Powers and consisting of an array of vassal states in the East subordinated to Germany within the *Mitteleuropa* scheme, Austria-Hungary, Rumania, and Bulgaria, with a vanquished and diminished France and Belgium in the West. The idea appealed above all to the politicians, and the Kaiser came to like it more and more, referring to it as the Imperial European Union, with German monarchs appointed by him for each of the member states.

The principal addressees of the *Mitteleuropa* scheme were to be the Poles inhabiting the hitherto Russian-ruled Kingdom of Poland. On 5th November 1916 the two Kaisers, Wilhelm II and Franz Joseph, created "their own" Kingdom of Poland. On the grounds of "the two Emperors' act" a Polish state was called into being, but to the end of the war no borders were demarcated for it. It had a Polish administration, judiciary, Polish universities and colleges including a university and polytechnic in Warsaw, and it had a Polish educational system and currency. The occupying powers set up a legislative body, the Provisional Council of State, which commenced operations in January 1917. No king was nominated: on this issue there was no agreement between the two Emperors, whether it should be a Habsburg or a Hohenzollern, and instead in November 1917 Germany and Austria-Hungary appointed an interim Regency Council of three, with Prince Zdzisław Lubomirski as its most active member. Lubomirski was a good organiser and had proved himself an efficient politician as Mayor of Warsaw. In December 1917 the Regents appointed a Council of Ministers, i.e. a government, which was gradually invested with more and more powers. The Kingdom of Poland was peculiar in that alongside its Polish authorities there were also civilian and military occupying authorities operating in it and conducting a policy of maximum economic exploitation until the very end of the war. Not many Poles were pleased with the November Act. Those who were banking on victory for Russia and the Western Allies were hostile to it. Those who were in favour of a triple arrangement, viz. the transformation of Galicia and the Kingdom of Poland into a third component of the Habsburg empire, in other words an Austria-Hungary-Poland, did not like it, either. The Poles living in the German partitional zone, Greater Poland, Gdańsk and Pomerania, and Upper Silesia, were inimical to it. The most vociferous in this respect was Wojciech Korfanty, a public figure and leader who came from Silesia and was a deputy to the German parliament representing the Poles. The establishment of a Kingdom of Poland under German control would mean that the prospective sovereign Poland would be deprived of its historic western regions. Not surprisingly the Poles living in the German partitional zone looked to the Entente and were pleased when a Polish army was established in France under General Józef Haller and politically under the command of the Polish National Committee, a kind of provisional government set up in alliance with the Entente. Neither was there a guarantee that lands to the east of the border of the Kingdom of Poland, including Grodno and Wilno (now Hrodna, Belarus; and Vilnius, Lithuania), with Poles as the majority population, would be part of a future sovereign Poland.

Another disputed question between the German occupying authorities and the Polish authorities in Warsaw was who commanded the armed forces of the Kingdom of Poland (*Polnische Wehrmacht*) which were being set up. Józef Piłsudski, the leader of the Polish independence movement, founder of the Polish Legions and future

Marshal of the Republic of Poland after 1918, saw these forces as the germ of a Polish army independent of the Powers that had partitioned Poland. But General Hans Beseler, Governor-General of the German part of the Kingdom of Poland, regarded the very modest *Polnische Wehrmacht* as a dependent army subordinated to Germany. Beseler also tried to gain control of Piłsudski's Polish Legions and incorporate them in the Kingdom of Poland's army. The Polish Legions had been founded in August 1914, and they were an independent Polish armed force, even though under Austro-Hungarian command. In July 1917 Piłsudski was summoned to take an oath of allegiance to the two Kaisers, and when he (and a large number of his legionaries) refused, he was interned and detained in the fortress of Magdeburg until the end of the war. This move aroused a hostile response from the Poles, an undeniable sign of the failure of German policy on Poland. On 10th November 1918 Piłsudski returned from Magdeburg and was given a hero's welcome as a providential figure and a martyr for the cause. The Regency Council invested him with the command and military authority over the Polish forces, and subsequently with supreme power over the civilian administrative authorities, which it had taken over from the occupying power a few weeks earlier.

The Act of 5th November was important because it made the Polish question an international issue, compelling the opposite side in the war to take up a position. Nonetheless London and Paris held their peace for a time, regarding the territories of the Kingdom of Poland as legally belonging to Russia. They changed their mind after the February Revolution, when the Russian Provisional Government and Council of Petrograd granted the Poles and other national and ethnic groups in Russia the right to cultivate their native language and establish their own national institutions and military forces in alliance with Russia. The ethno-national groups took advantage of this opportunity. They also made use of the principle of self-determination for the nations, which was constantly being emphasised by President Wilson. Following the February Revolution the Lithuanians, Latvians, Estonians, Finns, Azeris, Armenians, Georgians, Ukrainians, and even the Byelorussians started to set up structures for their own states within the framework of Russia. However, their territories were gradually being occupied by German and Austro-Hungarian troops. After the Bolshevik coup d'etat in November 1917 and the Treaty of Brest-Litovsk in March of the following year the Germans and Austrians were free to make arrangements in Central and Eastern Europe in accordance with their own interests and plans.

The most mature of these projects was the scheme the Lithuanians designed for their national state, encouraged by the Act of 5th November and the Russian Revolution. In point of fact, they had been making vigorous efforts on behalf of their national affairs, both in the belligerent countries and in America, ever since the beginning of the war. The Lithuanian diaspora in America – along with all the other diasporas of the "oppressed nationalities" – made up an excellent nursery for a national campaign. The leaders of the Lithuanian community in the USA lobbied Congress and the White House. They were just as efficient in the neutral countries of Europe, co-organising conferences in Berne, Lausanne, and The Hague of the nations oppressed by Russia, Germany, and Austria-Hungary. The Lithuanians were also active in Berlin, encouraging the Germans in their *Mitteleuropa* plans. Finally they got the Germans to consent to a conference of Lithuanian organisations, which was held in Vilnius on 18th–23rd September 1917. The delegates assembled at it elected a 20-member Lithuanian National Council (the Taryba) under the chairmanship of Antanas Smetona. On 11th November 1917 the Taryba declared "the restoration of the independent Lithuanian State in Vilnius," the Grand Duchy of Lithuania in alliance with Germany and ruled by a German monarch. This was the first Lithuanian declaration of independence. Encouraged by their success, the Lithuanians decided on a policy of *faits accomplis*, counting that their bid for independence would soon be recognised, and on 16th February 1918 passed a second declaration of independence. This time they made no mention of alliance with Germany, which resulted in Berlin failing to recognise it. Nonetheless the Lithuanians resolutely continued to build up their independent structures. The Sixteenth of February would later become Lithuania's Day of Independence, the national foundation myth. The first and second Lithuanian declarations of independence were announced in Vilnius, a city in which – according to a census carried out by the Germans – Lithuanians accounted for no more than 2% of the population. The majority in the city and its environs were the Poles, and hence the Polish population of Vilnius/Wilno and its region did not recognise the Lithuanians' right to the city and region – presaging a major conflict. Berlin did not consent to the establishment of new states in the East until the declaration of 5th October 1918 issued by its Chancellor, Prince Maximilian of Baden. Thereupon the Lithuanians hastened their preparations, and on 11th November 1918 appointed a government led by Augustinas Voldemaras.

There was a considerable amount of activity for Ukrainian independence, especially by the Ukrainians of East Galicia, which they had considered the nursery of an independent Ukraine even before the war. When it broke out the Galician Ukrainians started establishing national organisations of their own, including the Legion of Ukrainian Sich Riflemen modelled on the Polish Legions. In late 1914 there were 2,500 men serving in it, and only 1,400 in 1915. As it was so small it did not play a major part in combat. The Austro-Hungarian authorities did not trust the Ukrainians and did not encourage them to expand their units. It was not until late in the war that this attitude began to change when a friend of the Ukrainian cause, Archduke Wilhelm von Habsburg, aka Vasyl Vyshyvanyi, son of Archduke Karl Stephan (owner of the great estate of Żywiec in the Polish part of Galicia), took command of the Legion. In the autumn of 1918 the Ukrainian politicians were preparing to take control of the city of Lviv (Polish Lwów), where the majority of the population was Polish, and declare the independence of the Western Ukrainian People's Republic. This they did on the night of 31st October – 1st November 1918, triggering several months of fighting between the Poles and the Ukrainians. The Ukrainian Galician Army was composed of Sich legionaries and Ukrainian veterans from other units of the former Austro-Hungarian army. Eastern Galicia had a mixed population of Ukrainians/Ruthenians, Poles, and Jews. There could be two, three, or even four ethno-national groups living in the same village. Both the Poles and the Ukrainians regarded the whole of Eastern Galicia as theirs, and hence it was difficult to reach a solution that pleased both parties. Eventually the outcome of the Polish-Ukrainian war of 1919 determined the region's assignment to the Republic of Poland.

The building up of national structures in the part of Ukraine under Russian rule proceeded at a much slower rate, mainly because the local population did not have a well-defined national identity. The Ukrainians inhabiting that region were divided, into those from the west, from the area of Kamyanets-Podilsky and Rivne, and from the east, the left bank of the Dnieper. There were also divisions into Whites and Reds; anarchists and free Cossacks; Ukrainians who were decidedly in favour of a national state of their own and were making an effort to set up a free Ukraine, and Little Russians (*Malorossy*) who considered themselves one of the ethnic groups belonging to the Great Russian nation. These divisions showed that there were different levels of a sense of Ukrainian identity, and acceptance of the idea of a Ukrainian nation. The first structures of a free and independent Ukraine started to be established after the February Revolution. Their harbinger was the Ukrainian Central Rada (Council), founded on 17th March 1917 and headed by Professor Mykhailo Hrushevsky. On 28th June 1917 the Central Rada appointed the General Secretariat, its executive body, led by the Socialist Volodymyr Vynnychenko. In the summer of 1917 the Ukrainian Central Rada demanded the Russian Provisional Government grant Ukraine autonomy, allow Ukrainian to be established as the official language in its administrative authorities and schools, and introduce social reforms including the freehold of the land for its peasants. All of this was to be implemented within the framework of a democratic Russia. Although the Provisional Government did not meet all these demands, nevertheless a process of Ukrainisation commenced in the troops of the former Russian Imperial Army stationing in Ukraine. There were also new, strictly Ukrainian, Free Cossack forces formed, under General Pavlo Skoropadskyi. He was a descendant of a line of Cossack noblemen but not in sympathy with the aims of the Ukrainian national movement. The situation became even more complicated when the Bolshevik Revolution broke out. The Bolsheviks had a considerable following in Ukraine. Their adherents wanted to overthrow the existing authorities and establish a Soviet Ukraine. For a time the Ukrainian Central Rada had the upper hand and in November 1917 declared the foundation of a Ukrainian People's Republic "within the federation of the free and equal peoples of Russia." From June 1917 the Central Rada's General Secretary for military affairs was Symon Petliura, a 39-year old journalist – an eloquent orator and a talented organiser. In January 1918 the Central Rada declared the full independence of the Ukrainian People's Republic. The Bolsheviks did not acknowledge this and established a Soviet government for Ukraine at Kharkov (Kharkiv) in the east of the country. There was fighting and for a short time in February 1918 Soviet forces took control of Kiev (Kyiv).

However, the factor which sealed the immediate fate of Ukraine were the Central Powers, who signed a treaty with it at Brest-Litovsk on 9th February 1918, making Ukraine the eastern flank of *Mitteleuropa*. On the grounds of the second Treaty of Brest-Litovsk (with the Bolsheviks, on 3rd March 1918) the Soviet army was to withdraw from Ukraine and conclude an agreement with the Ukrainian People's Republic demarcating the border. The Central Powers assumed patronage over Ukraine, in the belief that it would furnish them with plenty of the raw materials they needed for the war and hundreds of thousands of tonnes of food supplies. The Treaty of 9th February stated explicitly that Ukraine bound itself to deliver 1 million tonnes of wheat to the Central Powers by June 1918. Visions of train upon train full of all kinds of freight making their way to Vienna and Berlin glowed in the mind's eye of the dominant contracting party. The Treaty entered on for the sake of victuals put Ukraine under the control of the Central Powers and allowed them to exploit Ukrainian territory, which they (chiefly the Germans) were quick to occupy. To win the support of the upper echelons of Ukrainian society they decided to set up a new state on a vast area. On the west they granted it the Chełm/Kholm region and Podlassia (Podlasie, both regions now in Poland), which had hitherto been part of the Kingdom of

Poland and had a Polish majority population. The upshot was a series of mass demonstrations on Polish territories and put an end to any expectations or trust the Poles still had in the Central Powers, even though in the end Chełm and Podlassia were not incorporated in the proposed state. It was the death-knell for the Polish concept of a triple monarchy of Austria-Hungary-Poland. After the dismissal of Foreign Minister Czernin Vienna did in fact speed up its work to separate off Galicia from the rest of Cisleithania and grant it far-reaching powers, but it did so not out of a sudden surge of sympathy for the Poles, rather due to efforts by the Austrian Germans to become the majority population in Cisleithania by segregating off the Slavs of Galicia and Dalmatia. Nonetheless the House of Austria was crumbling, and its debris crushing the landlords. It was too late for concessions of any kind, and these were pretty minor. Berlin and Vienna had lost in the rivalry to win support in Poland. But did they win it in Ukraine? It turned out they had not gained much. No trains laden with goods rolled for Germany and Austria-Hungary. Ukraine was plagued by domestic conflicts, its government was weak and did not even control half of its territory. Despite the presence of Central Power forces in Ukraine, fighting still went on with the involvement of Bolsheviks, White Russian generals, anarchists, peasant insurgents taking over large agricultural estates, and three Polish corps engaged in hostilities against German forces. Moreover, the railway network was too flimsy and devastated to allow for significant despatches. And finally, the peasants were obstructing exploitation by hoarding foodstuffs and selling them on the local market.

With a predominantly left-wing democratic membership, the Ukrainian Central Rada did not enjoy the confidence of the Germans, who put their money on General Skoropadskyi. On 29th March 1918 at a Peasants' Congress convened on a German initiative Skoropadskyi was appointed Hetman (a head of state with military and civilian powers; a title referring to the traditions of the Cossack state) of Ukraine. On the same day he conducted a coup d'état and installed a dictatorship. His aim was to restore "the old order." Supported by German troops, he appointed former tsarist officials to the administrative and jurisdictive offices, and dismissed Ukrainian nationalists. He also started to reprivatise property in rural and urban areas. But he did not make much headway, due to widespread resistance, chiefly from the Ukrainian peasants. He had not enjoyed much support from the very outset, and it waned from week to week. The Hetman's men were under attack from all quarters – Ukrainian nationalists, Ukrainian socialists, and Bolsheviks. His regime established neither a strong army to support its ventures, nor an efficient administrative system, and fell when the war ended.

The Byelorussians and Polish landed gentry living in Byelorussia voiced their national aspirations, too. On 25th March 1918 the Council of the Byelorussian People's Republic declared independence, with Minsk as the new state's capital. A diplomatic campaign for its international recognition was launched by Roman (Raman) Skirmunt, a Polish aristocrat. In October 1918 Anton Lutskevich was appointed Prime Minister of the Byelorussian government. The Germans were not too enthusiastic about Byelorussian independence, aware of the frailty of the Byelorussian educated classes and the anti-German tendencies of the Orthodox priests and peasants, nevertheless eventually they recognised it. In practice the Byelorussian People's Republic was more of an idea than a reality; no state structures had been established when the war came to an end. Nonetheless a handful of educated Byelorussians accomplished much in setting up Byelorussian associations, cultural and educational institutions, and schools.

For the first time in history the Finns started to set up their own independent state on the north-western peripheries of the Russian empire. On 6th December 1917 they declared independence. Pehr Evind Svinhufvud, who is known as the Father of Finnish independence, was the leader of a government referred to as the Independence Senate. Like other national groups in Russia, the Finns were riven by internal conflicts. The White Finns wanted to set up an independent Finnish state, while the Red Finns, under the leadership of Otto Kuusinen, wanted a Finnish Soviet republic. The Reds enjoyed the backing of Helsinki and the industrialised and urbanised south; the Whites were supported by the agrarian regions in central and northern Finland. Brutal hostilities ensued with much bloodshed. On the grounds of a decision issued by the Senate, on 27th January 1918 Carl Gustaf Mannerheim, a talented and energetic Russian army general, was appointed Commander-in-Chief of the White forces. With German assistance, the Whites took control of the country. In October 1918 the Finnish parliament put Prince Friedrich Karl von Hessen-Kassel, the Kaiser's brother-in-law, on the throne of Finland, investing him with the title of Grand Duke of Finland. Svinhufvud was appointed Regent. Finland was to defend the German *Mitteleuropa* on the north. The Finns claimed the right to the Åland Islands, even though they were inhabited by a Swedish community which in February 1918 had taken over the islands, expelling the Russians and Finns by force of arms. Later the Swedes were ejected by the Germans. The dispute had still not been settled by the end of the war.

Things were somewhat tougher for the Latvians and Estonians, who had been setting up autonomous structures ever since the February Revolution. An individual who made a particularly distinguished contribution to these was the Estonian Jaan Tõnisson. Both national communities started to establish their own armed forces, which were engaged in heavy fighting against the Bolsheviks at the turn of 1917 and 1918. Power passed from one party to the other. Finally, a reconciliation was effected by a swift and successful German offensive. After 200 years Russian rule on this part of the Baltic seaboard came to an end in early February of 1918. The Treaty of Brest-Litovsk carried an article confirming this and announcing the prospective creation of a Livonian state under German control. But it was not going to be a Latvian and Estonian state, instead it was to be governed by Germans, with a German prince, and German barons and townsfolk. The local German *landtag* assemblies lobbied in Berlin to have this plan implemented. After the war the country was to be intensively colonised by Germans and serve as a signal component of the *Mitteleuropa* system. Hence on winning their local victory the Germans did not recognise Estonia's declaration of independence and on 24th February 1918 arrested its Prime Minister, Konstantin Päts. On 25th April 1918 the Kaiser announced the forthcoming creation of a Baltic duchy which was to be united with the Kingdom of Prussia by a personal union, and have the Kaiser's brother Wilhelm Heinrich for its duke. However, the setting up of its structures went slowly, because the Baltendeutsche (Germans settled in the region) did not make up more than 10% of the population, and their efforts were sabotaged by the Latvians and Estonians. The task was not facilitated by subversive Bolshevik activities, either. It was not until 22nd September 1918 that the Kaiser issued an act declaring the independence of the United Baltic Duchy. The announcement was made at a session of the Baltic Landtag in Riga. Effectively, however, the Duchy never came into existence, and Adolf Friedrich, Duke of Mecklenburg-Schwerin, never came to ascend the throne. The war was drawing to an end and the Germans were preparing to put up the white flag.

3. Jews, Armenians, and Arabs

On the occupied territories of Central and Eastern Europe there were also numerous Jewish communities, most of whom wanted cultural autonomy. However, neither Germany nor Austria-Hungary had a crystallised opinion on what to do on the "Jewish question." Among the Jews there were also Zionists, who wanted freedom to travel to Palestine, which until 1917 belonged to Turkey, and to settle there. Finally there were also Jews who wanted Berlin and Vienna to establish a Judaeo–Polonia – a Polish–Jewish state – on the territory of the former Commonwealth of Poland and Lithuania. This idea did not take on a realistic shape and was not adopted by the occupying powers, either. Wartime was characterised by the emergence of very many, often contradictory national concepts, of which not much came. More often than not the belligerent parties shelved the accomplishing of such projects to after the war. There was a very influential Zionist, Louis Brandeis, active in the USA. He was a friend of President Wilson and a judge of the Supreme Court. But it was not the USA that had control of the occupied territories in the East. Brandeis drew attention to the risk of pogroms. Indeed, the atmosphere in Europe was becoming more and more hostile to Jews. They were generally blamed for all the material hardships and wartime setbacks, and accused of cheating on weights and measures, double-dealing, malingering, and serving the enemy.

The war motivated European and American Zionists to initiate a diplomatic campaign for the establishment of a Jewish state in Palestine, with its capital in Jerusalem. The movement received the active support of Jewish bankers in Europe and America, who financed their publicity drive and the dissemination of information on the not yet well-known Zionist movement and its ambition to settle Jews in Palestine. To augment their assets, they made an offer to the Turks to organise a Jewish legion under their colours and to assist them with espionage activities, but the Turks were not interested. They did not trust Jews, and deported over ten thousand of them, including David Ben Gurion, the future Prime Minister of Israel for two terms in office. The British victories in Sinai and Palestine induced the Zionist leaders to make Britain an offer of very far-reaching co-operation. The British authorities were more interested than the Turks. The original idea of a Jewish legion came from Chaim Weizmann, a British Zionist. A legion consisting of three battalions was set up under the command of a British officer. Ben Gurion served in the legion and distinguished himself for valour. The legionaries were recruited from the Jewish community settled in Palestine, which counted nearly 100 thousand. Jewish espionage organisations worked for the British, supplying important information, but they were eventually broken and their members executed. British politicians reached a conclusion that an organised Jewish community was a salient part of the international community which could not be disregarded, and Prime Minister David Lloyd George saw Palestine as the national home of the Jews. A Welsh Nonconformist by religion, Lloyd George loved the Hebrew Bible, and hence his sympathetic attitude to the Jews. For him the Scriptures were literally the Word of God. On 2nd November 1917 Arthur Balfour, Secretary of State and Foreign Minister in the British Cabinet, sent a letter to Lord Lionel Walter Rothschild, President of the Zionist Federation of Great Britain and Ireland, which financed the campaign for Jewish settlement in Palestine. In the letter, later called the Balfour Declaration, His Majesty's government promised to support the establishment of a "national home for the Jewish people" in Palestine, though not at the expense of other ethnic and religious communities. It called the Arabs, who constituted over 90% of the population of Palestine, the "non-Jewish communities." The Declaration started the Arab-Jewish conflict in Palestine.

Another issue associated with the Near East was the Armenian question. Armenians, Christians of the Eastern rite, lived in the eastern, mountainous borderlands of the Ottoman empire, around Lake Van. The new nationalist trends awoke their pride, and sense of identity and self-esteem. Their aim was to secede from the Ottoman empire and establish an autonomous state entity within the framework of imperial Russia. Hence their nationalist campaign earned the support of Russia, enemy number one of Turkey. From year to year tension grew between the Muslims and the Armenians. There were several pogroms. The coming to power of a Turkish nationalist group called the Young Turks in 1908 spelled serious trouble for the Armenians. The Young Turks announced that they would establish an ethnically homogeneous state, and promoted Pan-Turanian ideas. When the war broke out clashes occurred between the two communities in the towns along the Turkish-Armenian borderland. The Armenians sided with Russia and hundreds of volunteers joined the Tsar's forces. For the Turks it was a sign to put the programme of "ethnic cleansing" they had prepared even before 1914 into action. Their plan was to deport the Armenians to remote parts of the Ottoman Empire, to bring down their numbers to less than 10% of the population in the borderlands. The deportations were preceded by a series of pogroms Armenians refer to as the Great Slaughter. The Turks and Kurds who massacred the Armenians were openly supported by Islamic clerics, and discreetly by the authorities in Istanbul. Some of the mullahs actually said that if the Muslims did not kill the unfaithful, they would not go to paradise. On 27th May 1915 the Ministry of the Interior under Mehmed Taalat Pasha decided to deport thousands of Armenians to the area of the Upper Euphrates and the Syrian Desert. Those who resisted were murdered on the spot, and their houses and workshops were ransacked. The Turks seized Armenian property. The deportations lasted a long time, as the Turks did not have the means to deport a million people efficiently, even if they had wanted to do it in a civilised way. During the deportations, known as death marches or death caravans, Armenians were attacked, robbed, and murdered by Muslims. Some died as soon as they reached the concentration camps. After the Armenians had been deported from a given place, their church would be demolished, or turned into a mosque or a public lavatory, and some of the remaining Armenians would be forced to convert to Islam. Orders were given to conduct circumcision in public. Those who refused to convert, including Armenian priests, were tortured to death. They had horseshoes nailed onto their feet, their bodies were abused, their heads were stuck on poles. Husbands were made to watch while their wives and daughters were being raped and then bundled into a local church or monastery and burned alive. Armenian victims were forced to dig large pits into which they would then be cast and burned or scalded to death with hot tar.

The Germans, who had a strong influence over Turkey, turned a blind eye to the atrocities, saying it was a Turkish domestic affair. When begged to intervene, the German ambassador in Istanbul remained silent. In August 1915 the German Admiral Wilhelm Souchon said that it would be salutary for Turkey to get rid of the last Armenian, for then it would be free of the traitorous bloodsuckers. The German press referred to the Armenians with contempt, calling them "exploiters" and "Christian Jews." "The Armenian is like the Jew, a parasite living outside of his fatherland and devouring the marrow of the people hosting him… the patience of the Turks has really been praiseworthy," the German papers wrote. They often quoted a remark made by Taalat Pasha in 1916 published in the *Berliner Tageblatt*, "We are accused of not distinguishing between innocent and guilty Armenians. That is absolutely impossible, because those who are innocent today may be guilty tomorrow… Armenians are like animals, and animals may be chased away and killed with impunity." Enver Pasha, the Turkish Minister of War, held a similar view of the massacres and brutal deportations, blaming the Armenians for all the misfortune the Turks had suffered and arguing that the Turks had a right to put their national security plans into practice. At a time when fighting was going on in Gallipoli the Armenian massacres did not arouse much interest in Europe and America. The Armenians were left to their fate, just like the Jews in the Second World War.

According to the latest Turkish research, in 1915–1917 the Armenian population decreased by 972 thousand, in other words many more died or were killed than the earlier Turkish statistics had said (viz. 300 thousand), but fewer than the Armenian estimates say, which is 1.5 million. Half the Armenian national community was killed or died of exhaustion. Today the ordeal of the Armenians still lies on the world's conscience, but its memory is divisive. Debate is still going on whether it was a war crime or genocide. It has been recognised as genocide by the European Parliament, the US House of Representatives, Canada, Sweden, and France. The Turks defend their actions, saying they were provoked by the Armenians, who were to blame for their fate, and furthermore Armenians and Russian troops were robbing and murdering Turks.

There were also other Christian victims of Turkish purges. They included Catholics living in Syria and Mesopotamia, and Nestorians, speakers of Aramaic, the language of Jesus. In the space of a few months in 1915 armed units of Turks and Kurds killed hundreds of thousands of Christians. The Pope protested in their defence. The mass murders stopped, but Nestorians continued to be killed. The purges also affected Greeks, who were accused of espionage for the Allies. In 1915 hundreds of thousands were driven out of Thrace, and Anatolia to the islands and coastal areas. Hundreds of young Greeks and Armenians were castrated and sent to the harems. Germany protested against the deportations and murders of the Greeks, fearing that this could induce Greece to join the Allies. There were also pogroms of Jews, in places like Damascus and Istanbul.

The national aspirations of the Armenians or Greeks were no surprise for the Turks. What came as a shock was the conduct of the

Muslim Arabs. Not only did the majority of the Arabs refuse to support the jihad, but they also staged an armed insurrection against Turkish forces. Arab-Turkish relations had not been good in 1914, for nationalist ideas had reached the Arab communities, too. During the war Arab nationalism, which started in Alexandria, Beirut, and Damascus, spread further and further afield. The slogan of the power-craving sheiks and emirs was "Take from the Europeans and the Turks what they have taken from the Arabs."

The rebellion of the Arab tribes started in Hijaz. Under the leadership of the nearly octogenarian Hussein Abu-Ali and his sons, Abdullah (Abd Allah) and the ambitious Faisal of the Hashemite dynasty, the rebels took control of the vast territories of Hijaz including the road to Mecca. Although Turkish forces put down these revolts brutally, new ones kept springing up. Reprisals and outrages only exacerbated the conflict and made Hussein even more resolved to put up resistance. On 5th June 1916 he assumed the command of yet another uprising and declared himself King of Al-Hijaz. He dreamed of creating a large Arab state stretching from Hijaz to Syria. In July of the same year a handful of Arab insurgents took part in the capture of the port of Aqaba on the coast of the Red Sea.

Initially the Turks did not take the Arab insurgents seriously, thinking their rebellion was only a British intrigue, and the armed Bedouins merely British agents. However, there was a Briton who had a hand in the Arab rebellion. The historian, archaeologist, and army officer T.E. Lawrence persuaded the Arabs to take up arms against the Turks. He managed to do this thanks to his fluent Arabic and excellent knowledge of Arabian culture. Lawrence dressed in the Arabian manner, which won the confidence of the Arabs, but infuriated the British, earning him many enemies at home. He became famous in his lifetime and his swashbuckling exploits provided a plot for numerous novels and films. On behalf of the British government he promised to assist the Arabs of Hijaz in the establishment of their independent states, and gave them generous financial support for as long as he was in a position to do so. There was another British agent involved in the Arab national movement – Harry St. John Philby, Lawrence's rival, but unlike Lawrence he endeavoured to reach an agreement with the Saudi Wahhabists. His son Kim would later be a key Soviet spy. However, it soon turned out that London was not at all ready to help in the setting up of independent Arab states. What it wanted was to take over the territories seized from the Turks and make them part of the British empire. One of the British generals in the Near East wrote that it was convenient for him to give the leaders of the Arab movement the impression that Britain supported them, but the promise of independence was a house built on sand. The real intentions of Britain and France were formulated in a secret agreement negotiated by Mark Sykes and Georges François Picot in 1916, which envisaged the partitioning of the Ottoman empire after the war, but no creation of free Arab states. After the war the British were to take over Mesopotamia, the southern part of Palestine and what later became Transjordan; while France was to have Syria, Lebanon, and Iraqi Mosul. The area of Palestine between the Jordan and the Mediterranean, along with Jerusalem, was to be a condominium of Britain and France. Russia issued its consent to the Sykes-Picot Agreement, but received a guarantee that it would get Armenia and eastern Anatolia. In 1917 the Allies promised the Italians Smyrna/Izmir and south-western Anatolia. Thereby after the war Turkey was to be a rather insignificant country under the control of the victors. The Soviet government, which took over the Tsar's archives, published the Sykes-Picot Agreement, which of course infuriated the Arabs and caused a crisis in their relations with the Allies. Nonetheless some of the insurgents stayed with the British, expecting a revision of the Sykes-Picot Agreement and the emergence of a free Syria with Damascus as its capital, and a free Hijaz. When Arab fighters entered Damascus alongside Allied troops in the autumn of 1918, it was taken as a testimonial of Arab aspirations. The Arab force was under the command of Emir Faisal, who announced the establishment of a council of state of Great Syria. He was given an enthusiastic welcome in Damascus and Beirut both by the Muslims and by the local Christians, who made up 25% of the population. Eventually, in 1919–1920 the Allies were the ones who determined the future of the Arabs.

4. The Irish case

The Irish case was quite different from the ones I have described so far. The Irish national aspirations were the only serious problem of this kind in the West. The Irish people had never come to terms with the annexation of their island by the English. During the war the smouldering conflict between Britain and the Irish people erupted with an enhanced intensity, even though the Irishmen serving in the British forces were not giving any grounds whatsoever to be suspected of disloyalty. The Germans were counting on Irish support, and were sending weapons into Ireland for the Irish freedom fighters. Roger Casement, one of the leaders of the Irish partisans, was tracked by British agents and caught on the Irish coast as a consignment of arms was being delivered by a German ship. On 3rd August 1916 he was hanged. The English published his diaries, in which there was an account of his homosexual exploits. A debate went on for a long time whether the diaries were genuine.

The pragmatic Irish wanted independence but were afraid of the unforeseen consequences which might have arisen from an armed rising during the war, so they did not support the republicans. Instead they sided with the adherents of autonomy (home rule) for Ireland. The pro-independence republicans were irritated by their compatriots' lack of sympathy, and angered by the British putting the Home Rule Bill in cold storage. They decided to stage a rising in Dublin. They had arms purchased in the USA. On 24th April 1916 their insurrection – known as the Easter Rising – broke out. They occupied the General Post Office and other public buildings, hoisting Irish republican flags, appointing a provisional government and issuing the Proclamation of the Republic of Ireland. The leaders of the Rising were Patrick Pearse and James Connolly. Dubliners did not come out in support of the Rising, and some even hurled abuse at the insurgents. On the 29th in the General Post Office they surrendered. 100 British soldiers and policemen, 450 civilians, and 52 insurgents were killed during the hostilities. The Rising was brutally put down.

15 leaders, including all the signatories of the Proclamation of the Republic, were executed. 75 others had death sentences commuted to imprisonment. The severe reprisals infuriated the Irish people, who now switched their support from home rule to republicanism and independence. Michael Collins, one of the insurgents, founded the undercover Irish Republican Army (IRA). The insurgents of 1916 wanted to create a legion of martyrs for the cause, in the hope that their sacrifice would stir the nation's conscience. And to a certain extent that is what happened. It was not a question of winning, but of resisting for as long as possible. Of letting themselves be killed, just like the Christian martyrs in the heroic times. Their blood was the seed which sprouted, removing the pagan idols and replacing them with Christ the Redeemer. The blood shed by the Volunteers would also bring fruit, open up the eyes of the blind, and win freedom for Ireland, as Mario Vargas Llosa wrote in *The Dream of the Celt* (*El sueño del celta*). On 23rd April 1918 the Irish rose up again to fight, this time in another mode, a general strike. The British responded by bringing in the troops. The leader of the legal Irish independence movement was Éamon de Valera, who won the support of the Catholic Church in Ireland and led the Irish people to independence.

The renaissance of the national concept in Europe occurred during the war. So, too, did the concept of revolution. Hence in 1918 some had a social revolution on their mind, while others were absorbed by a national revolution which was to bring their national state to life. For the elites of the "oppressed nationalities" deprived of their own statehood, the war was good news. But if it was to bring the results they wanted it could not end too soon, it had to continue as long as possible, to debilitate and exhaust the chief belligerents as much as possible. Thus, at the end of the war the main enemies of national revolution were no longer the imperial powers, which were in a state of decline or imminent collapse, but the revolutionary movements which instead of national solidarity propagated an internationalist solidarity of the downtrodden proletariat.

Time to Conclude

In 1918 the German intellectual Oswald Spengler published his book *Der Untergang des Abendlandes* (*The Decline of the West*), in which he forecast that Europe would no longer be as powerful and as exciting after the Great War as it had been before. And indeed, by 1913 it had reached the peak of what it had been working for over the centuries, advancing more and more. It had colonised and subjugated the world. It was great and predominant in every respect, imposing its will on others and sweeping up almost the entire pool of international awards, especially the Nobel Prize. Nothing important could happen in the world without the knowledge and consent of Europe. But in August 1914 Europe lost its senses, as one British journalist wrote. Though perhaps that's what had to happen: once the Europeans had reached the summit, they had to climb down to make room for others. First of all for the Americans and the Japanese. After the war the Age of the Pacific started.

After such a bloodthirsty and gruelling war of attrition, Europe was no longer in a position to keep and exercise the political, cultural, and economic role it had enjoyed before August 1914. After November 1918 it was licking its wounds in the aftermath of a shattering experience of war, immersed in debt abroad and with respect to its citizens, struggling with a grim economic crisis, hyperinflation, an escalation of grievances, and the virulence of new political movements like Communism, Fascism, and Nazism. Due to this the order introduced in 1919 by the Treaty of Versailles survived only for 20 years. So we can hardly disagree with one of the contemporary French journalists, who said that Europe committed suicide – it fixed a war for itself out of fear of death.

Selected Bibliography

Abbal, Odon. *Soldats oubliés: les prisonniers de guerre français*. Betz-et-Esparon: Etudes et Communication Éditions, 2001.

Aubrée, Marion, and François Laplantine. *La Table, le livre et les esprits: naissance, évolution et actualité du mouvement social spirite entre France et Brésil*. Paris: J.C. Lattes, 1990.

Audoin-Rouzeau, Stéphane. *La guerre des enfants 1914–1918: essai d'histoire culturelle*. Paris: Armand Colin, 1993.

Badsey, Stephen. *The British Army in Battle and Its Image 1914–18*. London; New York: Continuum, 2009.

Bartov, Omer. *Mirrors of Destruction: War, Genocide and Modern Identity*. Oxford; New York: Oxford University Press, 2000.

Bauer, Ernest. *Der Löwe vom Isonzo. Feldmarschall Svetozar Boreović de Bojna*. Graz: Styria, 1985.

Becker, Annette. *Les Monuments aux morts: patrimoine et mémoire de la Grande Guerre*. Paris: Errance, 1988.

Becker, Jean-Jacques. *The Great War and the French people*. Leamington Spa: Berg, 1985.

Beckett, Ian Frederick William. *The Great War 1914–1918*. Harlow, Eng.; New York: Longman, 2001.

Binneveld, Hans. *From Shell Shock to Combat Stress. A Comparative History of Military Psychiatry*. Chicago: University of Chicago Press, 1998.

Black, Jeremy. *The Great War and the Making of the Modern World*. London; New York: Continuum, 2011.

Bourke, Joanna. *Dismembering the Male. Men's Bodies, Britain and the Great War*. London: Reaktion Books, 1996.

Bridgman, Jon. *The Revolt of the Hereros*. Berkeley: University of California Press, 1981.

Buitenhuis, Peter. *The Great War of Words. British, American and Canadian Propaganda and Fiction, 1914–1933*. Vancouver: University of British Columbia Press, 1987.

Calder, Kenneth J. *Britain and the Origins of the New Europe, 1914–1918*. Cambridge, Eng.; New York: Cambridge University Press, 1976.

Canini, Gérard, ed. *Mémoires de la grande guerre. Témoins et témoignages*. Nancy: Presses Universitaires de Nancy, 1989.

Chickering, Roger, and Stig Forster. *The Shadows of the Total War: Europe, East Asia and the United States, 1919–1939*, Cambridge: Cambridge University Press, 2003.

Coetzee, Frans, and Marylin Shevin-Coetzee, eds. *Authority, Identity and the Social History of the Great War*. Providence: Berghahn Books, 1995.

Cook, Tim. *No Place to Run: The Canadian Corps and Gas Warfare in the First World War*. Vancouver: UBC Press, 1999.

Cornwall, Mark. *The Last Years of Austria-Hungary: Essays in Political and Military History, 1908–1918*. Exeter: Exeter University Press, 1990.

Cross, Tim, ed. *The Lost Voices of World War I: An International Anthology of Writers, Poets and Playwrights*. London: Bloomsbury, 1988.

Darrow, Margaret H. *French Women and the First World War: War Stories of the Home Front*. Oxford; New York: Berg, 2000.

Davis, Belinda J. *Home Fires Burning: Food, Politics and Everyday Life in World War I Berlin*. Chapel Hill: University of North Carolina Press: 2000.

Douglas, Allen. *War, Memory and the Politics of Humor: The Canard Enchainé and World War I*. Berkeley: University of California Press, 2002.

Duroselle, Jean–Baptiste. *La Grande Guerre des Français. L'incomprehensible*. Paris: Perrin, 2002.

Eksteins, Modris. *Rites of Spring: the Great War and the Birth of the Modern Age*. Boston: Houghton Mifflin, 1989.

Farwell, Byron. *The Great War in Africa, 1914–1918*. New York, London: Norton, 1989.

Feldman, Gerald. *The Great Disorder: Politics, Economics and Society in the German Inflation, 1914–1924*. New York: Oxford University Press, 1993.

Ferguson, Niall. *The Pity of War*. New York: Basic Books, 1999.

Ferro, Marc. *The Great War: 1914–1918*. London; New York: Routledge, 1997.

Field, Frank. *British and French writers of the First World War: Comparative Studies in Cultural History*. Cambridge, Eng.; New York: Cambridge University Press, 1991.

Fuller, John G. *Troop Morale and Popular Culture in the British and Dominion Armies, 1914–1918*. Oxford: Clarendon Press 1991.

Gambarotto, Laurent. *Foi et Patrie. La prédication du protestantisme français pendant la Première Guerre Mondiale*. Geneva: Labor et Fides, 1996.

Gammage Bill, *The Broken Years: Australian Soldiers in the Great War*. Canberra: Australian National University Press, 1974.

Gatrell, Peter. *A Whole Empire Walking: Refugees in Russia during World War I*. Bloomington: Indiana University Press, 1999.

Gibelli, Antonio. *La Grande Guerra degli Italiani, 1915–1918*. Milan: Sansoni, 1998.

Gilbert, Martin. *The Routledge Atlas of the First World War*. London: Routledge, 1994.

Griffith, Paddy. *Battle Tactics on the Western Front: The British Army's Art of Attack, 1916–18*. New Haven: Yale University Press, 1994.

Gullace, Nicoletta F. *'The Blood of Our Sons.' Men, Women and the Renegotiation of British Citizenship during the Great War*. New York: Palgrave Macmillan, 2002.

Herwig, Holger H. *The First World War: Germany and Austria, 1914–1918*. London; New York: Arnold, 1997.

Horne, John, and Alan Kramer. *German Atrocities 1914: A History of Denial*. New Haven, CT: Yale University Press, 2001.

Joll, James, and Gordon Martel. *The Origins of the First World War*. Harlow, Eng.; New York: Pearson Longman, 2007.

Keegan, John. *The First World War*. New York: Vintage Books, 2000.

Keiger, John. *France and the Origins of the First World War*. London: Macmillan, 1983.

Kolko, Gabriel. *Century of War. Politics, Conflicts and Society since 1914*. New York: New Press, 1994.

Leese, Peter. *Shell Shock, Traumatic Neurosis and the British Soldiers of the First World War*. New York: Palgrave, 2002.

Lepick, Olivier. *La Grande Guerre chimique: 1914–1918*. Paris: Presses Universitaires de France, 1998.

Liulevicius, Vejas Gabriel. *War Land on the Eastern Front: Culture, National Identity and German Occupation in World War I*. Cambridge, UK; New York: Cambridge University Press, 2000.

Livesey, Antony. *Atlas de la Première Guerre mondiale, 1914–1918*. Paris: Autrement, 1994.

Lohr, Eric. *Nationalizing the Russian Empire: The Campaign Against Enemy Aliens during World War I*. Cambridge, MA: Harvard University Press, 2003.

Macdonald, Lyn. *To the Last Men: Spring 1918*. London: Viking, 1998.

Meigs, Mark. *Optimism at Armageddon: Voices of American Participants in the First World War*. Basingstoke: Macmillan, 1997.

Mombauer, Annika. *The Origins of the First World War: Controversies and Consensus*. Harlow, Eng.; New York: Longman, 2002.

Neander, Joachim. *The German Corpse Factory The Master Houx of British Propaganda in the First World War*. Saarbrücken: Universaar, 2013.

Offer, Avner. *The First World War: An Agrarian Interpretation*. Oxford: Clarendon Press, 1989.

Pourcher, Yves. *Les jours de guerre. La vie de Français au jour le jour entre 1914 et 1918*. Paris: Plon, 1994.

Rachamimov, Alon. *POWs and the Great War: Captivity on the Eastern Front*. Oxford; New York: Berg, 2002.

Ribhegge, Wilhelm. *Frieden für Europa: die Politik der deustchen Reichstagsmehrheit 1917/18*. Essen: Reimar Hobbing, 1988.

Showalter, Elaine. *The Female Malady: Women, Madness and English Culture, 1830–1980*. New York: Pantheon Books, 1985.

Smith, Leonard, Stéphane Audouin-Rouzeau, and Annette Becker. *France and the Great War, 1914–1918*. Cambridge, UK; New York: Cambridge University Press, 2008.

Soutou, Georges–Henri. *L'or et le sang. Les buts de guerre économiques de la Première Geurre Mondiale*. Paris: Fayard, 1989.

Steiner, Zara. *Britain and the Origins of the First World War*. New York: St. Martin's Press, 1977.

Stone, Norman. *The Eastern Front, 1914–1917*. New York: Scribner, 1975.

Sukiennicki, Wiktor. *East Central Europe during World War I: from Foreign Domination to National Independence*. Boulder; New York: Columbia University Press, 1984.

Weldon Whalen, Robert. *Bitter Wounds. German Victims of the Great War, 1914–1939*. Ithaca: Cornel University Press, 1984.

Winter, Jay, and Antoine Prost. *The Great War in History: Debates and Controversies, 1914 to the Present*. Cambridge, UK; New York: Cambridge University Press, 2005.

Winter, Jay. *Sites of Memory, Sites of Mourning: The Great War in European Cultural History*. Cambridge, UK; New York: Cambridge University Press, 2008.

Zeman, Zbyněk A.B. *The Break-up of the Habsburg Empire, 1914–1918: A Study in National and Social Revolution*. London: Oxford University Press, 1961.

Index of Persons

Geographical index

TECHNICAL EDITOR
Jadwiga Makowiec

PROOFREADER
Monika Skowron

TYPESETTER
Katarzyna Mróz-Jaskuła

Jagiellonian University Press
Editorial Offices: Michałowskiego St. 9/2, 31-126 Cracow
Phone: +48 12 663 23 81, +48 12 663 23 82, Fax: +48 12 663 23 83